The Life
and Times of
Mary Attenborough

1896–1961

RICHARD GRAVES

The Book Guild Ltd

First published in Great Britain in 2022 by
The Book Guild Ltd
Unit E2, Airfield Business Park
Harrison Road
Market Harborough
Leicestershire, LE16 7UL
Freephone: 0800 999 2982
www.bookguild.co.uk
Email: info@bookguild.co.uk
Twitter: @bookguild

Typeset in 12pt Adobe Jenson Pro

Printed and bound by CPI Group (UK) Ltd, Croydon, CR0 4YY

ISBN 978 1914471 148

British Library Cataloguing in Publication Data.
A catalogue record for this book is available from the British Library.

I dedicate this work to the memory of a very dear friend, Ruth David (1929–2020).

Ruth was a great inspiration and encouragement to me when I was originally researching the lives of Helga and Irene, the two young Jewish refugees from Berlin, and also the story of the Basque children refugees from the Spanish Civil War. Both these examples of desperate flight from murderous regimes in the middle of the twentieth century led me to the deeply humanitarian response of the Attenborough family, and to Mary Attenborough in particular, and determined me to undertake this work.

Ruth was able to flee to sanctuary in England as a nine-year-old from Nazi Germany on the *Kindertransport*, never to see her parents again, as they were both murdered in the horrors of Auschwitz. Ruth thus survived the Holocaust, but, alas, was not able to withstand the onslaught of the coronavirus pandemic, and she sadly passed away in Leicester in April 2020, just after her ninety-first birthday, while I was writing this work. Ruth enriched my own life beyond measure. I miss her greatly.

Richard Graves
April 2020

CONTENTS

LIST OF ILLUSTRATIONS

ACKNOWLEDGEMENTS AND COPYRIGHT

COLOUR PLATES

FOREWORD

BY DAVID ATTENBOROUGH

Dictionaries give the word 'zest' several meanings. One is 'an invigorating or keen excitement or enjoyment'. That exactly describes my mother's approach to life. She was zestful in everything she tackled, no matter how unappealing it might seem to others. Her domestic accounts were a prime example. They had to be done, so she dealt with them with a zest that demanded that they be both detailed and meticulously accurate. As a consequence, the last day of every financial quarter became a time of high tension for the rest of the family. An unidentified penny could not be simply dismissed. She used a particular brand of account book. It was the best she could find but it did not provide all the categories she needed for total accuracy. So she wrote to the publishers with detailed suggestions and after protracted correspondence they changed the layout to match her requirements.

Zestfully also describes the way in which she ran her household. Fridays were washing days. We lived in a large Victorian house in Leicester provided by the university college, of which my father was the principal. It had a cobbled yard with outhouses that had once been stables. One of them she turned into a laundry. Every Friday she disappeared into it. There she had installed a primitive top-loading washing machine, the size and shape of a large rainwater butt. Clouds of steam billowed from the door until eventually she would emerge carrying armfuls of damp sheets and pillowcases to hang them out to dry.

She certainly had a zest for motherhood. But she had to combine that with her responsibilities as the wife of the head of an academic institution, a magistrate, a founding member of what was then called the Marriage Guidance Council and the chair of Leicester's Little Theatre. This was theoretically an amateur organisation but it had highly professional standards, and it was there that my elder brother Richard started to learn his theatrical skills. She also had many other lesser responsibilities, but – large or small – she fulfilled them all with great vigour. She could not do all that as well as being a full-time mother. So she engaged a nanny to help her care for her three sons.

Neither I nor my two brothers, however, were in any doubt about her devotion to us. If, in retrospect, I had any uncertainty about whether she thoroughly understood the particular characteristics of each of her three sons – both their faults and their talents – they would have been dispelled by an extraordinary letter of which I only became aware long after her death.

It was a draft of one that she sent to a Canadian academic who, just before the outbreak of the Second World War, had volunteered to accept me and my younger brother John as refugees from the anticipated bombing of Britain by Germany. It was an offer that, in the event, was not taken up, but the letter remains. It is a long and penetrating analysis of us both, composed to enable our guardians-to-be to deal properly with each of us, and it could only have been written by a devoted parent, keenly aware of all the needs and failings of her offspring.

And she encouraged her sons to be equally zestful in their approach to life. In my early years, I was addicted to climbing trees. So when a distinguished mountaineer who had married her sister Margaret suggested that he might take me, then aged fourteen, to learn the skills of rock-climbing, she did not, as many a fearful mother might have done, dismiss the idea out of hand but gave it her approval. As a consequence, rock-climbing became the ruling and rewarding passion of my life for many years thereafter.

During the rummaging around needed to produce the raw material for this biography, my sister-in-law discovered a truly extraordinary document. It is a journal my mother kept when, aged seventeen, she went to Paris to perfect her mastery of the French language. The zest combined with innocence with which this young woman, left by herself in Paris, recorded what she saw makes quotations from it – for me at any rate – one of the high points in the pages that follow.

The suggestion that my mother's life should be researched and written about came from Richard Graves, one of Leicester's most enterprising local historians. He had become aware of her existence during his investigations into the story of the refugee children who had been taken in by Leicester people. The first group of them came in 1937 from the Basque country after the Germans bombed the Spanish city of Guernica. They were followed shortly afterwards by Jewish children from Germany who arrived in 1938. Among them were two sisters on their way to join their uncle in New York. My parents had offered to look after them here until they could get an onward passage which in those years could only be by ship. The declaration of war, however, prevented that, so they would have to stay here until the war was over. Accordingly, my zestful mother declared that they would become our sisters. And so they did.

Few sons know much of the detail of their parents' early lives or can escape the inevitable attitudes and prejudices of childhood. I certainly cannot. I might have discovered more in later years by persuading her to reminisce, but I never had the opportunity to do so, for soon after my father's retirement and while she was still in her early sixties, her life was cut short by a traffic accident. So I welcomed Richard's suggestion that he might research and write an account of her life. I am very grateful indeed that he has done so, for I have discovered many things about my mother's life from the following pages that until now, I never knew.

ACKNOWLEDGEMENTS

My very special thanks go to Sir David Attenborough, without whose enthusiastic support and encouragement this biography would not have been researched and produced.

Special thanks also to other members of the Attenborough and Clegg families for their willing assistance, patience and also hospitality, namely: Susan Attenborough, Janet Attenborough, Jane and Tom Muirhead, Michael Attenborough, Peter Clegg, Andrew Clegg.

Very special thanks to the family of Helga-Maria Bejach in the United States: particularly Beverly Waldman Rich, Hilary Waldman and Harlan Rich, for their absolute willingness to share and tell the story of their mother and aunt, and to provide access to a wealth of family papers. The close personal friendship and trust, which have followed naturally from eight years of contact, are priceless.

A huge debt of thanks is owed to Denise Hopkins, whose passion for preserving the historical legacy of Rye Hill Close, generous hospitality and friendship, and unconditional willingness to share her local knowledge of Sawley and Long Eaton, not to mention her eager pursuit of local 'primary sources' for me, are beyond measure.

During the course of my research, particularly in 2019 and the early months of 2020, I spent countless hours in the Archives and Special Collections at the David Wilson Library, University of Leicester, trawling through formal business papers, minutes etc. of the early university college, together with less formal papers relating to individuals. I am very grateful to Simon Dixon, Vicky Holmes and the entire team in the archives for their total support, co-operation and friendship during that process.

My thanks are due to staff at other institutional archives visited in person, particularly to Amanda Goode at Emmanuel College, Cambridge, and also staff at Royal Holloway, London, and at the University of Nottingham.

Thanks also to staff at other institutional archives visited 'remotely': Senate House Library, University of London, and Brunel University, London.

Other libraries visited in person where staff were always generous with their help include: Long Eaton Library, Stapleford Library, Derbyshire Record Office, and the Record Office for Leicestershire, Leicester and Rutland.

Special thanks to Martin Pantling JP, for enabling access to specific records of Leicester Magistrates' Court, also for his generous hospitality.

I wish to thank Carmen Kilner of the Basque Children of '37 Association, for sharing her personal family knowledge of the Basque diaspora and also for her hospitality.

I acknowledge the assistance of the following people I have met in person during the course of the research:

Volunteer archivists at the Little Theatre, Leicester.
Pamela and Helmut Popp, Sawley Baptist Church.
Maressa Mortimer, Eastcombe Baptist Church.
Sarah Osmik, Relate HQ, London.

And many people I have met only 'online', but who have been generous in their assistance, including:

Daniel Herlinger, Santa Barbara, California, USA.
Dr Peter Cunningham, University of Cambridge.
Professor Cathy Burke, University of Cambridge.
Debbie Meredith, Bisley-with-Lypiatt Parish Council (Eastcombe), Gloucestershire.
Patricia Mansfield, Soroptimist International, Leicester.

Gillian Weston, National Council of Women.

Susan Hare, Alpine Club.

Rev Esther Rachma Abbott, Clyffe Pypard, Wiltshire.

Peter Gantlett, Clyffe Pypard Parish Council, Wiltshire.

Closer to home I would like to acknowledge the many hours of work devoted to proof-reading my 'final' draft by my daughter-in-law, Jennifer Graves, not an easy task when coping with the demands of an active five-year-old son. Many of Jenny's suggestions are writ large throughout this work. Many thanks, Jen.

And finally, I owe a huge debt of thanks to Hazel for her unconditional support, patience, wisdom and encouragement throughout, and for many suggestions after the checking of drafts. In particular I recall the countless hours spent during the 2020 'lockdown' when Hazel typed up as I was unravelling and transcribing Mary's Sorbonne diary, entrusted to us by David. This was one of the most rewarding and privileged tasks either of us have ever undertaken.

PREFACE

When I first suggested to Sir David Attenborough in September 2019 that I would very much like to research and write a biography of his mother he was at first mildly surprised at the idea, but then very quickly, upon reflection, thought it was a 'wonderful idea' and, crucially for me, said, 'There is a story to be told.' These last seven words provided the confirmation and supportive background for me to proceed. Without the wholehearted endorsement of the family I would not have gone ahead with the project. Family sensitivities are paramount, and I would never attempt to write about anyone who has died within living memory without the genuine agreement of their close family. In the event I cannot speak highly enough of the enthusiastic backing of both the Attenborough and Clegg families for this work.

In most instances I have referred to Frederick Attenborough as simply 'Fred'. In case readers may feel this sounds disrespectful, I agreed this with Sir David Attenborough, who was perfectly happy with this usage as his father was always known as Fred within the family.

I will draw on primary sources of evidence, and where evidence or family knowledge is lacking I will occasionally speculate on a basis of 'reasonable probability' to fill in a few gaps in order to create a generally chronological biographical portrait, but I will always distinguish between evidence and speculation. Mary lived in the East Midlands 'Lace Triangle' (the area bounded by the major cities of Leicester, Nottingham and Derby) in two separate periods, for around forty-six of her sixty-five years. The first of those periods, from her birth in 1896 until her marriage in 1922, was spent in Sawley and Long Eaton in Derbyshire. I hope to demonstrate the many and complex social factors present at the time, which in turn may have influenced Mary Clegg (the future Mary Attenborough). Mary's second spell in the East Midlands, from 1932–51, was spent in Leicester as the wife of the principal of the then University College of Leicester. This was arguably the time when Mary had the most energy, drive and passion to achieve so much and make a difference in the humanitarian spirit, which has characterised both the Attenborough and Clegg families in the twentieth and twenty-first centuries. Inevitably, therefore, there may appear to be a considerable East Midlands 'bias' in drawing this portrait of Mary.

I believe that it is timely to write this biography when we have so recently celebrated the centenary of the Representation of the People Act 1918, which led within ten years to the full electoral emancipation of women. The University of Leicester is also currently celebrating the centenary of its foundation and is very keen to uncover and emphasise the role of some of the female pioneers in the early years of its development.

My aim is to allow the reader to draw their own conclusions about the place of Mary in history. I began the research thinking I was piecing together the life of Mary Attenborough, but as the story has unfolded it became clear that I was also unravelling the story of the remarkable Clegg family, and, as a result, the considerable contribution of Mary to the equally remarkable Clegg–Attenborough partnership.

So, Mary Clegg or Mary Attenborough? In the end it matters little, the key point here is that 'there is a story to be told'. I hope to tell that story as fully as possible, to unveil a little of the life of, in my opinion, a remarkable woman of the twentieth century.

Richard Graves
March 2020

Mary's Family Tree showing the four generations mentioned in this book

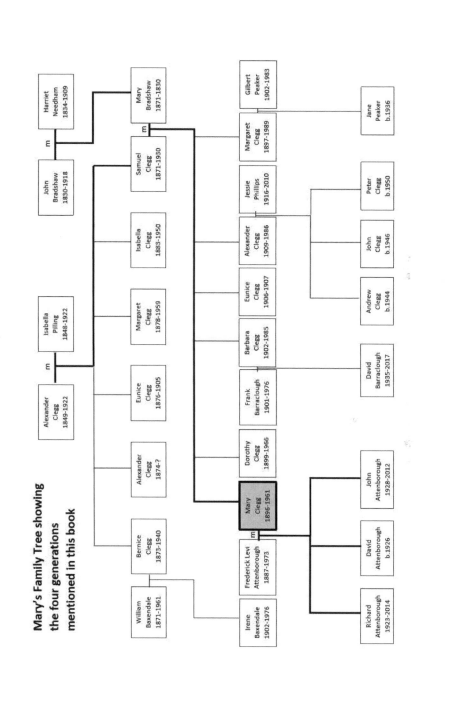

1896 MAP

From Ordnance Survey One-inch Revised New Series,
England and Wales: Sheet 141 Loughborough (Outline).
(Reproduced with the permission of the National Library of Scotland
https://maps.nls.uk/index.html)

This shows the old settlement of Sawley by the River Trent (the county boundary then and now with Leicestershire). In 1896 Sawley was clearly separate from the expanding Long Eaton.

The first signs of a new development are just visible to the south of what was then Sawley Junction Station (now Long Eaton Station). This was Mary's maternal grandfather, John Bradshaw, developing his land in what became known as New Sawley, in effect a third settlement between Sawley and Long Eaton (see Chapter 9).

1946 MAP

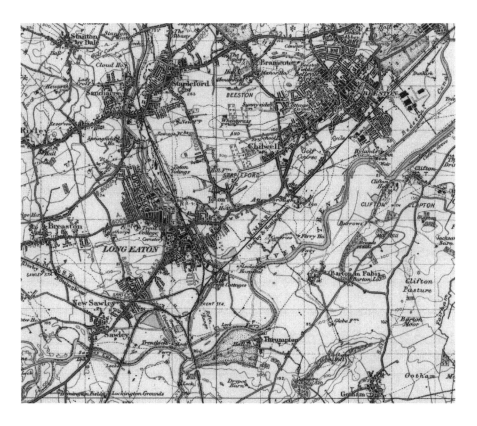

From One-inch New Popular Edition, England and Wales:
Sheet 121 – Derby, Nottingham and Leicester.
(Reproduced with the permission of the National Library of Scotland
https://maps.nls.uk/index.html)

This shows in particular the development over fifty years of the settlement of New Sawley around the railway station, almost but not quite joining Sawley with Long Eaton into a single mini-conurbation.

It also shows a northward growth of Long Eaton towards Sandiacre and Stapleford, the birthplace of Frederick Attenborough. Just to the east of Long Eaton is the small settlement of Attenborough, from where the family name originated.

PRESENT DAY

| *(Sourced from Ordnance Survey OpenData)*

Showing Sawley, bottom left, now completely joined with New Sawley and Long Eaton, which in turn forms a mini-conurbation with Sandiacre, Stapleford, Attenborough and Beeston, just to the south-east of Nottingham.

SECTION ONE
INFLUENCES ON MARY'S EARLY LIFE

CHAPTER ONE

NONCONFORMIST ROOTS IN THE EAST MIDLANDS

Mary Clegg, later Attenborough, was born on 8 April 1896 to Samuel and Mary Clegg senior of New Sawley, Derbyshire, the first of six siblings, and the first Clegg child of her generation and family branch to be born in the East Midlands.

In 1882 the Clegg family had arrived in Sawley, a settlement in the south-eastern corner of Derbyshire, within a stone's throw of the River Trent, which at this point forms the boundary with Leicestershire and flows east in a broad flood plain on its way to nearby Nottingham. Sawley is very much at the heart of the 'Lace Triangle', formed by the cities of Leicester, Nottingham and Derby.

In the first section of this work I hope to demonstrate how the young Mary Clegg's character and personality were in part influenced by the milieu in which she grew up and also by the gifts of her own remarkable family. Although this will of necessity delay the start of the main narrative about Mary until Section Two, I believe it is worth first outlining some of the factors which both influenced Mary's father, Samuel Clegg, and also provided fertile ground for his educational philosophy to flourish. I will, therefore, write a little about the particular development of Sawley and Long Eaton, about the influence of Dr John Clifford and about Samuel Clegg's meeting of minds with the educationalist, Michael Sadler (later Sir Michael Sadler). By the end of the work the reader will hopefully see the relevance of this background to the story of Mary's life.

Alexander Clegg (Mary Clegg's paternal grandfather), a schoolmaster aged twenty-one, married Isabella Pilling, a weaver aged twenty-two, on the 16 April 1870 in the Baptist Chapel at Astley Bridge in Bolton, Lancashire. Alexander had been born in Tonge, and Isabella in Sharples, neighbouring districts on the northern edge of Bolton. More than half of all persons with the family name Clegg were living in Lancashire at this time. Less than a year later the young couple were living in Astwood Bank, Feckenham, near Alcester in Worcestershire, close to the border with Warwickshire, where Alexander had taken a post as a schoolmaster. Isabella had given birth to their first child, Samuel, shortly after they had moved to the West Midlands.

Within a couple of years Alexander and Isabella had moved back to Lancashire, and in 1881 they were living in Helm Croft, Haslingden, about twenty miles north of Manchester. Alexander was described in the 1881 Census as an 'Elementary Teacher (Certificated)'. By now they had four more children, Bernice, Alexander, Eunice and Margaret (these would be the future Mary Attenborough's aunts and uncle), who were all born in Haslingden. Also living with the family at the time was Sarah Pilling, a niece of Isabella, a cotton weaver aged twenty-two, who was unemployed at that time, with her own son, Samuel, aged two.

It was the next move for Alexander, Isabella and their young children in 1882, which brought the Clegg family to the East Midlands, when Alexander accepted the post of schoolmaster at the Baptist School in Sawley, next to the Sawley Baptist Church. So what attracted Alexander Clegg to the East Midlands, and to Sawley in particular, at that time and at that stage in his career? Two factors may have attracted him and influenced his decision to move when the position of schoolmaster became vacant. Firstly Sawley Baptist congregation was thriving in the latter half of the nineteenth century, and secondly one of the most important figures in the history of British Nonconformism, Dr John Clifford (1836–1923), had strong associations with Sawley.

In the late eighteenth and early nineteenth century Sawley was a prosperous settlement. Many families were involved in the lace-making trade and home-based hosiery manufacture. The nearby River Trent also provided employment for many as boat builders, bargees, and in the warehouses along the banks of the river and canal system. According to the

1811 Census Sawley had a population of 823 compared to Long Eaton, its 'daughter' settlement almost two miles to the north, with a population of 580. Around 1836 the first machine-made lace was introduced to the area by makers from Gotham near Nottingham and possibly from Whitwick in the north-west of Leicestershire. However, during the next decade the balance of power shifted decisively north from Sawley to Long Eaton with the opening in 1839 of the Midland Counties Railway line between Nottingham and Derby and a new station (later called Sawley Junction Station and eventually Long Eaton Station as it is today) which was located where the line crossed the old turnpike road midway between Sawley and Long Eaton. In 1847 the Erewash Valley branch opened, taking the line from Leicester on to Chesterfield and Sheffield without the need to call at Derby or Nottingham. This created a major railway complex just east of Long Eaton, which came to be known as Trent Junction, with the associated Toton Sidings just to the north.

In 1849 a new wagon works in Long Eaton was developed by Messrs S.J. Claye & Co., and became a major local employer. Three years later the first large factory opened, eventually housing a substantial lace-making plant. In his book *Co-operation in Long Eaton* (1901) Samuel Clegg wrote:

> *Our Long Eaton of 1867 was an old-time village in process of spoiling, and was beginning to take on itself some of the unlovely features of a manufacturing town of mushroom growth.*

The population of Long Eaton grew from 859 in 1841 to 3,204 in 1871. Sawley, by comparison, saw no new development or population change during this same period. The local lace-making industry witnessed a rapid growth between 1870 and 1900. Lace workers moved into Long Eaton from the north of Leicestershire, and hosiery workers from villages on the Derbyshire–Nottinghamshire border also joined them. The development of Toton Sidings and the continued growth of the wagon works, which employed between 600 and 800 workers, swelled the Long Eaton population to 13,045 by 1901. In 1902, an infant Harry Godwin, who would later become one of the notable alumni of the Long Eaton County School, moved with his family from Rotherham to Long Eaton, illustrating precisely how and why the rapid growth of the town was occurring around the turn of the twentieth century. As a grown man Sir Harry Godwin recalled:

> *My father, a young grocer and licensed victualler, was taking advantage of the considerable local development of railway siding and associated wagon building alongside a great Nottingham-centred expansion of the machine making of lace.* [The new industries] *attracted a rootless population of nearly 20,000 with little in common save initiative, working-class determination and strong adherence to the numerous non-conformist sects represented locally.*

In the 1890s the younger generation of Sawley started to develop new housing in the area close to the Sawley Junction Station, so that within a few decades the map shows three distinct settlements: Sawley, New Sawley and Long Eaton. Among those moving into New Sawley were Mary Clegg's parents, as we will see later. A century on in 2020 there are no green gaps between the three settlements, which now merge as a mini-conurbation.

Sawley Baptist Church in Wilne Road (formerly Back Street) dates from 1801. Constructed of brick with a slate roof, the church has its own attached graveyard, a feature which would have been absent if the church had been built in the later nineteenth century as land became scarcer. Immediately adjacent to the church and within the same precinct is a later building, which was originally the Sunday school and then became the full-time Sawley Baptist School. As the Baptist community was thriving in the 1870s and 1880s when Alexander Clegg arrived, so too was the Baptist school with an attendance of around 100 to 120 pupils, which would have filled the two large rooms of the school building.

Sawley Baptist community, whose membership had grown from ninety-nine in 1859 to 164 in 1874, now felt in a position of strength to break away from its mother church in Castle Donington and appoint its own minister. However, one of the reasons for the recent growth in the Sawley congregation was the rapid industrial expansion and population growth of its own daughter settlement, Long Eaton. In 1876 the latter congregation announced its intention to appoint its own minister independent of Sawley. In the space of two years, therefore, Sawley Baptist community underwent two seismic shifts, but when Alexander Clegg arrived in 1882 the community and the school were still flourishing and must have represented an interesting challenge for the new schoolmaster.

Alexander Clegg's predecessor as schoolmaster was John Stenson, who retired aged sixty-three, and who had served the school for many years. Stenson was also the local Baptist preacher and lived at 73 Back Street, very close to the church and school. John Stenson was a maternal uncle of John Clifford. It is possible that Alexander Clegg, as a dedicated Baptist, may have already met Clifford or heard him preach at some stage, but in any case he would certainly have been aware of Clifford's Sawley connections and his importance in the British Nonconformist movement.

John Clifford was born on 16 October 1836 in Sawley, where a blue plaque commemorates this event on the house now known as 52 Wilne Road, just a few doors from the church and school. When he was around four years old the family moved from Sawley to Beeston some five miles away. John Clifford attended Sawley Baptist School for a short time at the age of four before the move to Beeston, where, perhaps surprisingly, he attended the local national school. National schools were voluntary schools providing elementary education, so-called because they were founded by the National Society for Promoting Religious Education. They promoted the principles of the established Church of England. Although by the age of eleven John Clifford was working in a local lace-making factory, his horizons had already been broadened by his former schoolmaster at Beeston, Mr Godler, who talked of Oxford and of life outside the village. This, combined with his experience of a sixteen-hour working day in factory conditions, helped to develop Clifford's social conscience.

Soon the leaders of the local Baptist congregation recognised John Clifford's potential and sent him to the Academy of the New Connection of General Baptists, then located in Humberstone Gate, Leicester, and later to the Baptist College in Nottingham, for training for the ministry. In 1858, aged just twenty-two, Clifford started work at the Praed Street Chapel in Paddington, London. At the same time he registered for a BA degree course at University College, London. The Praed Street Chapel, founded some thirty years earlier by a Leicestershire Baptist, Alice

Ludford, was in decline when Clifford took over. His vision for the role of the chapel, in addition to spiritual care, was to encourage a range of self-help activities in an effort to fight the social evils of the time. These included the establishment of a benefit society, sickness benefit, a labour bureau for job seekers, a building society and free adult education facilities. These activities necessitated a move to larger premises, and in 1877 the Westbourne Park Chapel was opened near Royal Oak train station with seating for a congregation of around 1,400 people and many function rooms to accommodate the varied activities of the community, in effect a mini 'welfare state' well before its time.

John Clifford was passionate about the role of education in achieving social justice and also self-improvement. Legislation evolved in the latter decades of the nineteenth century to establish the principle of universal elementary education, to be managed by local school boards on a non-denominational basis. This was a move away from the earlier voluntary school structure where the national schools promoted the principles of the established Church of England, and British schools, founded by the British and Foreign School Society (BFSS), promoted non-denominational teaching and consequently tended to be favoured by Nonconformist parents. The move towards non-denominational education was not welcomed by the established Church of England.

The key Education Acts of 1870 and 1876 established a compromise whereby religious teaching in the new board schools, while still based on the Bible, nevertheless excluded all aspects of sectarianism. Clifford was a strong supporter of the new compromise, but there was a major backlash over the next thirty years by the Established Church, which argued against so-called undenominationalism and in favour of support through the rates for voluntary schools. A bill introduced in 1896, which conceded some of the key demands of the Established Church, was withdrawn after strong opposition by Clifford and others. A new Education Bill in 1902 proposed the establishment of local council control of schools but also brought back state funding of voluntary schools. Despite major popular resistance to the bill it was enacted, and this eventually led to the development of the Passive Resistance Movement. Dr John Clifford was later mentioned by Mahatma Gandhi in a paper written in 1928 explaining the origins and definition of passive resistance:

When the British Parliament passed the Education Act some years ago, the Nonconformists offered passive resistance under the leadership of Dr. Clifford.

I will return to this subject in more detail later when I examine the life and achievements of Samuel Clegg, Mary's father, in the field of education.

The struggle to achieve non-denominational universal schooling for primary and secondary pupils inevitably politicised John Clifford. He involved himself in a range of major issues of conscience for the rest of his life, including opposition to the Boer War (1899–1902) and its terms of settlement, extension of the suffrage, Irish Home Rule, reform of the House of Lords, the rights of conscientious objectors in the First World War, calls for the disestablishment of the Church of England, and the championing of the major trade union campaigns of his day. Gradually the legislation of the late nineteenth and early twentieth centuries did lead to universal and compulsory education at primary and secondary levels, but Clifford remained firmly opposed to the state financing of sectarian education for the rest of his life.

It is very likely that Alexander Clegg would have known Clifford either personally or indirectly through family connections in the Sawley area. It is also no coincidence that his eldest child, Samuel Clegg, Mary's father, later embraced much of Clifford's liberal philosophy and proactive involvement in many issues of conscience and humanitarianism around the turn of the twentieth century. In turn we shall see how this transferred through the generations to Sam Clegg's own family, who absorbed the importance of equal educational opportunities for children and passionately embraced humanitarian issues and a deep sense of justice. John Clifford also played a direct role in the life of Mary Clegg later, just one year before his death in 1923 at the age of eighty-seven.

Alexander Clegg took up his new post as schoolmaster at the Sawley Baptist School at the start of the new academic year 1882/83. The school had been built in 1860 to serve the significant Nonconformist community in the village. Alexander's own children all entered the school as pupils at the start of the new term. The school register shows that the five children joined the school on 4 September 1882. Samuel, Bernice, Alexander, Eunice and Margaret Clegg, listed in the register as pupils 231–235, were then aged eleven, nine, eight, six and four years respectively. The youngest sibling, Isabella, later known affectionately in the family as 'Bell', was born in 1883.

Bernice was the first to leave Sawley Baptist School in March 1886, aged thirteen, for 'home duties'. Alexander left in April 1888, aged almost fourteen, 'to work'. The 1891 Census shows Alexander living at 83 Draycott Lane, Sawley, with Thomas Bowmer, a farmer, and his family. Alexander is described as a 'farm pupil'. It is known that Alexander later emigrated to Canada. He does not feature in the 1901 Census, so it is likely that he emigrated sometime in the last decade of the century as a young man in his twenties to seek opportunities in what became known as the 'third wave of immigration' to Canada. The Canadian government at the time was fearful that an influx of settlers from the United States might 'overrun' British territory and advertised in Britain and Europe for new settlers. This third wave would take advantage of the new transcontinental railway network to open up and create new farms, towns and cities in the Prairie Provinces. Eunice left school in March 1888 at the age of twelve to stay at home, and Margaret left in May 1891, aged thirteen, also to stay at home. Samuel Clegg left school at the end of May 1888, aged seventeen.

In 1896, after fourteen years at Sawley Baptist School, Alexander Clegg, aged forty-seven, took up the post of headmaster at the British school in the small settlement of Eastcombe, near Stroud in the Cotswolds. Although Eastcombe was essentially a rural village by nature and location, it was also 'industrialised' in the sense that much of the population worked in and depended on the cloth factories in the nearby Chalford Valley. This probably accounts for the strong Baptist tradition in the village, and by the late nineteenth century there was considerable pressure from Nonconformist families for the village to have a British school with non-denominational principles as an alternative to the already existing national school. The new Baptist school (a British school) was duly opened in 1879.

When Alexander moved to Eastcombe in 1896 the family lived at a house known as 'The Firs', now called 'St Mary's'. As a keen enemy of alcohol Alexander apparently took pleasure in the fact that The Firs had previously been Eastcombe's unsuccessful nineteenth-century public house, 'The Bear'! At least two of Alexander's three youngest daughters moved to Eastcombe with him. In the 1901 Census Eunice, then aged twenty-five, was still living with her parents, with no occupation listed. Less than four years later, at the age of twenty-nine, Eunice was dead. On 31 January 1905 she died in Liverpool following a recent operation. The death certificate does not list her occupation, describing her simply as the 'daughter of Alexander Clegg, Schoolmaster, Eastcombe, Stroud, Gloucestershire', so why she was in Liverpool at the time is a mystery. Her address was given as 18 Bedford Street, on the edge of Liverpool's Georgian Quarter. It is possible that Eunice was living with a family as a nanny or governess, but this remains speculation, although we do know that her younger sister, Margaret, was working as a governess to her niece, Irene, on the Wirral, just across the Mersey, according to the 1911 Census. Eunice was buried on 3 February 1905 in the Nonconformist section of the Victorian Toxteth Park Cemetery in Liverpool.

Isabella, aged eighteen in 1901, was also still living at home and described as an 'articled pupil teacher'. Isabella pursued a career in teaching and, at Kesteven and Grantham Girls' School, the future Prime Minister, Margaret Thatcher, was one of her pupils. As well as being the Baptist school's headmaster Alexander was also a deacon at the chapel. Although Alexander was apparently known for being a disciplinarian, one of his granddaughters, possibly Mary or just as likely Margaret, remembered country holidays at The Firs and recalled Alexander as a gentle person:

I only once saw him slightly angry and that was with me. He kept bees and one of his bees stung me. He was angry – not with the bee for stinging me but with me for being responsible for the death of one of his bees.

When the schoolmaster from the local national school went to fight in the First World War his pupils were transferred to the British school for education. Alexander Clegg had recently retired, but he came out of retirement to teach both groups, and by so doing he eventually presided over a reconciliation and merger of the two schools. After the war this temporary arrangement was made permanent and the schools were combined. The Baptists retained full rights over their building out of school hours, but the county education authority took on the cost of repairs and maintenance.

CHAPTER TWO

THE ESTABLISHMENT OF THE CLEGG FAMILY IN SAWLEY

By the time Mary's grandparents, Isabella and Alexander Clegg, left Sawley in 1896 their eldest child, Samuel (hereafter referred to generally as Sam), was already married to Mary Bradshaw and the couple had settled in Sawley. They had married on 2 August 1894 at Sawley Baptist Church, both aged twenty-three. The *Derby Daily Telegraph* described the occasion thus:

> *Sawley. Fashionable Marriage. The bride, who was given away by Mr. W.I. Baxendale, was attired in a trained bridal gown of blue and gold silk brocade. The bridesmaids were Miss Bernice Clegg (sister of the bridegroom) and Miss E. Needham, of Rotherham, (cousin of the bride). The Rev. G. Needham (uncle of the bride) officiated. Later in the afternoon the happy pair left for Ilfracombe, where the honeymoon will be spent.*

Mary Bradshaw was the only child of John and Harriet Bradshaw. John was a retired baker, originally from Sawley, born in 1830, while Harriet was born in Queniborough, just north of Leicester, also from a village bakery background. The 1851 Census shows John Bradshaw, aged twenty-one, living with his mother, Catherine Bradshaw, in the village of Hathern, just north of Loughborough in Leicestershire. Both are described as bakers. Catherine was a native of Sawley, so why they had moved just nine miles

Mary Bradshaw, seated centre, on the day of her marriage to Sam Clegg, 2 August 1894, with her father, John Bradshaw, outside the Bradshaw home in New Sawley

away from home to Hathern is a matter of speculation. By 1861 John had met and married Harriet, and they were living at 38 Bath Street, Syston, the neighbouring settlement to Harriet's native Queniborough, just outside Leicester. John was a 'baker and flour seller' and Harriet was also a baker. Their daughter and only child, Mary Bradshaw, was born in 1871. By 1876 John had retired from the bakery business apparently on health grounds, and the family moved to John's native Sawley.

In 1876 John Bradshaw had acquired an almost triangular piece of land bounded to the north by the Midland Railway line from Derby to Nottingham and to the south-east by what was then referred to as the 'turnpike road' between Sawley and Long Eaton and beyond. The railway station now known as Long Eaton, then Sawley Junction, was adjacent to John Bradshaw's land at the intersection of the Midland Railway with the turnpike road. John's land was in the heart of the area that would become known as New Sawley and was to develop rapidly over the next few decades as an aspirational area of choice for many people benefitting materially from the sudden industrial growth of Long Eaton. John Bradshaw acquired the land, an area of 3.15 acres, with the help of a mortgage of £500 secured, according to the conveyance, from:

John Atkin Clarke of the town of Nottingham Trimming Manufacturer
and Thomas Samuel Dobson of the same town Lace Manufacturer.

John Bradshaw lost little time in starting to develop the land, and by 1881 the first developed plot is shown on the Ordnance Survey Map as Woodbine Cottage. This is the substantial property variously described as 119 Nottingham Road, 26 Nottingham Road and now 192 Tamworth Road. It was the new home of John (now retired) and Harriet Bradshaw and their daughter Mary, who would later become Mary Attenborough's mother. The Bradshaws, like many families of their financial means, employed domestic staff at various times, as we can see from a 'small ad' in the *Nottinghamshire Guardian* on 15 January 1886:

WANTED at once, a Nurse; also General Servant – Apply by letter,
Mrs. Bradshaw, Woodbine Cottage Sawley.

When he was at Sawley Baptist School Sam Clegg had become a 'pupil-teacher' at the age of thirteen. His lifelong belief in the importance of education for all and the right of all children to the best available preparation for life, whatever their social background, probably stemmed in part from the Nonconformist tradition to which he had been exposed from an early age at home and school. After four years of his apprenticeship Sam moved in 1888, at the age of seventeen, to Forster Street School in Radford, Nottingham, a larger school with opportunities for Sam to broaden and develop his skills. At Sawley his father, Alexander, had been responsible for up to 150 pupils in a very popular school, with just one female teacher to share the load. It is possible that both Sam and his father felt that Sam could not be given enough individual attention in this environment. After two years at Radford Sam gained a 'first-class' in the scholarship exams and, after a medical examination due to concerns about his health, he was admitted to Owens College in Manchester in October 1890. Owens College had been founded in 1851 with the help of a major legacy to create a college for education on non-sectarian lines. The college was a direct precursor of what eventually became the University of Manchester. At Owens College Sam studied a general course, which included elements of English, law, science, history, the arts and pure mathematics. In 1891 he passed a 'preliminary exam' but never gained a degree, and after just two years he left Owens. Whether this was due to concerns about his health or about finance we do not know.

It is possible that Sam took a short break for health reasons as he was next teaching at Nun Street School in Derby in 1893. He only stayed there for almost two years before joining the staff at the High Street Board School in Long Eaton, closer to home, in late 1894, around the time of his marriage to Mary Bradshaw. The Long Eaton School Board was one of the earliest school boards to be formed, in 1873, much against the wishes of the local Anglican clergy, but probably due to great pressure from the growing Nonconformist community. Despite the success of the Baptist school at Sawley no similar school was established in Long Eaton. The doubling of the population in Long Eaton during the 1870s, including a proportionate increase in the Nonconformist population, probably outpaced the potential long-term planning process for such a school. Nonconformists, therefore, apparently preferred to send their children to the national school or to no school at all, preferring home education. The last school built by the Long Eaton School Board was opened in 1894, known as the Sawley Road Board School.

Sam Clegg joined the staff at the new Sawley Road Board School on 2 March 1896 when he moved from the High Street Board School. This was also the date when the Sawley Road Board School officially changed its status from elementary to 'higher grade' because more pupils, and particularly their parents, wanted their children to stay in formal education beyond Standard VII (age thirteen, the highest official level of elementary schools), especially if the higher education could equip pupils with the range of skills to reflect the demands of an increasingly sophisticated and diverse local labour market. From the outset Sawley Road Board School had offered a broader range of subjects than others in the town. The broader curriculum in turn demanded better educated and qualified teachers above the level required for elementary schools. The school naturally started to attract teachers with ambition and interest in the opportunity to extend beyond the basic subjects. Sam's appointment to the staff on the day the school officially became higher grade seems to have been an early recognition and endorsement of his ability and ambition to teach to a higher level than that normally demanded by elementary schools.

Like John Clifford, both Sam Clegg and his father-in-law, John Bradshaw, were supporters of the Passive Resistance Movement. They objected on principle to the fact that an element of their local authority rates was now used to support state-funded denominational voluntary schools, as required under the Education Act 1902, despite strong opposition before it was enacted. On 25 September 1903 the *Derby Daily Telegraph* reported on a:

> *sale by auction of the goods seized from the 29 passive resisters at Littleover, Long Eaton and Sawley,* [which] *took place in the large yard at the County Police Offices, St. Mary's Gate, Derby, and passed off without any disturbance. The proceedings were of rather a farcical character, and possessed none of the features of a bona-fide auction.*

Twelve of the twenty-nine lots at the auction involved goods seized from Sawley men. They included 'Lot 22 silver watch Mr. John Bradshaw Sawley', and 'Lot 27 plated tea service Mr. Samuel Clegg Sawley'. The newspaper reported that the Sawley goods were 'bought in' for £8. 17s. 11d.

One month after Sam Clegg started work at the Sawley Road Board School, his wife Mary (Mary Clegg senior) gave birth to their first child, also Mary Clegg, later Mary Attenborough, on 8 April 1896. The birth certificate does not give a home address but describes Sam and Mary senior as 'of New Sawley'. It is almost certain that when they married in August 1894 Sam and Mary Clegg senior initially lived with John and Harriet Bradshaw, Mary's parents. Mary Bradshaw (later Mary Clegg senior) had been an only child, and her parents, having built a house in around 1881 on the land they owned near Sawley Junction station, would have had adequate room in their new house to accommodate the young newly-weds. Over the next thirteen years Sam and Mary Clegg senior had five more children, four girls and a boy: Margaret, Dorothy, Eunice, Barbara and Alexander. I shall talk more about Mary's siblings later.

No information survives about Mary's early childhood. Around the time of Mary's birth or shortly afterwards the young family moved into the house where Mary would grow up, known as Rye Hill Close. The new house had many features designed by Sam Clegg, and was next door to the Bradshaws. The house is mentioned by Nikolaus Pevsner, art historian and architectural historian, in the Derbyshire volume of his county-by-county guide: *The Buildings of England (1951–74)*. Rye Hill Close is described as:

1895–1900. Domestic Revival style with Dutch gables and some interesting stained glass.

As a result of the ownership history many of the original features have been retained by subsequent owners, and this will be described in more detail as it fits in chronologically with this work.

When it came to a choice of schools for Mary and her siblings, the obvious choice was the new Sawley Road Board School where Sam had been appointed just a month before the birth of his first child. In New Sawley and Long Eaton this school was a popular choice for Nonconformist families in the absence of a Baptist school such as the one at Sawley, particularly following its elevated status as a higher-grade school where aspirational families could see wider opportunities for their children. The Sawley Road Board School was conveniently only a five-minute walk from the Clegg family's new home. Given the proximity of the new school there would have been little incentive to continue the 'family tradition' and send Mary and her siblings to the old Sawley Baptist School almost a mile away. When Mary was fourteen years old she moved to another brand-new school, which was officially opened on 29 October 1910, and where her father had been appointed as headmaster, a post he was to hold until his untimely death in 1930.

CHAPTER THREE

SAMUEL CLEGG, SIR MICHAEL SADLER AND THE NEW LONG EATON SCHOOL

The pupil-teacher system had started in 1846, but its success depended very much on the attitude, ability and whims of the supervising teachers. The gradual broadening of the elementary curriculum in the second half of the nineteenth century in turn demanded better educated staff and began to highlight the deficiencies of the existing pupil-teacher system. The solution was deemed to be the establishment of dedicated pupil-teacher centres. In Long Eaton the local board opened central classes in November 1894, which met in the evening in the Derby Road schools, but evening classes were not an ideal solution for students who had already spent a long day in school. The board quickly accepted that the increasing numbers of pupil-teachers and the higher curriculum demands of the Sawley Road Board School in particular required further action. In November 1896, just eight months after joining the staff of the school, Sam Clegg was appointed as a full-time instructor in sole charge of the pupil-teacher classes. Sam taught the pupil-teachers himself and personally supervised their teaching practice in class. Gradually the new generation of pupil-teachers were treated with more respect in their own right by other staff.

Sam Clegg's belief in the development of the personal strengths of pupils demanded an ability on behalf of the teachers to identify those strengths in individuals and to nurture them. One of his students at the Pupil-Teacher Centre was William Bullock, born in 1889, from a working-class family in the village of Breaston, two miles from Long Eaton. Harry Godwin recalled the interaction between Sam and his student:

> *Mr. Clegg's unsparing services to his early pupil-teachers are illustrated by the way in which he helped to launch the education of another local boy, then acting as railway clerk on the Erewash Valley line. Sam would go up the line in the evening to sit with the young Will Bullock, and coach him in the slack intervals of the ticket office. This was Will Bullock who in due course became gold medallist of the Edinburgh Medical School and achieved great distinction through and after the First World War. There can be small wonder at the affection as well as respect with which Sam Clegg was locally regarded.*

William Bullock later adopted his first wife's surname of Gye, and as William Ewart Gye went on to become a highly respected pathologist and cancer researcher. He became director of the Imperial Cancer Research Fund's laboratories in Mill Hill from 1934 until his retirement in 1949. He was elected as a Fellow of the Royal Society in 1938.

By 1904 there were twenty-seven students at the Long Eaton Pupil-Teacher Centre; however, not all planned to pursue a career in teaching. At the same time there were around 400 pupils in Long Eaton alone who had stayed in elementary schools beyond the minimum age limit, and it was clear that the future direction for senior schools was a pressing problem for the newly established Derbyshire County Council to resolve. Even at a national level government thinking was rather unclear at this time and the debate continued. The county council appointed Professor Michael Sadler to carry out a review, and his report *Secondary and Higher Education in Derbyshire* determined the future direction of educational development in Long Eaton. At the time Sadler was the foremost authority on secondary education in England, and he produced similar reports for nine education authorities in the wake of the Education Act 1902. Derbyshire compared unfavourably with other counties in the provision of secondary schools; however, Sadler believed that the answer was not simply to provide more school places but to develop more vocationally relevant forms of further education to better suit the requirements of the local economy. His strong view was that specialisation should follow a good basic education and not replace it:

School ought to be something higher than a knowledge factory,

but he also believed in the development of 'character':

What a man is matters a good deal more than what he knows.

Sadler proposed a three-year course, from the age of twelve to the age of fifteen, with an emphasis on a thorough grounding in English. To start with a basic two-year course would be taken by all pupils and would include:

geography, begun earlier with the study of the home district, nature study, which should be connected with art teaching, practical physics, elementary mathematics, including arithmetic, algebra and geometry, drawing, handicraft exercises, class singing and carefully graded physical exercises. The course should also include French taught on the best modern methods.

After the basic course four optional one-year courses could be offered, according to local demand: a general course, an industrial course for boys only, a mixed commercial course and a household management course for girls only.

Professor Michael Sadler and Sam Clegg would have had a series of meetings, and it is interesting to speculate now the extent to which the one influenced the other in terms of educational philosophy, but it was presumably, and fortuitously, a meeting of minds from the outset in many ways. Theirs was seemingly a symbiotic relationship, with mutual respect and much in common, but at the same time they were strong-minded individuals with their own visions. Sadler once described Clegg as a 'high-voltage cable'. Both men were in agreement about the wider effects of education beyond the strict curriculum demands and the importance of 'non-examinable gains'. Throughout his career Sam Clegg placed great importance on intangible assets for the development of character, such as perseverance, social awareness and manual dexterity. Sam was a person of wide interests and tastes, hence his belief in a liberal education. In order to broaden his own knowledge and experience he left in October 1906 for a three-month 'sabbatical' to visit the United States, returning in January 1907. In his absence his assistant, Miss Taylor, deputised as head of the Long Eaton Pupil-Teacher Centre. He believed that the acquisition of good taste and the ability to appreciate beauty were key to a full enjoyment of life. In his pupils he tried to develop a lasting 'sincerity and a respect for the finer things in life', which in turn would hopefully permeate every aspect of character.

In his report for Derbyshire County Council, Sadler suggested that the Long Eaton Pupil-Teacher Centre should be retained and that a new higher-grade elementary school should be built on the same site, allowing the two institutions to share common facilities and some staff. His specific ideas for Long Eaton suggested a form of further education suited to the social and industrial needs of the area. Some were disappointed that a secondary school had not been proposed, which may have been a more appropriate route for parents aiming for more academic careers for their children via a university education, but Sadler felt there were other options available for such pupils locally in all three counties of Derbyshire, Leicestershire and Nottinghamshire. The future of higher elementary schools was still unclear at this stage and the very name itself confused the issue in the minds of some.

Sadler was clearly impressed by Sam Clegg as a natural leader, not only in education circles but also in the broader civic and cultural life of the town. Sam was proactively involved in the co-operative movement in Long Eaton and was also a member of the local Liberal Party. He had been the secretary of a committee leading a campaign to purchase a piece of land known as Parkin's Close, or more anciently Gorseholmes, adjacent to the Erewash Canal in the centre of the town for the purpose of building a public library. Eight men pledged the sum of £1,150 before approaching Andrew Carnegie, the wealthy Scottish-American industrialist and philanthropist, through the local MP, Sir Walter Foster, for a grant. An offer of £3,000 was forthcoming, conditional on Long Eaton Urban District Council adopting the Public Libraries Act 1850, the full library rate (1d.) being levied and the promised land being made available. The land had been presented to the town to fulfil a key condition of the application for a 'Carnegie grant' to provide a public library. The application was successful, and the new library was eventually opened in June 1906. The first librarian, Mr Hooper, appointed on an annual salary of £80, said that Clegg's:

> great-hearted vision, intense enthusiasm, and genial personality overcame what to others might have been insuperable.

Long Eaton Library still occupies the same building and site today.

Professor Michael Sadler's report was accepted by Derbyshire County Council, and the remainder of the Gorseholmes site, adjacent to the library, was chosen as the site for the new school. Construction work began in May 1908. When the foundation stone was laid in February 1909 without any formal ceremony, the school governors, possibly to mark the occasion but certainly to mark the head's additional responsibilities, recommended a salary increase from £225 to £260 per annum. Derbyshire County Council compromised at a new figure of £240.

Meanwhile Sam Clegg's belief that language teaching must involve direct contact with another country had led to the appointment in 1908 of the first native French speaker, Mlle Marie Martin. Sam took a day's leave, with the support of the governors, to meet and greet the new member of staff. Marie only stayed for one year, but she was succeeded by M. Georges Michellet, who stayed for three years. These appointments were the first in a long line of French *assistant(e)s* on the staff. Sam's belief in the need for close contact with another country and culture would be put into practice later in regard to his eldest child, Mary, the subject of this biography.

The new school, then named Long Eaton County School and Pupil-Teacher Centre, built at a cost of £14,900, was opened in time for the start of the 1910/11 academic year, although the pupil-teacher centre was able to use the wing closest to the library from January 1910. An excellent source of information for this period is a publication produced in 1960 by a group of former pupils and current and former staff to celebrate the golden jubilee of the school and is known simply as the *Long Eaton Grammar School Jubilee Book 1960*. In April 1910 a performance of *Twelfth Night* was given in the almost completed chemistry laboratory. We know that the part of Malvolio was played by Mary Clegg, just turned fourteen. Apparently the weather was cold, and the new building, still under construction, was draughty. Sam Clegg, in the audience to see his eldest daughter, first caught a cold and then developed a serious illness, thought to be pneumonia, which kept him off work from 28 April until the start of the next school year in September 1910. The *Jubilee Book* quotes one of the pupils at the time, Mr Adams, recalling:

How Miss Taylor, who had taken over responsibility for the school, relied on me to call at Mr Clegg's house in Sawley, since I passed the house twice each day, and either read the bulletin issued or inquire how Mr Clegg was. During the crisis of the illness I cycled down between lessons for the latest news and when Mr Clegg was recovering I was allowed in to see the headmaster, with 'untrimmed beard and thin, pale face' looking very ill indeed.

Sadler's recommendation for leadership of the new school was accepted by Derbyshire County Council, and Samuel Clegg was appointed as head of the new combined higher elementary school and pupil-teacher centre from September 1910, coinciding with his return from illness. The formal opening took place on 19 December 1910, when Professor Michael Sadler spoke on 'The Realisation of a Dream'. Sam Clegg was thus given a unique opportunity to organise a new school with no history or tradition and to shape higher education locally according to his own clear views and principles. Harry Godwin, who entered the school in 1913 at the age of twelve, later described an early sense of joining a new venture, which potentially offered a glimpse of broader horizons:

I exchanged the Board School with its atmosphere of corduroy trousers and heavy boots as worn by all my friends, for the wider territory of a progressive new school, drawing its pupils from a radius of several miles.

Both Clegg and Sadler agreed on another significant point within education and within local communities: the value of art and artistic development, and the appreciation of art and beauty in all aspects of life. Clegg was concerned not so much with the final outcome or product of art but with the mastery of certain skills and the self-confidence such processes can develop in a child. In his own book *Drawing and Design: A School Course in Composition* (1918), Sam Clegg describes five main aims for his art course:

1. *At the outset, provisions for the exercise of the play instinct in the child.*
2. *The development of muscular control, and concurrently mental and moral control.*
3. *The training of the powers of observation, memory and representation.*
4. *The giving of full liberty to the powers of expression.*
5. *The encouragement of appreciation and the acquisition of a right sense of values.*

These principles again reflect Sam Clegg's view of education as something far broader and more permanent than the purely 'examinable' benefits. *Drawing and Design* sets out a three-year course for children over ten, an age at which it was felt appropriate to channel the liberty of the early years into a more formal discipline. Within the course he always advocated variation to maintain interest and focus and also encouraged experimentation and the development of personal strengths. He believed that art should be integrated into all aspects of schoolwork and the application of skills across the curriculum, particularly the sciences and humanities. He demanded the development of powers of careful observation and pictorial memory, both especially important in a number of disciplines:

In Botany and Zoology [observation and representation] are an essentially important part of the subject, in Petrology and Palaeontology hardly less so. In History it is becoming increasingly evident that picture memory as well as story memory, must be cultivated.

Sam Clegg believed strongly that 'taste and sensitivity' are absorbed through the environment, and, translating this to basics, he believed that:

the schools of childhood should in every sense be pleasing and attractive, in the schools in which years of adolescence are passed, refining and stimulative surroundings are the first essential.

| *Sam Clegg teaching at Long Eaton County School, 1912/13*

He strongly urged the 'de-cluttering' of classrooms and railed against the:

> *bewildering mess of useless litter which disgraces the walls of so many schools and* [which] *is surely responsible for much untidiness of mind and perhaps for the low standard of public taste.*

He believed that a school should be an aesthetically pleasing environment for young people during their impressionable years.

Within a couple of years of the new Long Eaton County School and Pupil-Teacher Centre opening a clash over the status of the school was looming with the Board of Education. Under the existing school codes for higher elementary schools the upper age limit for pupils was supposed to be fifteen, but as the new Long Eaton School was also a pupil-teacher centre where the minimum age for apprenticeship as a pupil-teacher had been raised to sixteen, the school had to take into account the codes for both types of establishment. A 'bridging course' for ages fifteen to sixteen along the lines suggested by Professor Sadler was therefore introduced. From 1902 the Board of Education had encouraged future teachers to complete a secondary school course before starting their teacher training. Education at a combined higher elementary school and pupil-teacher centre was increasingly seen as a less desirable route by ambitious pupils and their parents.

French was being taught at the new Long Eaton school in line with Sadler's recommendation, but Latin was considered suitable only for secondary schools. As pupil numbers quickly increased additional staff were required. The first appointment was a woman as deputy head, reflecting the disproportionately higher number of girls entering the pupil-teacher centre, and then a teacher of French and Latin was appointed. Sam Clegg had decided that in his school Latin was an appropriate option, even if this risked a clash with the national Board of Education. The clash soon occurred when in 1912 the school inspectors asked for an explanation of the curriculum, which had not been approved by them, as it was in effect a secondary-school curriculum and thereby circumventing the governing codes. The school governors realised that they either needed to formally apply for a change in status to a secondary school or radically re-organise the set-up to comply with the higher elementary school code. After a year's deliberation the school governors decided to apply for a change of status to secondary school, which in practice it already was:

> *Its contraband Latin was now lawful; its justification would be the success with which it trained pupils for the professions and the universities.*

Where an establishment with secondary status was available the need and demand for pupil-teacher centres declined. The change in status, however, raised another issue. In accordance with the increasing expectation of higher-quality teaching staff generally, the Board of Education stated that, unless a special case could be made to the contrary, the head of the new secondary school should be a graduate. Sam Clegg was not a graduate as such as he had left Owens College after passing only a preliminary exam. The school governors, however, were unanimous in their support for Sam, and the Board of Education accepted their

Mary's sister, Margaret Clegg (centre), with friends, Form VI Long Eaton County School, c.1913

recommendation. Another hurdle had been overcome, and Sam now had renewed support and a vote of confidence in his vision for the future.

Sam Clegg's belief in the importance of an aesthetically pleasing environment within the school was a key theme in its design, and a number of original artworks were acquired for the school. Several murals were painted by artistic members of staff, sometimes with the assistance of senior pupils. Sam also carried the theme into the grounds of the school, planting thousands of bulbs in the borders and describing this activity as 'buying hyacinths to feed the soul'. When the first edition of the school magazine was produced in 1912 the emphasis was on producing:

a beautiful object rather than a record of school events,

and so the usual formal record of sports events and exam successes was replaced by a wide range of projects carried out by senior pupils from Form 3 upwards, individually or in groups, on topics which had caught their imagination. The head explained that:

In most cases the work has been unaided, in others, done under the direction of the teachers, but everything here is shewn ... with all faults.

In that first edition Sam Clegg's eldest two daughters featured heavily. A fifteen-year-old Margaret Clegg wrote an article about:

The use of the indefinite article before words beginning with 'u'.

Meanwhile sixteen-year-old Mary Clegg showed a mature grasp of both French and English to produce a verse translation into English of the lyrics of a well-known French song, 'Ma Normandie', written in 1836. Mary also showed her interest in history by researching and writing a local history article of around 600 words about 'The Hundred of Sawley'. In 1913 there are also mentions in the magazines of both sisters in terms of academic success and progress. Mary gained the London Matriculation 2nd Class, while Margaret achieved the Oxford Senior Level 3rd Class Honours.

Sam Clegg always encouraged an overlap of subjects rather than strict compartmentalisation, and in this way he hoped to nurture independent thinking in his pupils, placing emphasis on the ability to think in a deductive way, to take disparate elements and combine them to produce innovative ideas. Science teaching in the school was restricted in range partly due to a shortage of laboratory facilities. One former pupil said that:

> apart from Botany we did very little science. There was only one small lab anyway, for Chemistry and Physics together.

Despite this a number of former pupils went on to have distinguished careers in scientific research, such as Harry Godwin and William Bullock (later William Gye). Sam Clegg's democratic outlook, his background in Nonconformism and in the co-operative movement seem to have produced an environment for staff and pupils alike where the usual rigid hierarchies were absent. He encouraged pupils to reach their full potential, but he also applied this to staff, and where their abilities seemed to suggest greater potential he supported them to continue their studies while at the school and in some cases on to university and higher academic positions. Respect seemed to be mutual throughout the school. He enabled every opportunity for staff to broaden their own knowledge and interests in the hope and belief that they would become educators in the true sense of the word. One such staff member with higher aspirations would eventually go on to marry Sam Clegg's eldest daughter, Mary.

SECTION TWO

MARY'S EARLY YEARS AND MARRIAGE

CHAPTER FOUR

MARY AS A YOUNG WOMAN

As Mary entered her teenage years and continued her school career at Sawley Road School she would have been aware of debates about and changes afoot in the field of education in Long Eaton, as discussed in the previous section. As an intelligent young woman she must have been aware from family talk within the home, and perhaps even from one-to-one discussions with her father, of the evolution of his views on education and educators in the broadest sense. She would have watched the construction of the new school a mile up the road from home on land next to the new Long Eaton Library, and would have been aware of her father's role in the planning of the school. She may have even had a 'sneak preview' of some of her father's vision, plans and aspirations for the school. By her fourteenth birthday in 1910 Mary may have had thoughts and dreams about her own future, trying to work out her own pathway in life and how she might fulfil her dreams. In discussions with her family Mary would probably have already decided that the new school in Long Eaton would be the place for her when it opened later in the year.

Before she changed schools Mary had experienced death in her immediate family for the third time in two years. In 1907, on 9 November, when Mary was eleven years old, she had witnessed the death of her baby sister, Eunice, who had died at home aged just seventeen months old from diphtheria, still a major killer of the young at the time. Eunice had been born just sixteen months after the untimely death of her aunt of the same name. It is quite likely she was named in tribute to her aunt. Baby Eunice was buried at Sawley Baptist Church, where a stone still marks her burial close to the main church door. And then on 10 March 1909 her maternal grandmother, Harriet Bradshaw, who lived in the house next door, died. June 1909, however, brought the birth of Mary's youngest sibling and only brother, Alexander Bradshaw Clegg, to become known as Alec, about whom more later. In the space of four years in her early adolescence Mary witnessed the highs and lows of family life.

In the 1911 Census we can see that Sam and Mary Clegg senior not surprisingly employed a live-in 'mother's help', Nellie Gaskin, at a time when Mary Clegg senior would have been very taxed trying to cope with five children aged fourteen, thirteen, twelve, eight and one. Nellie Evelyn Gaskin, aged twenty-three, was (according to the 1901 Census) the eldest of four children living in Burton-upon-Trent, just twenty miles away, where her father, Frank Gaskin, was a bricklayer. Domestic service was the largest employer in Britain on the eve of the First World War, with around one and a half million people working like Nellie and representing a remarkably mobile working-class labour force.

Postcard photo, c.1912, Tamworth Road, New Sawley, from outside Rye Hill Close, looking north towards Long Eaton, Midland Railway station by the bridge crossing

Postcard photo, c.1912, Tamworth Road, New Sawley, looking south towards Sawley. The Dutch gable of Rye Hill Close is just visible behind the Bradshaw house, right, behind the children

Mary Clegg, aged around 16, c. 1912, in the oak room at Rye Hill Close

By 1913, if not before, the seventeen-year-old Mary would also have been aware of a young man in his mid-twenties, nine years older than her, living literally just around the corner in a house now known as Salisbury House, Bradshaw Street, but which was then known as 118 Nottingham Road. The owner or tenant of the house was Mary Jane Potter, born in Leeds, and by now a widow aged sixty-four. In 1901 Mary Jane had been living at 114 Victoria Street, the next side street down from Rye Hill Close (the Cleggs' home) with her husband, Frederick, eighteen years her senior, and three sons. Frederick Potter had been born in Coleorton in north-west Leicestershire, and had moved to the Long Eaton area probably as a young man to take advantage of the new employment opportunities offered by the opening of the Midland Railway. In 1901 he was aged seventy but was still employed as a foreman on the railway. The two eldest Potter sons, Frederick and Horace, were also working for the railway, while the youngest, Arthur, was still at school. At some stage between 1901 and 1911 the family had moved the short distance to 118 Nottingham Road. Frederick Potter senior seems to have died in late 1905, and by 1911 the two older sons had left home, leaving Mary Jane and her youngest son in the house. Arthur was by then aged twenty-three and was a gas engineer for the Long Eaton Gas Company in the days when utilities were provided by local companies. As frequently happened in under-occupied homes Mary Jane had taken in lodgers to supplement her income and to provide short-term accommodation for younger people in 'respectable' occupations and professions. In 1911 she had two lodgers, John Drury, a schoolmaster aged twenty-three, and William Vaughan from Worcestershire, who was a railway clerk aged twenty-two. By 1913 one of her young single male lodgers was Frederick Levi Attenborough (Fred), born in Stapleford, just four miles away, to the west of Nottingham. Fred had been a pupil at Sam Clegg's Pupil-Teacher Centre and had now joined the teaching staff at the new Long Eaton school where Sam was head. Latterly Fred had been living at 82 Selborne Street on the edge of the Toxteth area in Liverpool where he was a 'Certified assistant schoolmaster at elementary school', according to the 1911 Census. Fred taught at the Long Eaton school for almost two years before he left for Cambridge, as we shall see later.

Mary had changed schools in 1910, aged fourteen, to join the new Long Eaton school where her father was in charge. If she hadn't known Fred Attenborough from the days when he was a pupil-teacher under Sam Clegg she would by 1913 have known him as both a teacher in her school and as a neighbour. Apparently Mr Attenborough also taught dancing after school on Fridays, and for a while there were dancing sessions at the school on Saturday evenings. These events may well have endeared Fred Attenborough to quite a number of female pupils at the time!

The new school may have had several attractions for Mary when she went there in 1910. She would certainly have been attracted by her father's own educational philosophy, and she may have considered teaching as a future profession for herself and known that she could become a pupil-teacher in 1912 when she was aged sixteen without changing schools again. She may already have considered the possibility of even higher education by way of a university degree and realised that the pupil-teacher route enabled her to stay on in higher education closer to the age at which she could then apply and enrol for a degree. Mary seems to have had an early aptitude for learning languages and had taken advantage of the French available on the curriculum. By the start of her final school year in 1913 she probably took up the option available to start learning Latin, seeing that this could be advantageous if she later hoped to study modern European languages at degree level. By the autumn of 1913 Mary must have already decided to apply to take a degree course, but where and how?

CHAPTER FIVE

DAWN OF 1914

On New Year's Day 1914 the radical weekly literary publication *The New Age* published an article penned by 'A Rifleman', who argued that success in war:

> *carries with it the potentiality of the highest form of economic development ... [and] the highest degree of physical and moral development.*

Just seven months later the First World War erupted, resulting eventually in some thirty million military casualties, dead and wounded, national economies and former empires shattered, expectations and dreams changed forever – hardly an opportunity for 'physical and moral development'. However, as the new year dawned in 1914 there was no clear indication or suggestion of impending major conflict. Warning signs were there for those who chose to look, with the rise of nationalism and the constant clamouring of the many and diverse ethnic groups within the Austro-Hungarian Empire for recognition and self-determination, and the rapid militarisation of Germany, unified under the dominance of Prussia after the Franco-Prussian War in 1870. In Britain, however, these seemed to be very distant distractions, and the view was that the domestic front was if anything more unstable than the international situation. Politics and the general population were more introspectively concerned with ongoing matters like the struggle for Home Rule in Ireland, the rise of the organised labour movement and the suffragette campaign. Sylvia Pankhurst had proclaimed in a speech in December 1913 that:

We will make the Cabinet members shake in their shoes until they are afraid for their very lives.

Trade union membership was growing rapidly amidst a wave of strike action and considerable social change. Even in Europe, despite the underlying agitations, the new year was welcomed in an atmosphere of relative calm. The British Army and Navy, we are told, had plans in place, but were seemingly talking about 'what if' rather than 'when'.

During the course of my research, I was initially lacking in hard information and evidence about what Mary was doing between the years 1914, when she finished her formal schooling, and 1922, when she married, in other words a significant part of her life between the ages eighteen and twenty-six. I have seen references to Mary described as a 'suffragette'. Whilst it would be almost a given that Mary would have been sympathetic to the long-term aims of the suffragist movement there is no hard evidence that

she was an active participant in the suffragette campaign, which in any case was largely suspended during the war years.

Mary's family knows very little about this period, apart from the suggestion that at some stage during the war she may have helped on local farms in the equivalent of the later Women's Land Army. A faded photograph of a group of young people, including Mary, working on a hayrick, with the note 'Costock 1916' on the back, seemed to confirm Mary's participation in this particular aspect of the war effort at some stage. Costock is a village in

Mary Clegg, aged around 18, c.1914, by Edwin Hadley, photographer, Nottingham

south Nottinghamshire about twelve miles from Mary's home. An article in the *Leicester Evening Mail* on 4 June 1943 about a Miss Dorothy Elliott, then organising secretary of the Women's Land Army in Leicestershire and Rutland, mentions the fact that during the First World War it was on her father's farm that:

> *the experiment was made of employing women on the land, and following the success of the experiment, his farm in the Midlands was used as a training centre for members of the Women's Land Army. …* One of the first trainees on the farm was Mrs. F.L. Attenborough [then Mary Clegg], *wife of the principal of Leicester University College.*

By January 1915 more than 100,000 men who worked on British farms had gone to war, causing serious disruption to vital food production and seasonal work. A number of young women began to volunteer to work on the land, but there was a reluctance in some quarters initially to encourage the use of female labour on the land. It was thought that women would not be able to cope with the physically demanding work. Volunteering by various groups of young women nevertheless became more organised throughout 1916. In January 1917 Meriel Talbot (later Dame Meriel Talbot, DBE, in recognition of her civilian war work) became director of the newly established Women's Branch of the Board of Agriculture and Fisheries. Two months later she co-ordinated the various groups of volunteers into the Women's Land Army and established a formal recruitment and training system for young women over eighteen. By 1918 it is estimated that around 300,000 women were working on the land.

Home Farm in Colston Bassett, a village east of Nottingham and about twelve miles from Costock, was owned by Mr M Knowles in 1914 and was tenanted by his agent, Mr Elliott, father of Miss Dorothy Elliott, referred to in the above article. Home Farm soon became one of around 250 training centres across the country for the volunteers, including Mary Clegg (Attenborough) according to the 1943 article. To what extent Mary was trained or how many hours she was able to offer at a time when she was continuing her higher education studies (see Chapter 7) we do not know.

Whilst I was following up a different strand of the research I came across the one and only reference I have seen to 'Mary Attenborough B.A.' (in a document dated 1942). When I asked Sir David Attenborough about this in early 2020 he said that the family had always 'assumed' that their mother had a degree, but had never really thought about how, when and where she may have obtained it, other than the knowledge that she had spent some time at the Sorbonne in Paris and possibly also in Bologna, Italy:

> *I never remember her mentioning that she had a degree. It was simply assumed that she had one but whether that was in Paris or Bologna I don't know.*

In the event the degree came at neither of these famous institutions. I assumed, therefore, that Mary had perhaps spent a few weeks or a term in Paris at some stage, and possibly also in Bologna, in order to enhance her linguistic skills. The facts which subsequently emerged revealed very different intentions and outcomes.

In the new year atmosphere described above, on 8 January 1914, Mary Clegg, still only seventeen, set sail from Folkestone for France to enrol at the Sorbonne in Paris. Whilst in Paris Mary kept a detailed daily diary. The journal covering the period 8 January to 9 February 1914 in Paris was discovered in late 2019 by Janet Attenborough, David's sister-in-law, around the time I began the research in earnest. The diaries for the other months in Paris have yet to be found, if indeed they still exist, but the journal for January to February 1914 alone provides a wonderful insight into the character and personality of Mary as a seventeen-year-old from a small industrial town in the East Midlands, finding her way and observing in minute detail the life and characters of Paris on the eve of a conflict which would change the world for everyone, forever. It is also a remarkable piece of writing in its own right.

CHAPTER SIX

THE SORBONNE DIARY OF MARY CLEGG,
8 JANUARY TO 9 FEBRUARY 1914

Mary's one surviving diary covers the period from 8 January to 9 February 1914. It is written in a hardback notebook 20 x 13cm in size with 100 pages top copy and 100 pages intended for carbon copy. The extant diary is 100 pages of the carbon copy with blank facing pages. Sir David Attenborough suggested that the top copy would have been sent home by Mary at regular intervals with family correspondence to both inform and reassure her parents. That allowed Mary, on a handful of occasions, to write notes in pencil on the blank facing pages about incidents or thoughts, which she presumed best to keep to herself as a private memorandum. The variable quality of the carbon copy, coupled with Mary's own very distinct handwriting style and the passage of time, makes it an interesting task to transcribe. Mary seems to have decided to change the carbon paper at the start of each new calendar month. So the entries from the first day, 8 January 1914, are initially fairly clear, the main challenge being the tight handwriting style, but as January progresses and the carbon becomes over-used the copy becomes more faded. The most difficult sections to read are often the bottom few lines of each page, which seem to have faded most through age. On occasion they have almost disappeared completely. On 1 February, after a mere 18,400 words, Mary thankfully started to use a new carbon sheet, but even then by the end of the diary nine days later the new carbon sheet is showing signs of heavy wear!

In total the diary is a document of just under twenty-five thousand words for a single month. From a research point of view the diary is a priceless source in so many ways, even though it covers a mere thirty-three-day snapshot in time, but it is also a beautifully constructed account. Mary writes in great detail about everything she experiences, and consequently the document reveals much about her personality and character, her intellect and her almost forensic examination and total absorption of the new world she was experiencing in Paris. We therefore have not only a valuable personal account of a seventeen-year-old woman but also a fascinating piece of social history about the Latin Quarter in Paris on the eve of the First World War.

Mary seems to slip almost seamlessly from life at home in a middle-class household in a small East Midlands industrial town to life in a very fashionable and cultural quarter of one of the world's great capital cities with quite remarkable maturity for her age. From the off she has only one thought in mind – to always look forward and to embrace the new experience completely with self-confidence and with a positive work ethic, a trait that causes her frustration when she sees it lacking in others around her. She anticipates, and has no fear of, hard work. This constant drive is a feature of Mary's personality, which will be demonstrated again and again in later life.

In the diary we see so many elements of Mary's personality and character in such a short time frame. When she left home for France in January 1914, Mary was three months short of her eighteenth birthday. As such she was of an age where she was at times very much still a teenage girl and at others very much a highly sophisticated young woman finding her own way in the world and announcing her arrival as Mary Clegg, a woman with a right to be taken seriously. Consequently we see Mary as a seventeen-year-old having fun with her co-lodger, the twenty-one-year-old English student Beatrice Prynne, always referred to as 'B.' or later 'Bee' by Mary. She always respects the older women in the milieu she finds herself in, but Mary also observes and occasionally pokes gentle fun at her elders' more quirky traits in the manner of all young people but with a deeper perception than most. Occasionally Mary seems to display a certain naivety, although this could be deliberate to reassure her parents. On the other hand it may have alarmed them!

We see the serious student and bibliophile, determined to absorb, learn and take as much as she can from her time as a student, not just in a purely academic sense, but also as a total life and cultural experience, assimilated and observed in minute detail in the diary. Mary clearly starts her Sorbonne experience as an already gifted student of languages, French in particular, well-trained at her father's school in Long Eaton where Sam made a point of employing French native speakers as teachers or assistants. Sam Clegg was a strong advocate of language learning as a complete cultural experience. He would have been very keen to offer his eldest daughter the opportunity to continue her studies in the most famous university in France, and in Mary he found a very willing taker. As a gifted student she sets herself very high standards, and in return she naturally enjoys and appreciates the praise she often receives from the adults and young people around her. However, she can also on occasion be self-effacing and self-mocking. We see Mary using her new 'freedom' away from home to experiment as one would expect, even within the closely chaperoned and controlled environment she lives in. She tries new drinks when offered and clearly enjoys some more than others, she experiments with smoking, but she mostly acts with sobriety out of choice, from an instinct of not wanting to miss out on any detail of her new experience. She always enjoys finding bargains, particularly when buying clothes, and usually notes in detail and with obvious delight the prices paid and the English currency conversion in many cases. This may have been a feature of home life in Long Eaton. Although Sam Clegg was head of a senior school his salary was not enormous for the time, and it is likely that budgets at home were very closely monitored. This trait certainly features in Mary's later life. She kept detailed daily household accounts for every year of her married life. Most of these accounts books have also been preserved and were discovered along with her Sorbonne diary.

Mary's frequent detailed observations and descriptions of the people and characters and the social mores of the Latin Quarter in 1914 are remarkable for her age. Her joyful physical descriptions of the city of Paris are like paintings in words, a feature which again echoes her father's ethos of art pervading all aspects of life. It must be assumed that Mary maintained the diary for the remainder of her stay in Paris, and we can only speculate, therefore, on what has been lost. In the quoted sections below I have been faithful to Mary's own version and style. For example, Mary almost always uses a dash on occasions where we would mostly use a comma.

In the diary Mary tells us that on Thursday, 8 January 1914, she left home 'at 7 o'clock', presumably by train, arrived in London 'at 11 o'clock', left London again 'at 2 o'clock', and arrived at Folkestone 'at 4.30', whence the boat sailed 'at 5.00'. She was:

horribly ill

all the time on the boat, and was then sick again on the train from Boulogne. She arrived in Paris 'at 11.30',

got to the Hopkins about 12.30 and to bed about 2am.

Although she doesn't say so initially her father evidently travelled with her to see her settled in, and then thirty-six hours later on Saturday, 10 January, she:

said goodbye to father at 2 o'clock.

Sam presumably arrived home on Sunday ready for school again, possibly the start of the new term, on Monday. Mr and Mrs Hopkins seem to have been the key contacts and the link between Mary and her family back home while she was living in Paris. Quite how they became known to Sam Clegg in the first place to establish the connection and the base for Mary is not recorded. Sir David Attenborough also has no idea who they were or how they came to be involved. My best speculation is that Sam may have discussed the matter with his French staff at Long Eaton, possibly M. Michelle, later mentioned by Mary in the diary, and they may have known people in Paris, who helped to establish the connection. Mary stayed for four nights with the Hopkinses and then moved to rooms in a house rented by the two Misses Redfearne, Selina and Berthe, and owned by the Princesse de Monaco. The other key adult characters who feature greatly are a Mrs and Dr Austin and Mrs Fearing. All have varying roles in overseeing and sometimes chaperoning Mary to give assurance to her family back in England. All seem to have been long-term British expatriates in Paris and all are clearly well-heeled. Mary has been transported in the space of twenty-four hours from a comfortable but still modest home in Long Eaton, not just to ordinary 'digs' in Paris but to rooms in an exclusive quarter of the city on the Left Bank close to the Sorbonne and the Boulevard Saint Germain. All the more remarkable that she has the self-confidence and equanimity to take it all in her stride and to immediately and enthusiastically embrace it.

Mary did not start her first term at the Sorbonne until Monday 19 January, so she had ten days in which to acclimatise, to register for her course and to prepare for her meeting with her co-lodger, Beatrice Prynne, who arrived from England on Sunday 18, the day before term commenced. During that first week Mary was invited out several times to sample some of the cultural life on offer, always accompanied by at least one of the adults, and she was determined to take advantage of every opportunity available to her. On the evening after her arrival the Hopkinses took Mary, and presumably her father, on his only full evening in Paris before returning home, to one of their regular haunts, La Rotonde Café, a famous venue to this day in the Montparnasse Quarter, founded in 1911. In 1914 it was frequented by Pablo Picasso, who had a studio nearby, and in the interwar period it became renowned as a gathering place for intellectuals, artists and writers. When Mary visited for the first time, less than twenty-four hours after her arrival in Paris, she calmly observed the girls, who:

> sat at the tables and let the men treat them to drinks – when one left them many just sat still and waited until someone else sat down beside them. All the drinks were served on plates on which was printed the price. If no one paid for a girl she would gather up her collection of plates and walk round until someone accepted them. La Rotonde evidently a place where it would be impossible to go unchaperoned – as seems to be the case with every café and restaurant in Paris.

Very different from Nonconformist nightlife in Long Eaton, one suspects! Did Mary understand what was going on here? We can only speculate.

Two days later Mary went with Mr Hopkins to see *La Tosca* at the Opéra Comique. Later they were joined by Mrs Fearing, who says:

Yes, I saw you, I have been watching you.

In the diary Mary notes, in a slightly amused tone of self-mockery:

We wondered what on earth we had been doing but couldn't think of anything very awful – by her manner afterwards we judged that we had passed muster.

On this same day, twenty-four hours after her father had left to return home, Mary was at pains to stress her independence:

Mrs F ... thought I might see as much as I could before my studies began so asked what I would like to go to and if my father minded what I saw. I said not in the least – I saw or read what I liked.

Her empathy with the independent, even rebellious, spirit in others is hinted at on 2 February in one of her observations of life on the streets of Paris:

Everywhere you go in Paris you meet soldiers – either a very shabby company of foot-soldiers in their navy blue coats and dirty red trousers or else a very smart company of horse soldiers with most wonderful head-dresses. It is amusing to notice a young soldier when he meets his superior officers – the first one he will salute – the

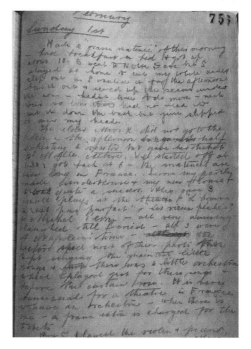

A sample page of Mary's Sorbonne Diary, Sunday 1 February 1914

same with the next, but when he meets a third it is beginning to get rather boring so he studiously keeps his face turned the other way while the officer glares at the back of his head.

Mary has a particular fascination with prevailing fashions of the time, one of the features which make the diary such an important piece of social history. She has an eye for detail and records it in the manner of an artist capturing an image on canvas. At the Opéra Comique she notes that:

it is the fashion at present to enter soirées, operas and theatres wearing no outdoor wraps but carrying a huge muff. Was very amused to see 2 young girls of about eleven years old walking up and down talking and gesticulating in a very grown up manner each carrying a large muff. And the children here seem to be women at about seven years old.

Mary also noted on this occasion that:

If a lady wishes to rouge or powder she does so quite unceremonially as she walks along as it is no longer chic to hide the fact that one makes up but rather to advertise it. I seldom see anyone over fifteen, English, American or French, who does not powder.

When Mary moved from the Hopkinses after four nights to her new rooms in the house of the Misses Redfearne, she explored the house and quickly found the piano to play and a large collection of music, but:

alas no Gilbert & Sullivan – will have to get a copy of the Mikado somehow.

Combining her language and musical skills she then:

Found a book of Schubert's songs – in French – I learnt one or two.

At lunchtime, or 'luncheon', as Mary always calls it:

> *Miss R. gave me some Muscat – as it was sweet – I liked it very much but one can only drink a little as it is so strong. Also had a drop of Triple-sec Cointreau which is stronger still. The Misses R. are evidently connoisseurs in wine.*

These little experiments are recorded with a very understated and matter-of-fact sobriety. For Mary they are nothing to get overly excited about. Similarly we hear very little from Mary about French cuisine. For Mary there are simply more interesting things to observe and absorb in Paris, although she does record:

> *Tried some salad made of endives at dinner but couldn't stand the taste of the oil.*

In the week before term starts Mary has her first taste of shopping in Paris and visiting the large stores. With Mrs Hopkins she visits a sale at the Bon Marché, an institution where:

> *A person can begin as a floor sweeper and rise to the position of director.*

A social comment perhaps with echoes of the co-operative movement with which Mary would have been very familiar from home. In the store itself:

> *I have never seen a shop so crowded and looking down from the upstairs the ground floor was just black with people like a beehive.*

Also lodging in the same house as Mary was a lady from Alsace, aged about thirty-five, a former governess, who spoke French and German equally well:

> *While in Germany once she learned manicure and massage and finding that it paid very much better than teaching gave up her situation and now has a large clientele of society ladies.*

This may have made rather depressing reading for Mary's father. The same lady explained to Mary that fashions in nails change as much as anything else:

*It used to be the fashion to cut the nails an oval shape to follow the lines
of the finger ends but now the nails must come to a point in the middle.
I don't like it a lot, have noticed that all the 'chic monde' have their nails
trimmed in that way.*

The culture change from life in Long Eaton to lodging in a house belonging
to the Princesse de Monaco in the most fashionable Quarter of Paris must
have been immense, yet Mary calmly observes life and takes it all in her
stride:

*Miss R. happened to be talking of some Duchess one day and on
enquiring it seems that this Duchess – the sister of the King of Belgium,
comes to see her whenever she comes to Paris.*

On Wednesday evening, 14 January, Mary, making full use of the week
before term begins, went to the Opéra Comique again with Mrs Hopkins
to see Massenet's *Werther*. Emerging from the theatre at a quarter to
midnight Mary notes that:

*The street seemed almost as crowded at 12 o'clock at night as in the daytime
– taxis whizzing about and all the trams at work. Seems to be quite the
thing here for the ladies to walk to the theatre in the high heeled evening
shoes and thin silk stockings although it is freezing hard. At 12 o'clock
all the theatres, the operas and the cinemas are disgorging people and the
restaurants are full – many of the cinemas are being filled up again.*

The following day, Thursday 15 January, was the day for students to
immatriculate and register for their courses at the Sorbonne. At this stage
it becomes clear that Mary was planning to study for the *Licence ès Lettres*
(French equivalent of a British bachelor of arts degree) over three to four
years. She was given set book lists for 1914 and 1915 and refers to an:

exam a year next July

i.e. July 1915. She would be taking a languages course with elements
of French, Latin, German and English. On the following day she was

again at the Opéra Comique with Mr Hopkins to see *Manon*, and at an interval Mary talked with Mrs Fearing, who was to give her 'diction' classes and:

> it was understood that I should stay with her until a year next July [1915] – after that she didn't promise anything.

Mrs Fearing asked Mary:

> if I'd be able to go to Fontainebleau with her in the summer or if I should want to go home. I said I'd love to go with her. Told her I had a week's holiday at Xmas, a fortnight at Easter and all July, Aug, Sept and Oct in the summer.

Mary was calmly and carefully planning the next three years of her life in Paris in what seemed like the halcyon days of early 1914 just seven months before Europe would explode into a conflict, which would shatter and reshape lives and dreams forever.

On Friday 16 January, whilst Mary was with Mr Hopkins to see Massenet's *Manon*, she delighted in a detailed description of the sets and costumes, but in particular she:

> liked the music a lot better than that in 'Werther' – most of the time it was very light and ripply and the loveliest little airs kept coming in over and over again. Mr Attenboro' would just have delighted in it – he certainly would have wanted to get up and dance.

This is the first of two references to Fred Attenborough in this diary. At that date Fred was twenty-six and was teaching under Sam Clegg at the school in Long Eaton that Mary had just left, and we know that he gave dancing lessons after school and arranged social dances at the school. The seventeen-year-old Mary obviously had an insight into Fred's personality and musical tastes by this stage.

Mary enjoys being praised and flattered, not unnaturally, and writes about it. On Sunday 18 January, after several visitors to the house have departed, Mary writes:

When Miss R. tells people what I am doing they hold up their hands in surprise and say I am very very young. I tell them I am nearly 18 – they are again surprised and say I look about 15 – everybody who comes says the same – I don't get tired of hearing it.

However, the reality also sets in:

Most people seem to think I am flying very high at my age – to take the L ès L in a language which is not my own – I've resolved not to think of the awfulness of it.

Later the same day Mary is introduced to her new co-lodger, Beatrice Prynne, three years older than Mary, just returned from home in England to resume her studies. During the period covered by the remainder of the diary Mary and Beatrice appear to develop a close friendship of mutual support, although in outlook the two young women seem to be poles apart. Mary writes that:

she is a sweet girl – can dance the Tango and all the latest dances – says she lives for tennis in the summer and dancing in the winter – says she doesn't like work of any kind – only thing she can bear in the shape of work is her drawing – didn't want to come back to France a bit, she had been having such a good time in England.

As she helps her companion to unpack Mary notes that she:

has a most lovely and fashionable wardrobe – her boots even have beaded tops, has four evening dresses … a wine-coloured opera cloak and a long string of real pearls given to her by an aunt many years ago – wears either white embroidered or black satin underskirts.

Mary started term at the Sorbonne on Monday 19 January 1914. The first lecture she attended was in the *Amphithéâtre*, a monumental hall, inaugurated in 1889, with seating for almost a thousand people. Mary does not describe the magnificence of the venue, perhaps because she is so focussed and attentive to the lecture on her first day. In the afternoon, after some confusion over changed timetables, Mary asked a *professeur* where she could find out about the changes. The *professeur* repeatedly explained that Mary would first have to take the *baccalauréat* and refused to listen when she said she had already done so. Mary's frustration manifested itself when:

> *I stamped my feet … and he gave a patient sigh as if to say I was absolutely past redemption. I don't think he believed me even then so I turned on my heel and left him.*

Mary is determined that she will be taken seriously from the start, possibly the first time she has encountered such a negative attitude from adults, and a lesson for the future. Her efficient and very organised approach to life and her expectation of the same efficiency in others was once more offended on her second day when she again found timetable alterations:

> *Strikes me they spend their time there in altering room, hour and lectures for each subject – if you don't keep your eye on the affiches [notices] every day you are sure to go wrong.*

By the third day of term, despite yet more timetable alterations, Mary has relaxed sufficiently for her to be able to paint a wonderful picture of life at the Sorbonne:

> *I never saw such a place as the Sorbonne for rushing about – everybody runs into the lectures and runs out – no one is ever seen walking down a corridor – always rushing and hurriedly scanning the notice boards as they rush by – if one is in a courtyard one sees people rushing from all the entrances and making a dash for a certain door. The way the students dress who attend these lectures is amazing. Quite half the girls wear velvet silk or satin dresses with draped skirts and extravagantly low necks – pendant bracelets and rings galore – and of course earrings and jewelled ornaments in their hair – then they wear very smart hats and beautiful furs and without exaggeration I can say that half of them have lovely fur coats – not only seal and coney but all kinds – it seems very funny to see such a girl take off her furs and sit down with a*

notebook and a fountain pen and scribble away for dear life for an hour. A fact that has struck me very much in Paris is that nearly all the girls and women can have lovely furs and many have fur coats – irrespective of their social position.

Later that day Mary had a diction lesson with Mrs Fearing and Mlle Even, who:

told me to work hard at my French for it would be worth the trouble – said I had a very good accent and read well.

Another compliment for Mary, and good reading for the folks back home. Mrs Fearing is very generous and often bestows fancy gifts on Beatrice, but practical gifts on Mary, to help with her studies. In later married life in particular Mary was meticulous about keeping detailed accounts and monitoring her domestic budget, and at this stage she notes with amusement quirky traits in others relating to economy:

It seems so funny that Mrs F. should be so wildly extravagant in some things and so economical in others – she has fits of economy – she thinks it is a great sin to waste a stamp on a letter destined for Paris when you can always find someone to take it.

In the entry for Saturday 24 January, Mary describes social etiquette, which she has observed in Paris:

Have just noticed that everybody in France shakes hands at any available opportunity. All the men and girls shake hands with their friends when they come and when they leave in a morning and the same in the afternoon. If a workman meets a comrade in the street he shakes hands with him and does the same when he leaves him – so do all the market women and servant girls. When introduced to anybody it is not correct just to bow – you must shake hands. I shake hands with the Misses R. when I get up in the morning and when I go to bed at night and whenever I enter or leave the house. I hear much about the politesse of the French but don't see much of it in the streets, metro and tramways. Have never yet seen a Frenchman get up and offer his seat to a lady – the men all remain seated no matter how many ladies are standing. If a man and his wife enter a tram or the metro and there is only one available seat lots of the men take it and the women look upon it all as a matter of course.

Although Mary likes to record other people's foibles this is often done in a light and humorous manner, particularly regarding the characters closest and most important to her in Paris, and she is also generous in her praise of those same figures in equal measure. Mary's ability to throw herself wholeheartedly into her academic work, while at the same time having the sheer intellectual energy to observe and record the people and the world around her in minute detail, is remarkable for a young woman of her age. As she gets to know her co-lodger, Beatrice Prynne, she is well aware that the two students are very different in their attitude and application to work, but she understands that if she makes compromises and accepts Beatrice for who she is then their friendship and indeed partnership can be mutually beneficial. In later life Mary was not always willing or happy to compromise, particularly when she was absolutely convinced of the justice of her argument, but in her present position she had the common sense to do so. In some ways she has a genuine admiration for her slightly older and possibly more worldly-wise companion. On the Saturday at the end of the first week of term Mary and Beatrice go together to the Vieux Colombia (now the Vieux Colombier), a small and new theatre at the time, opened in 1913. Mary comments:

B. looked lovely in an evening dress of black satin with red tulle in her hair, bands of red satin over her shoulders and a huge red rose at her waist – she really is a lovely girl and such a dear.

This occasion was the first time Mary had been to the theatre unchaperoned:

B. and I had to walk home at 11.30 by ourselves – not far by any means but through rather lonely streets – am sure the Austins and the Hopkins won't like it when they know.

Her tutor, Mrs Fearing, thinks it is ridiculous that a girl cannot go out without a chaperone, but Mary comments:

That is all very well carried so far but Mrs F. doesn't know everything.

Occasionally there are comments in the diary when it appears maybe Mary has not quite yet crossed the threshold from teenage girl to young woman. When Beatrice went to a *croquis* (life class) at the school of art one afternoon Mary writes:

Anyone can go to these croquis and can stay for the two hours – everybody has to pay 50 centimes (5d) as they come out. B. says that it is at night that she sees the queerest people there – it is much freer too than in a morning. In the morning no one is allowed to speak to their models but at night the models have a good time. One of these nights I am going with B. just to see what it is like.

Unfortunately Mary's visit must have been after the end of this diary!

On Tuesday 27 January, Mary finished at the Sorbonne at half past three, and walking back home she was able to observe and paint a picture of aristocratic life in Paris:

When I went out people were just arriving to pay their calls. There were private carriages or motors all down both sides of the Boulevard and a bit later on they would be waiting down all the side streets. Many of the carriages had Coronets and Coats of Arms on them and had two footmen in livery. The Boulevard St Germain is in the most aristocratic quarter of Paris – there are nobles sprinkled all over the place – all the houses are very old – Miss R. has to pay 110 francs a year for the rent of her plot mainly because of the quarter it is in.

Just occasionally we see a 'provincial' side to Mary, even though she normally accepts people for who they are. On Wednesday 28 January, Mary was attending a lecture when:

A most awful fop came into the lecture – he had a suit of dark heliotrope

coloured cloth – the coat cut in very much at the waist – a big black satin
bow for a tie with ends streaming down nearly to his waist – nobody
seemed to take much notice of him – such freaks are quite common in
Paris.

The subtext seems to be 'but not in Long Eaton'.

We also see the girl who loves a bargain. Mary loves to browse the large
and colourful stores in Paris, especially when the sales are on. She visits
a store called Le Printemps with Mrs Hopkins, intent on looking for a
blouse in the sale as 'they are all awfully dear'. After much searching with
Mrs Hopkins, Mary:

was just giving up in despair when we found a very pretty little yellow
satin blouse which was only 12 francs (10 shillings) and all the others
that were at all decent had been from 15 francs upwards. This blouse
was originally 20 francs and had been marked down once to 15 francs
and then to 12 francs. Mrs H. seemed to think it was a great bargain
and she said you generally get a very ordinary looking blouse for 12
francs – this was really a very swanky blouse so with one last lingering
look at my 12 francs I bought it.

The pair then went on to the Galerie Lafayette in search of some trimming
for a dress. Despite causing much amusement Mary was able to laugh at
herself:

I caused a great laughter amongst several of the shop women when we
discovered that my hat was trimmed with a pair of fancy garters – how
on earth they got on my hat is a mystery.

Mary's relationship with the small group of English adults seemingly
entrusted with her welfare in Paris, the Hopkinses, the Austins, the two
Misses Redfearne and Mrs Fearing, is interesting. All of them at regular
intervals check with Mary that she has all the books and study materials
she needs, and they also seem to act as her 'bankers', making sure she has
sufficient cash for her daily needs. Mr and Mrs Hopkins seem to be the
anchor point, the initial link between Paris and Long Eaton. Sir David

Attenborough asked me if I knew who the Hopkins were. So far I have not been able to find any information about them whatsoever. The impression gained from Mary's diary is that they, and indeed all the other members of this small group, were by then long-established expatriates. Mary is clearly fond of the Hopkinses and especially the Austins. Mrs Fearing can be quite unpredictable at times and possibly more 'intimidating'. Mary handles this very calmly, does not allow herself to be intimidated and finds it humorous at times. On one occasion Mrs Fearing asked Mary if she wanted any more money:

> *I said I still had some left but took this opportunity to tell her what a lot it costs on tram fares – often a franc a day which is atrocious. Mrs F. said 'Oh yes' she knew it would cost me a lot what with my books and everything else … whereupon she sighed and looked very resigned. Of course on these occasions Mrs F. rambles on in French and nearly has a fit if you show you don't understand something she says. She got up and asked B. to tell her quite bluntly if I had proper meals – she evidently thought I wasn't getting any fatter – I told her that I eat much more than I used to eat in England – which pleased her very much.*

Mary herself comments that Beatrice on the other hand, despite being three years older than Mary, 'gets flustered' in Mrs Fearing's company and retreats into her shell, once again just the opposite to Mary. Mrs Fearing:

> *was very anxious to know if I was alright and said B. was a lovely girl, very sweet etc. etc. but was much too silent – such a pity – never had anything to say for herself – she can't say that of me – Miss R. said she didn't find B. very silent – perhaps she was shy with Mrs F. – Mrs F. said she had no reason to be shy with her. B. is not at all silent really but she has let herself get frightened of Mrs F.*

At seventeen, just three months short of her eighteenth birthday, Mary is very much at a transitional phase in her life between provincial teenage girl and urbane sophisticated young woman. Her experience of Paris possibly accelerates the transition as Mary responds to the signals around her. She has already observed and remarked upon the fact that in Paris, as we might analyse it today, the over-sexualisation of young girls makes them seem like women at the age of seven. On the last day of January a Mlle d'Acosta came to lunch:

> *I happened to have my hair done straight back in one plait – after some time she said that before when I had my hair done in the plaits at the back of my head I looked about 14 but now I looked no more than 11.*

Five days later we note that:

> *am doing my hair in plaits round my ears as a preliminary to doing it up.*

She still cannot hide her almost childish joy and feels 'very triumphant' when she finds a bargain, but she is happy to do her own alterations to clothes to make herself feel and look more sophisticated. On account of her maturity when it comes to her approach to her work Mary is often treated, and is expected to act like, an adult. This, however, also allows her to recognise aspects of her own personality and even smile at them. On the first day of February Mary and Beatrice pay a visit to a wealthy American, Mrs McNally, and her daughter in their suite of rooms:

> *in a very swanky hotel … from the McNallys' drawing room window you have a most lovely view – can see right across the Jardin des Tuileries and a good deal of Paris.*

Shortly after making Mary's acquaintance Mrs McNally recognises that Mary's tendency to be 'bossy' when she feels it to be appropriate might make her an ally in disciplining Beatrice and Mrs McNally's own daughter. Mary notes with amusement:

> *Mrs McN said she hoped I'd discipline B. – B. said there was no need to tell me as I tried to discipline everybody I came across. The McNally [daughter] and I got into a long argument over English professors – hadn't time to finish or else B. and I would have been late for dinner – Mrs McN said I must come again very soon and finish the argument*

and I must be sure to sit on the McN. B. and the McN say they are
going to join forces and stand up against me – they have a strong
objection to being sat upon.

In the first week of February Mary started Italian lessons and clearly
enjoyed them. Mary would eventually 'major' in Italian when she finally
obtained a degree in modern languages. By the time she started Italian
she was looking for justification and a good reason to drop or reduce the
amount of time spent on learning German:

Had my German lesson at night – am sure I shall never know German
if I learn for ever – when there are about a dozen ways of writing each
letter and how each form must be used for one special thing what is a
body to do? – and I can't remember a bit what letter is which.

Two days later by contrast after an Italian lesson Mary is full of joy:

The professor was delighted with the way I answered his questions –
Mrs F. was too. At the end of the lesson he praised me up to the skies
and said I should know Italian in no time – and I was by far the best
scholar he had ever had. Mrs F. said yes – he certainly hadn't been spoilt
in the way of scholars and said to me you know they were all so stupid
and never paid any attention – that included poor Bee who hated it and
Miss Payne who hated it even more and in the end refused to learn it
and I don't know how many more unfortunates. The professor is really
a wonderful teacher – it is his fault that I get on not mine.

The last point is interesting and probably rings true for many people.
Good teachers at senior school often have a significant influence on
pupils' later subject choices and even careers. Two days later again Mary
admits:

have almost decided to take Italian instead of German for my Licence
because it is much easier and I shall therefore learn it much quicker,

but one of the reasons for this is:

The Austrian girl isn't a good [German] teacher. Mrs F. asked me if she was and I really couldn't say anything but yes! She served simply as a reference. I learned my work and if there is anything I don't understand she explains – she gives me new words and certain parts of the book to learn for the next lesson – she follows the book all the time. However she is going away for good these summer holidays and so I shall have another teacher – by then anyhow I shall have got a good start in my German which is better than nothing.

Less strong-minded individuals than Mary could well have been influenced by the knowledge that her older roommate, Beatrice, absolutely hated Italian, but Mary had made up her own mind and nobody else would distract from her own decisions. Two very contrasting teachers had helped her to make her choice.

On 2 February Mary detects early signs of spring and makes more observations of features of the capital:

Paris is lovely just now – it is very much warmer and we get quite a lot of sun. I enjoy very much coming back at night from Mrs F. on the top of a bus – never tired of seeing the Seine surrounded with hundreds of little lights and the big open square of the Place de la Concorde. One of the great beauties of Paris is that it possesses so many of these large squares which seem so open and free in spite of all the traffic. There are so many wide streets too – the Cours la Reine is a beautiful street – it is divided into four parts by lines of trees and banks of grass – the widest division is for ordinary traffic and is as wide as one of our widest streets – then there are two divisions for pedestrians and one for horsemen. So many of the Paris streets are divided up in this way. The streets always look so clean for at intervals along the gutters are water taps which are turned on every so often and thus all rubbish in the gutters is washed away.

As previously mentioned Mary almost certainly sent the top copies of her daily entries back to Rye Hill Close with her regular letters to her family. An interesting feature of the diary in the carbon copy version which survived is that on four occasions Mary wrote notes in pencil on the blank facing pages. Sir David Attenborough suggested that these were in the form of 'notes to self', which she wanted to record but did not necessarily want her parents to see. With each note there is an intriguing air of mystery. Opposite the entry for Tuesday 19 January, she writes:

> *Saw my nice dark man for the first time – sat opposite him in the library – wonder if I shall see him again?*

In this diary there is no further mention of the 'nice dark man'. Opposite Saturday 31 January, she writes:

> *Wonder if I shall ever get to know this man. Have found myself somewhere near him at almost every lecture. He has always got his eyes glued … am interested in him but don't know why.*

On Tuesday 3 February, Mary writes:

> *Went to the lib. but didn't see my nice man. Dreamt that I got engaged to Mr A – and that I didn't mind half as much as I thought I should.*

The final such entry is two days later when Mary records another incident in the library:

> *Went into the lib at the college this afternoon. There was no one sitting facing me and opposite for about 4 tables. At the 5th there were 2 fellows. They were always looking at me and laughing and talking to each other. At last one got up – walked right down the room – of course I looked up and he grinned – he walked up and at the back of me and coming back stood stock still behind me and looked at what I was doing – then went and engaged in animated conversation with the other.*

Mary immersed herself in the total experience of Paris with her eyes wide open and her brain receptive to every stimulus – one reason why we see many wonderful images and descriptions of people and places. She makes hardly any references to the folks back home, only briefly when she receives a letter about every two weeks and when she once shops for presents for her sisters. From these we learn the familiar names of her siblings. Margaret is referred to as 'Mag', Barbara is 'Bab' or 'Babs' and Dorothy is 'Doll'. There are no references to homesickness; Mary is so absorbed by the Paris experience that there is no time for sentimentality, and she perhaps senses that any concerns her parents may have would be best allayed by her positive outlook and the humorous touches in the diary entries she sends back home. Sam Clegg's own views on art and beauty would be vindicated by his daughter's writings and records. Only in the very last words of this journal, written on Monday 9 February 1914, do we see a moment's reflection of home when a photo arrives with a letter:

> Got the home letter at night. The picture of Alec is just lovely – it makes me want to see him and hug him all the more.

Alexander, or 'Alec', Mary's youngest sibling and only brother, was four years old at the time.

CHAPTER SEVEN

AFTER THE SORBONNE

We cannot know for certain the chain of events after 9 February 1914 when the diary finishes. Presumably Mary continued with her courses at the Sorbonne until the end of June when term would have finished. Her plan, as mentioned in the diary, was to spend the summer in the village of Samois, near Fontainebleau just outside Paris, where Mrs Fearing had a country home and regularly arranged Italian classes out of term time. Mary did not even originally plan to return to England to visit family during that summer. Whether she made it to Samois or not we cannot be certain, but if she did she would not have spent the whole summer there as planned. On 4 August 1914 Britain officially declared war on Germany after a rapid chain of events during the previous week. It is likely that Mary returned to England at some time during July 1914 when the threat of war was becoming a reality.

On returning home from Paris, presumably in great disappointment at the unavoidably premature termination of her Sorbonne adventure, Mary and her family had to act quickly if she wanted to pursue a

Mary Clegg 1915-17

degree course, with the start of the new academic
year only weeks away, and with war potentially
disrupting the status quo. Despite the upheaval
caused by the outbreak of war academic terms
did continue on time in the autumn of 1914.
However, courses were disrupted or suspended
for many young men, who answered the call for
volunteers on the Western Front, and many never
returned to complete their courses.

My first hunch regarding Mary's path after
the Sorbonne fortunately proved to be correct,
and with the efficient help of the University of
London and University of Nottingham archives
and records teams I was able to confirm that Mary
took an external University of London degree.

Mary Clegg 1915-17

A number of early universities or university
colleges in the first half of the twentieth century
were not able to award their own degrees until
they achieved the necessary status to do so.
It was possible to take University of London
degrees at several institutions, including the then
University College Nottingham, and this was the
closest higher academic institution at the time to
Long Eaton. Enquiries through Senate House,
University of London, revealed that Mary Clegg
was awarded a BA (Hons) degree in Italian
in 1921 as a 'day student at University College
Nottingham and by private study'. In discovering

*Mary Clegg, "A giddy
Saturday night" 1915*

Mary's 'academic career' I also found out that Mary's closest sister in age,
Margaret Clegg, was awarded a BSc (Hons) degree in botany, also in 1921,
and also as a day student at Nottingham.

University College Nottingham had been founded in 1877, built on
land owned by the City Corporation in Shakespeare Street in the city centre
and opened in 1881 to meet an increasing demand in the late nineteenth
century to make university-standard education available for those unable
to attain or afford Oxford or Cambridge. Initially day students were

admitted from the age of fourteen to give those leaving school at the age of thirteen a chance of secondary, rather than higher, education, and the opportunity to take 'university extension' courses. This changed after the Education Act 1902. The Clegg family home in New Sawley was a two-minute walk from the railway station, and it is reasonable to assume that both Mary and Margaret would have travelled in to the college daily by train, a twenty-minute journey.

Mary had 'matriculated' at the Long Eaton School in 1913 and then enrolled at University College Nottingham as a day student for the 1914/15 academic year, within weeks of the disappointment of having to leave Paris. The annual fee for all day students attending not less than four hours weekly was just five shillings (5s.), or twenty-five pence in modern currency. The local fee for a final exam in courses administered by the University of London was £1.10s. (£1.50). For the first three years Mary was enrolled for an intermediate arts course with a range of subjects at differing levels all leading to a three-year BA course and honours degree by 1921. Subjects available to students included English, Latin and Logic at intermediate level, plus French at BA level and Italian at honours level. German was also available. Classes in Italian, Spanish and Portuguese were arranged if sufficient numbers of students were interested.

The head of modern languages was Professor E. Weekley MA, and one of the German teaching staff was L. Biach, an interestingly similar name to one which plays a major role in this story later. We learn that Mary studied, amongst other things, classic authors such as Victor Hugo, Racine and Corneille, plus mediaeval classics like *La Chanson de Roland* and *Vie de Saint-Alexis* to illustrate Old French and Historical Grammar.

Mary's sister, Margaret, meanwhile had 'matriculated' in 1915 at the Long Eaton school and enrolled at University College Nottingham in the autumn to study biology and zoology. The head of department was Professor Carr. Fees per term were 15s. (seventy-five pence) for the intermediate work and 22s.6d (£1.12) for the BSc. elements. Subjects studied included zoology, evolutionary biology, geology and botany as well as mathematics.

Sir David Attenborough told me that Mary became friends with an Italian fellow student at the Sorbonne by the name of Lia Benuzzi and that Mary spent some time at Bologna University. In August 2020 Sir

David 're-discovered' a certified copy of Mary's birth certificate translated into Italian. This was certified as a true copy (in Italian) of Mary's original birth certificate, at the Italian Consulate in London on 20 April 1920, as requested by Samuel Clegg. Whether Sam and Mary visited the consulate in London in person, or whether the request for a copy was made by post is not clear. Either way the assumption is that the document was requested to enable Mary to register at Bologna University. The date of the certificate may have been too late for a summer-term course, so it is possible that Mary spent much of the following full academic year 1920/21 in Italy. We do not know for certain, but time spent in Italy at that stage would have been well spent before taking her final exams in the summer of 1921.

Both Clegg sisters received their respective honours degrees at University College Nottingham in 1921. A note evidently pencilled in perhaps two years later in the final column of the 'Records of Students – Day Classes – Women', tracking alumni, against the entry for Mary Clegg reads simply: 'Now Mrs Attenborough of 45, Tenison Road, Cambridge'.

CHAPTER EIGHT

REFUGEES OF WAR

In October 1914, less than three months after Britain had declared war on Germany in order to honour its obligations to defend Belgium, and around the time that Mary started her degree course at Nottingham as a day student, the front-line impacts of war were brought home to many communities across Britain. Not only was the civilian population witnessing military casualties returning from the theatre of war, but many communities also saw the arrival of civilian refugees from Belgium. Both cities and smaller towns initially welcomed the refugees and sympathised with their plight.

On 16 October 1914 *The Derbyshire Advertiser* reported the arrival of a party of refugees at Long Eaton:

Twenty-four Belgian refugees who left Antwerp on Tuesday afternoon arrived at Long Eaton on Saturday afternoon. There were nine families – men, women and children – who were met at Trent [Junction] Station by the Rev. H.T.C. Swingler, Chairman of the local Refugee's Committee, Mrs Swingler and Madame Guilbert. The visitors carried small bundles containing all the belongings they possessed. As they stepped out of the train their appearance touched the hearts of many people, who bestowed money and kisses upon the children. After a formal reception at the Y.M.C.A. Rooms at Long Eaton the families left for their new homes cheered by a large crowd.

A young woman of the party, who carried a baby 7½ months old, stated that when shells began to fall in the village in which they lived she and her husband rushed out of the house, and had not met since. Another young refugee from Eerchot said both his father and brother (civilians) had been shot by the Germans.

Mary would certainly have been aware of this event as she was home from Paris and again living at Rye Hill Close. Also around this time a number of the male teaching staff from the Long Eaton School had joined the war effort. Sam Clegg managed to partly make up for this loss by the appointment to his teaching staff of two young teachers, Belgian refugees, who may have arrived with the party mentioned above or on a separate occasion. One was Mlle Verachtert, appointed to the modern languages department. She stayed for one year:

plagued unmercifully by a heartless middle school, and haunted by the school's cat, she was a very courageous young lady

according to an article by former pupil, Canon J.D. Hooley, in the excellent *Long Eaton Grammar School Jubilee Book 1960*. The other was Mlle Rosa Vaerwyck, later Mme Pauwaert.

In 1911 a French artist, M. Bissiere, had been on the staff for a short time as an art master, and Sam Clegg persuaded him to paint a mural of the Canterbury Pilgrims in Room 6 at the school. The room thereafter became known as the Chaucer Room. Rosa Vaerwyck, a former professor of figure-painting at the University of Ghent, extended this work and also created new murals of her own, with the help and 'dizzy experience' of senior pupils and some staff. She was, according to former pupil, Harry Godwin:

now expressing nostalgic affection from the Flanders countryside as she remembered it free from the defilement of war. It was she also, with fellow refugees from Belgium, who introduced into our language classes a stream of relatives of miscellaneous size, age, shape and vocalisation for conversation and 'dictées', so enlarging our familiarity with spoken French that at the ensuing Oxford Local Examinations, the class was awarded, throughout, distinction in the spoken language.

Although Mary was no longer a pupil at the school by the time the refugees arrived it is almost certain that, through her father, she would have been introduced to Mlle Verachtert and Mlle Vaerwyck. Mary would have relished the opportunity to practise her French with them, but also her experience of knowing these women and their background would have given her a deep insight and empathy into what it meant to be refugees, forced to flee their homeland by war and invasion. This would remain in her consciousness, and some twenty years later, while living in Leicester, Mary would spend ten years of her life actively and passionately involved in rescuing, assisting and defending first-hand, young refugees from the tyranny of Franco and later Hitler.

CHAPTER NINE

JOHN BRADSHAW, MARY'S MATERNAL GRANDFATHER

On 27 March 1918 the fourth close family death to occur in Mary's lifetime was that of her maternal grandfather, John Bradshaw, aged eighty-eight. There is a story within the Clegg family that John died after falling off a ladder. He may have had such an accident, but the death certificate simply records the cause of death as 'senility'. John had spent his working life since childhood in family bakeries at different locations, mainly in Leicestershire, where he had met and married Harriet Needham, whose family background was also in village bakeries. Harriet, Mary's grandmother, had already died, aged seventy-four, nine years earlier when Mary was twelve. John had retired from the bakery business apparently on health grounds in his early forties. His doctor 'ordered' him to give up work, giving him six months to live, and the couple had moved back to John's native Sawley with their only child, Mary (Mary Clegg senior, Mary Attenborough's mother). From humble beginnings John and Harriet had evidently managed to accrue and save money to the extent that in 1877 John had purchased, with the aid of a mortgage of £500, and probably with a degree of calculated risk, just over three acres of land adjacent to the railway embankment and station in the newly developing and expanding area, which came to be known as New Sawley. He had the foresight to stake an early claim in an area, which was rapidly becoming an aspirational area of choice for the new dynamic middle classes of Sawley and Long Eaton. The intention from the outset was presumably to build a new and substantial home for himself and Harriet in their early retirement and also to provide similarly for their daughter and only child, Mary, when she made her choice in marriage.

Having acquired the land in 1877 John first built the house originally known as Woodbine Cottage, with a frontage facing the former Sawley to Long Eaton turnpike road, now known as Tamworth Road, for his family. The house was completed by around 1880 or 1881. Very shortly after the birth of his eldest grand-child, Mary Clegg, in April 1896, John Bradshaw conveyed another piece of land of the original three-acre plot, adjacent to Woodbine Cottage:

> *in fee simple by an Indenture made the Twenty sixth day of February One thousand eight hundred and ninety seven*

to Samuel Clegg only, interestingly omitting his daughter from the formal conveyance title, presumably in accordance with normal custom and practice of the time. The formal transfer of the land to Sam Clegg was probably made when the new house, to become known as Rye Hill Close, was completed and ready for occupation, almost as a deferred wedding present for his only daughter and her spouse. The young couple and their one-year-old daughter, Mary, moved from the Bradshaws' house next door into a new house with many features designed by Samuel Clegg himself, following his own tenet that beauty should permeate all aspects of life. The house was built in red brick beneath a graduated slate roof. It had external features of note including 'Dutch gables' and many internal features redolent of the Arts and Crafts movement in vogue at the time in Britain. The movement had evolved as a reaction to the perceived loss of appreciation and downgrading of the decorative arts. Sam's own quest for beauty in all things fitted in perfectly with, and was no doubt in turn influenced by, the aims of the new movement. By a remarkable sequence of coincidence and good fortune of the subsequent ownership of Rye Hill Close many of the original features of the house have been preserved and lovingly cared for, which will be described in more detail later. The house is featured in the Derbyshire Volume of *The Buildings of England* series (published between 1951 and 1974), which was researched and written by the art and architectural historian Nikolaus Pevsner and a team of collaborators and co-authors. The house is also included in Erewash Borough Council's list of 'Buildings of Local Historical Interest' on account of its special architectural interest and its inclusion in Pevsner's work.

John Bradshaw had made a will on 21 August 1901 in which his daughter, Mary Clegg senior, was:

immediately before the First day of January One thousand nine hundred and twenty-six entitled during her life to the possession of the land [Rye Hill Close].

Subsequently:

By virtue of the Law of Property Act 1925 *the land ... vested on the First day of January One thousand nine hundred and twenty-six in* [Mary],

an interesting technical switch of ownership from Sam to his wife Mary Clegg senior in 1926.

By around 1906 John Bradshaw had developed another part of his three-acre plot by building on as semi-detached to the house called Rye Hill Close another substantial property at right angles to it, the two properties together forming an overall L-shape. The new property was built to face onto the lane which led under the Midland Railway line and out to the fields to the north-west of Sawley. The developed part of the lane was eventually named Bradshaw Street – the name it still bears. The new property was designed by Alfred Edward Lambert FRIBA, a Nottingham-based architect who worked on many large and prestigious projects in Nottingham itself, and particularly on Nonconformist churches across the country, including in London and Manchester. For Lambert to accept this commission to design a private house would have been a considerable coup for John Bradshaw. It was built in purple brick beneath a slate roof in the Arts and Crafts style as a doctor's house and surgery, incorporating a consulting room and a waiting room. This house also features in Pevsner and on the Buildings of Local Historical Interest list of Erewash Borough Council.

The 1911 Census shows this new property, then known as 116 Nottingham Road, as being occupied by Dr Chester Hugh Latham, aged thirty-two, Medical Practitioner (General), originally from the village of Holbrook just north of Derby, his wife, Margaret Emily, aged twenty-eight, from Saxilby near Lincoln, and their young daughter, Dorothy Margaret, aged one. Also in the household were Dr Latham's brother-in-law, Henry William Bathurst, from Gerrards Cross in Buckinghamshire, aged thirty-nine, already a widower, described as a Student (Theological), Edith Aldridge, twenty-eight, a House maid (domestic) from Woodville, South Derbyshire, and Ada Smedley, twenty-eight, a Cook (domestic) from Burton-on-Trent.

Records suggest that there were only three doctors residing in the house over the course of the following eighty to ninety years, Dr Latham, Dr Lee and Dr Hay-Heddle.

John Bradshaw's gradual development of his land was not without incident. A clash of interests with the highways authority of the time is recorded in a local newspaper. John was evidently a man of principle, who was prepared to fight his corner when he felt that common justice was on his side. On 16 July 1909 the *Derbyshire Advertiser and Journal* reported the outcome of a civil court case between the plaintiff, John Bradshaw, and defendants, Derbyshire County Council, in a dispute over alleged 'encroachment' onto the highway:

On July 8th, at Long Eaton County Court, Judge Lindley gave judgment in the Sawley boundary dispute, which has been before the Court on two occasions previously. Two months ago Mr. Bradshaw, of New Sawley, brought an action against the Derbyshire County Council to recover £6.5s. damages for the knocking down of a fence at a point at which he was building a house at New Sawley. The dispute arose through the County Council contending that plaintiff's fence encroached four feet on the highway. The facts were placed before a special jury, who found that the fence was constructed on the highway. A new trial was asked for, and his Honour granted this application, stating that the verdict was not satisfactory. Accordingly his Honour tried the case at Derby on Monday week without a jury, and on that occasion reversed his decision. His Honour, in giving judgment on July 8th, said the defendants relied on two main points, first that the fence was on the highway or turnpike road, and that it was an encroachment. After exhaustively dealing with the evidence he held that the ditch had been made by the plaintiff in pursuance of the Highways Act 1875, and that the parish award set forth that the ground owned by Mr. Bradshaw must be mowed and fenced against the turnpike road. Building had gone on until 1903 without opposition to the boundary line, and the County Council claimed that the fence was on the highway. His Honour gave judgment for the plaintiff, with costs on the higher scale.

John Bradshaw was thus vindicated, and the front boundary of Rye Hill Close seen today is the result of his action. His principled and determined stand against higher authority when he was prepared to defend what he saw as natural justice was a character trait, which would be manifested in great measure some thirty years later by his eldest granddaughter, Mary Attenborough, when she was fighting to save the lives of refugee children against the threats of a fascist dictatorship in Spain.

CHAPTER TEN

FREDERICK LEVI ATTENBOROUGH

The surname Attenborough originates from the village of the same name near Beeston, just to the south-west of Nottingham. Frederick Levi Attenborough was born in Stapleford, at the time a small town five miles west of Nottingham on the border with Derbyshire, on 4 April 1887, to Mary Attenborough senior and Frederick Augustus Attenborough. He took his middle name from his maternal grandfather, Levi Saxton. Frederick Levi's parents, Frederick Augustus and Mary (née Saxton), were both from Nonconformist Methodist families. They had married on 14 February 1882 in the parish church of St Mary Magdalene at Hucknall Torkard, the church where Lord Byron and his daughter, Ada Lovelace, and other members of Byron's family are buried. Since 1915 the town has been known simply as Hucknall. Just north of Nottingham, the town had initially developed in the eighteenth and nineteenth centuries as a centre for the hosiery and stocking frame industry and later as a coal mining town. Hucknall Torkard was Mary Saxton's hometown, where her father, Levi Saxton, was a textile manufacturer. Mary Saxton was the second of five siblings, with three brothers and a sister.

Levi Saxton is first listed as a maker of fine shawls in 1864, and we know that he was a member of the United Framework Knitters Society in the 1860s. He later joined the Hucknall Manufacturing Company as a partner with William Calladine, who had founded the company in 1856, and Andrew Radford. This company had its factory almost next door to the Saxtons' home in Albert Street. The building was only demolished in recent years to make way for an inner ring road in the town. In August 1877 the *London Gazette* reported that the company:

> *was this day* [4 August] *dissolved by mutual consent, so far as relates to and concerns the said Levi Saxton. The said business will in future be carried on by the said William Calladine and Andrew Radford, under the style aforesaid, and they will receive and pay all debts owing to or by the said firm.*

Despite his financial embarrassment Levi was soon back in the trade familiar to him, and in the 1881 Census he is described as a Manufacturer of Shetland Wool falls and shawls.

In the 1880s Levi was a member of the local Liberal Party, and he was an elected member of the Hucknall Torkard Local Board, which had responsibilities for local issues such as highways, markets, lighting and water. In later years Levi was seemingly less liberal when dealing with an incident in September 1899 of 'scrumping' from his apple trees. Three local youths were taken to court by Levi for taking apples worth 10d. According to the *Nottingham Evening Post* on 16 September 1899:

> *He had practically had his garden stripped of fruit in this manner. John M ... was dismissed on account of his youth, and each of the others ordered to pay 7/6d.*

This was the equivalent of almost £50 today.

The family business of Frederick Augustus Attenborough in Stapleford was a bakery and grocery store, with living accommodation above, located in The Roach, the main crossroads at the centre of the town, so the business would have been familiar to everyone in the town due to its prime location. Young Frederick Levi was the third of five children, with two older sisters and eventually a younger sister and brother. At the time of the 1891 Census the family also employed a 'general servant domestic', thirteen-year-old Edith Mansfield from Hallam Fields in Derbyshire. Sir David recalled that he understood there had been a 'major rift' between Frederick Levi and his parents when Frederick was around twelve. Frederick's sister,

Laura, three years his senior, had allegedly become pregnant and was told to leave the family home. Frederick said that if Laura goes he would go too. I cannot dispute this, but similarly I can find no hard evidence to support the story. According to the 1901 Census both Laura, then aged sixteen, and Frederick, aged thirteen, were still living in the family home in Stapleford. It is possible that if Laura had a baby 'out of wedlock' it may have been adopted, but if she had been asked to leave home the family must have quickly relented. In 1911 Laura was still at the family home, still single, and with all her siblings at home, apart from Frederick. Another version I have heard within the family believes this story related to the oldest sibling, Ada, who was eighteen in 1901 and was also still living at home.

Reading between the lines it may also have been the case that Frederick (Fred) had disagreed and argued with his father about education. His father may have been of the view that for his daughters formal education was unnecessary as their role would initially be as assistants in his business and then as homemakers, but this is speculation. Fred had a longer-term vision of the value of education, and crucially he could also see that education could help to forge a future career beyond the village bakery business.

Eventually, in 1903, Fred, aged sixteen, found his way to Sam Clegg's new Pupil-Teacher Centre, opened in nearby Long Eaton in 1896. He remained there until 1906 when he was nineteen. At some stage Fred also

| *Street scene in The Roach, Stapleford, c.1911, outside the Attenborough family bakery (left)*

attended classes at the People's College in Nottingham. The college had opened in 1847, initially as a day school for boys and girls, but within a few years it was also running evening classes for adults in employment, so it is quite possible that Fred was attending classes in both Long Eaton and Nottingham concurrently for a while. According to former Long Eaton alumnus and lifetime friend of the Attenboroughs, Harry Godwin, in his autobiographical account *Cambridge and Clare* (1985), Fred's next move was considerably influenced by Sam Clegg, even though he initially ignored Sam's advice. According to Godwin, Sam Clegg's love of the visual arts was matched if not exceeded by his love for the English language:

> *its superb legacy of poetry and prose, and those inherent qualities of flexibility and strength that have given it such overwhelming importance to the world.*

Sam took on much of the teaching of English to the upper forms himself, and Godwin believes that it was Sam's instruction in English of 'that gifted pupil', Fred Attenborough, that took the latter to university, even though Fred initially ignored Sam's advice to seek a place at Cambridge.

Instead Fred applied, unsuccessfully, for admission to Borough Road Training College in London with a view to a career in education. He then successfully applied for entry to Bangor Normal College in North Wales. The college in Bangor had been founded in 1858 through the efforts of The British and Foreign School Society (more of which later). It was an independent teacher training college, the term 'Normal' taken from the French concept of an *école normale*. The epithet originated in sixteenth-century century France where the intention was to provide a model school with model classrooms to teach model teaching practices to its students, thereby acting as a teacher-training institute. Bangor Normal College was eventually absorbed into the University of Wales Bangor in 1996. Fred's stay at Bangor was short-lived, however, as, according to Godwin, he 'acknowledged heart-brokenly that he already knew more English than did his new teachers'. By 1911, aged twenty-four, Fred was living and working in the suburbs of Liverpool as a 'certificated assistant schoolmaster' at an elementary school. He may have gone to Liverpool straight from Bangor. In 1913 he linked up again with his mentor, Sam Clegg, when at the age of twenty-six he joined the teaching staff at the Long Eaton school. Fred was apparently a talented amateur footballer, to the extent that he had a trial for the England international amateur team. It was a long-term football injury, which exempted him from military service.

Mindful of Sam Clegg's original encouragement to apply for Cambridge, and having saved enough from his salary at Long Eaton, Fred successfully applied and was admitted to Emmanuel College to finally pursue his university education on 1 October 1915 at the age of twenty-eight. Fred entered the college to sit the Modern and Mediaeval Languages Tripos, which he successfully completed. The *Emmanuel College Magazine* records:

> *F.L. Attenborough (B.A. 1918), formerly Scholar and Graduate Research Student of the College, was placed in the First Class of the Mediaeval and Modern Languages Tripos, obtaining the mark of distinction in Section A in 1917 and in Section B in 1918.*

Having given an undertaking to assist with college teaching he was then accepted as a research student in 1918 by H.M. Chadwick, holder of the

| *Freshmen at Emmanuel College, Cambridge, 1915, Fred Attenborough back row, third left*

university chair of Anglo-Saxon studies. In January 1920 Fred, aged thirty-two, was elected as a Junior Fellow for three years specialising in Anglo-Saxon studies. He gained an MA following his publication *The Laws of the Earliest English Kings*, which established his academic reputation. Financially he was assisted by an exhibition worth £30 for 1916/17 and by a research studentship in English philology worth £150 for 1918/19 and 1919/20. One of Fred's early new friends at Cambridge was Mansfield ('Manny') D. Forbes, a Fellow of Clare College. Forbes was passionate about the visual arts, and, like Sam Clegg in Long Eaton, Forbes was promoting them in Cambridge. It followed, therefore, that Forbes was very interested in Clegg's educational philosophy when it was explained to him by Fred Attenborough. Fred and Manny became lifelong friends. Forbes was instrumental in the founding of the Cambridge School of English in 1919.

At Emmanuel, Fred was an active member of the debating society, and from October 1919 to January 1921, when he resigned mainly due to pressure of work after his first year as a Junior Fellow, he was a member of the debating society committee during what seems to have been a 'golden era' for the society. The *Emmanuel College Magazine* for 1922/23 reports that:

> *The past academic year has not been too favourable to the Debating Society, which has had to pass through a period of reaction after the brilliance of the years immediately following the close of the war.*

Perhaps illustrating the fact that Fred was a 'mature student', who had made it to Cambridge the hard way by his own efforts and had little patience with the frivolousness of some of the motions debated, it is recorded that on 15 February 1919 he spoke in opposition to the proposal:

> *That this House disapproves of the modern tendency in this university to work in the afternoon.*

The Cambridge that Fred entered in 1915 was very different from the noisy, bustling scene he might have anticipated had he gone up to Emmanuel even two years earlier. By the start of the First World War, according to Elisabeth Leedham-Green (*A Concise History of the University of Cambridge*, 1996), the colleges:

were reduced … to echoing shadows of their former selves with fewer than half the usual number of men in residence in October 1914.

The *Magazine* for August 1915 explains:

As soon as it was realised that the finances of the town must suffer considerably from the absence of undergraduates, a joint Committee of the Town and University made representations to the War Office that some of the distress might be relieved by the presence of troops in the town. The position of the landladies of licensed lodging houses was particularly serious … The War Office accordingly arranged that an entire Welsh Territorial Division should be billeted in Cambridge and troops began to occupy the town just before Christmas.

Striking a note of rather desperate idealism and optimism the same edition of the *Magazine* says:

We must ask those men who have served their country in her hour of need to think well if they should not serve their University also, and this will be best done by their coming back to wipe out memories of the war by cherishing the old ideals and pointing the way to the younger generation.

Two years later in August 1917 the *Magazine* reports that:

The general aspect of the College has undergone no change during the last year. The Hostel has been closed since June 1916, and it is possible that some of the other staircases will be closed down during the coming year. The property of absent members is still carefully stored in expectation of their return.

Many, of course, never would return to collect their belongings. The war claimed the lives of 130 Emmanuel men, most of the casualties occurring in 1916 and 1917.

CHAPTER ELEVEN

1922 – ONE WEDDING AND TWO FUNERALS

As 1922 dawned Europe was still coming to terms with the social and economic consequences of the First World War. British Prime Minister David Lloyd George was soon to lead a conference of thirty-four nations held in Genoa, Italy, in April and May, intended to resolve outstanding economic and political issues within a shattered Europe. Key issues on the agenda were: how to rebuild a defeated Germany, and to negotiate a new relationship between Europe's capitalist economies and the Bolshevik regime in Russia. Ultimately the conference ended in stalemate, with the questions of German reparations and a potential financial aid package to Russia unresolved. Already the seeds for future conflict in Europe were being sown.

This was the early backdrop to a year, which, in the space of two months, witnessed three significant events in the family life of Mary Clegg. During the war, as we have seen, the young Mary Clegg was studying for the different stages of her eventual University of London external BA (Hons) degree, taken at the University College Nottingham. Although travelling most days into Nottingham for her coursework she was still living at the family home in New Sawley during this time. She would have kept in touch with local news and would have been aware of what was happening at her former school where her father was headmaster and where the young teacher, Fred Attenborough, had joined her father's teaching staff in 1913 and lived for a while just around the corner from the

Clegg family home in lodgings. A close friendship must have developed between Mary and Fred before the latter moved away to Cambridge in 1915. There is a hint of a close friendship in Mary's 'Sorbonne diary', and the young couple must have kept in touch for the next few years while they each focussed on their respective university courses, separated most of the time by a hundred miles.

On Thursday 23 March 1922, Mary Clegg, aged twenty-five, and Frederick Attenborough, aged thirty-four, were duly married in the Westbourne Park Baptist Chapel in Paddington, West London. Neither Mary nor Fred were particularly religious despite their strong Nonconformist family backgrounds, so the fact that they chose to marry in one of the largest Baptist chapels in the country may at first seem surprising. Fred was based in Cambridge at the time, where he had been elected as a Fellow of Emmanuel College, and Mary was still at home in New Sawley after graduating from University College Nottingham the previous summer, so London was a neutral choice of venue. However, the neutral location was far from a random choice. Westbourne Park Baptist Chapel had been established by John Clifford, originally from Sawley, who later became a nationally important figure in Nonconformist and political circles, as previously described. It is highly likely that the Clegg family had been in contact and on friendly terms with Clifford over many years. When Alexander Clegg had taken up his post as schoolmaster at the Sawley Baptist School in 1882 his predecessor in the post had been John Clifford's uncle, John Stenson. It is no coincidence that much of Sam Clegg's liberal philosophy, proactive involvement in issues of conscience, and belief in education as an essential route to achieving social justice and equal opportunities, reflected the thinking of John Clifford, irrespective of religious commitment. One can only speculate, but it could be the case that if a neutral venue was a deliberate choice of the young couple, Westbourne Park Baptist Chapel was chosen out of deep respect for a family acquaintance, John Clifford, who by then was aged eighty-five.

John Clifford was present at the wedding and almost certainly led the service in his own chapel. The registrar, whose presence was required at all marriages outside the established Church of England, was Mr Percival E. Kirk. The two other witnesses were Mary's father, Sam Clegg, and Mary's uncle, William Baxendale, who had married his second cousin, Sam's youngest sister, Bernice. It is not known whether any of Fred's immediate family were present, or indeed invited. However, Sir David told me that his father's rift from his own family after the alleged arguments about his sister, Laura, was 'profound', to the extent that Fred never talked about his family and David never met or knew any of them. It must be assumed, therefore, that the Attenboroughs were not present and not invited to the wedding. There are no surviving wedding photographs.

Less than five weeks after the wedding, on 25 April 1922, Mary's paternal grandmother, Isabella Clegg, died of a heart attack, aged seventy-four, at The Firs, the couple's home in the village of Eastcombe, near Stroud, in the Cotswolds. It seems that after the funeral Alexander Clegg probably went to stay for a while with his eldest daughter, Bernice, and her husband, William Baxendale, witness at Mary's wedding just a few weeks earlier, at their home in West Kirby on the Wirral Peninsula in Cheshire. There, just a few weeks later, on 28 May 1922, Alexander Clegg, Mary's grandfather, died from a heart condition, aged seventy-three. Both Isabella and Alexander are interred in the burial ground at Eastcombe, opposite the Baptist church. Their tomb is in a prominent position, next to the village war memorial, and directly opposite what is now Eastcombe Primary School, the former Baptist school, where Alexander was headmaster for over twenty years in total before his delayed retirement after the First World War. The house and spacious grounds where the Cleggs lived in Eastcombe, formerly The Firs, is now known as St Mary's. It has been empty since about 2018, and at the time of writing (2020) it is looking sadly derelict.

SECTION THREE

EARLY MARRIED LIFE

CHAPTER TWELVE

MARY AND FREDERICK ATTENBOROUGH IN CAMBRIDGE, 1922–25

As Mary joined her husband in Cambridge in 1922 the town and the university were still adjusting to life after the First World War. Of the students who came up to Cambridge after the war many had seen active service, and many were returning to complete courses interrupted by the war. These men were very anxious to get their degree and then move on quickly to get on with their lives. There was a gulf between them and the 'new boys' fresh from school. In the excellent publication *Emmanuel College Cambridge, An Historical Guide* (2017) college archivist Amanda Goode writes:

> After the end of the War men returned in great numbers to complete their degrees and the College was full as never before. The inter-war years are often regarded in retrospect as a halcyon period at the University and the image of golden youths drifting along the Cam in punts has achieved an almost mythical quality. The truth, certainly as far as Emmanuel was concerned, was that few students could afford the luxury of indolence.

One issue which may have been expected to be resolved quickly in the post-war era, however, was the anomaly that women were still not allowed full membership of the university. Oxford University quickly made some progress towards this, but, despite several attempts in the interwar years

The Hostel, Emmanuel College, Cambridge, (probably 1920s)
where Fred Attenborough had a room/office as a Fellow

to rectify the position at Cambridge full membership for women was not achieved until after the Second World War in 1947.

After their marriage Mary and Fred rented a house at 45 Tenison Road, Cambridge, near the railway station, about a mile from Emmanuel College. Fred had lived in college up to that point, in New Court as an undergraduate, and later in Front Court as a research student, but married Fellows were normally expected to find accommodation outside college, and the young couple presumably preferred the additional privacy anyway. From 1922 to 1925 Fred had a room in the hostel within the college grounds in Parker Street, but as he was by then married and living off-campus this room would have served as an office base and for the occasional overnight stay. In January 1923 Fred was re-elected as a Fellow for three more years.

There appears to be no evidence of Mary's reaction to her new way of life in Cambridge and the dramatic cultural shift from life in Long Eaton. As the wife of a college Fellow Mary would probably have been expected not to have a career of her own unless she already had an established academic career in her own right. Academic wives were expected, however, to contribute to the social life of the college and the university, assisting with the organisation of many functions. At Emmanuel as elsewhere in Cambridge a key role was to assist with the organisation of the annual May Ball. The tradition of May Balls at Cambridge dates back to the first half of the nineteenth century. The events normally take place actually in June to celebrate the end of the academic year, and they are elaborate and formal black-tie events.

On 29 August 1923 Mary and Fred's first child was born, Richard Samuel. The Parlour Club at Emmanuel, a group for members of college which was dedicated to:

> intellectual and other forms of entertainment with frequent bets to enliven proceedings,

recorded that the master donated:

> a bottle to congratulate Attenborough on attaining his proud position.

Richard Samuel Attenborough was the first of the new generation of very gifted 'Cleggs' and their variously adopted names through marriage. Mary now had a new focus, new priorities, new responsibilities.

| *Mary with Richard Attenborough, 1923/24*

CHAPTER THIRTEEN

BOROUGH ROAD COLLEGE, ISLEWORTH, 1925–1931

In 1925 the young Attenborough couple moved on, when Fred was appointed as principal at the Borough Road College, a teacher training institute in Isleworth, West London, just a few months before his extended three-year tenure as a Fellow at Emmanuel would have been reviewed. The *Emmanuel College Magazine* for 1924/5 recorded Fred's departure and made reference to his reputation as both a singer and a photographer, not to mention the photogenic qualities of Cambridge:

> *If Isleworth can provide as appreciative an audience for his songs, it is to be doubted that Mr. Attenborough will find to his hand so much at which to point his camera.*

For Fred this move ended a ten-year association with Emmanuel and Cambridge, but it proved to be an opportune moment for his career to progress on its own track outside the protective atmosphere of academia, and ultimately it opened up opportunities for his own family. Also it is quite likely that the Clegg family, through Mary, would have been financially helping to support the couple after their marriage for the first three years, and this was a chance for Fred to be truly financially independent for the first time, at the age of thirty-eight.

For Mary the next six years would again be a time where she would be supporting her husband's career, whilst her own family-orientated 'career',

| Borough Road College, Lancaster House with Principal's Lodge (undated)

equally if not arguably more significant, is not recorded by history. The key events for Mary during the time at Isleworth were the birth of her second and third children, David Frederick, in May 1926, and John Michael in January 1928. The year 1930 was also a pivotal year in the lives of Mary and her siblings, and this will be dealt with in a later chapter. Apart from these key 'headline' events during the time at Isleworth nothing is really known or recorded about Mary's own life there, her reaction to the move from Cambridge or her busy role as a mother of three young sons. History was not in the habit of acknowledging women's lives or recognising their role in society.

Borough Road College dates back to 1798 when a school for the children of the poor was set up by Joseph Lancaster, a Quaker, in his father's house in Southwark. Fairly soon a larger building was required to meet demand, and premises were rented in Borough Road, Southwark. Lancaster was unable to afford to pay for an assistant and so developed a 'monitorial' system along the lines of the French écoles normales whereby older pupils (monitors) taught the younger ones. Lancaster's pioneering work was formalised with the establishment of the Royal Lancasterian Institution for the Education of the Poor of Every Religious Persuasion in 1808. Shortly afterwards it was renamed the British and Foreign School Society (BFSS), one of whose fundamental tenets was that religious instruction in its schools should be completely non-denominational. By 1817 much larger and more spacious premises were needed for the school, and these were built, also in Borough Road, to accommodate 500 boys and 300 girls.

Under the BFSS a separate teacher training establishment had also developed, and this became known as the Borough Road Normal School, following the nomenclature of the écoles normales, later Borough Road College. The teacher-training period in the early days was typically between three and six months. Numbers of students at the normal school stood at 207 by 1840 and regularly included a few students from overseas, including Russia, Greece and Sierra Leone. By 1846 the government recognised the need for properly trained teachers and introduced the Teacher's Certificate, whereby at age thirteen boys and girls of the right calibre could become pupil-teachers for five-year apprenticeships, examined annually by Her Majesty's Inspectors (HMIs). At the Borough Road establishment the first students sat for the Teacher's Certificate in 1851. The Education Act 1870 established state-maintained and locally rate-aided board schools administered by locally elected school boards. This move was welcomed by the BFSS, together with the instruction that religious education in the new schools was to be non-denominational. The Act also created an immediate demand for more trained teachers as only certificated teachers would be appointed to board schools. For Borough Road College this meant an immediate deluge of applications for places. In 1890 the college moved out of Southwark to a new site in leafy Isleworth, West London, but retained the Borough Road name.

In 1924 and 1925 the two longest-serving staff members, with eighty years of service between them, retired, one of whom was the principal, Dr Miller. Frederick Attenborough was appointed as the new principal of Borough Road College in 1925 at a pivotal moment in the life and direction of the establishment. He took charge of the very college which had earlier rejected his application as a student before he went instead to the BFSS sister college in Bangor. In his book *A History of Borough Road College* (1976), G.F. Bartle, referring to the new principal, wrote:

Still only 38 at the time of his appointment … he was, in spite of a certain aloofness of manner, which made it difficult for him to achieve easy relations with students, the right man to carry through the much-needed modernisation at Borough Road. Yet even Attenborough could not have achieved what he did if economic recovery had not made possible the Society's heavy expenditure during the next six years.

Developments during Fred's tenure included much-needed improvements to the college's buildings and student facilities and the extension of university work by establishing a regular three-year degree course. By 1928 the public examinations taken at secondary schools, such as London Matriculation and the Oxford and Cambridge School Certificates, became the normal criteria for selecting candidates for college training. A major national debate had been taking place about the role of ordinary residential teacher-training colleges such as Borough Road College in terms of university-style education. The Board of Education's view was that universities should prepare graduates for teaching in secondary schools, while training colleges should continue preparing teachers for elementary schools. After much debate within the BFSS and the college committee at Borough Road the decision was taken to continue and in fact expand degree work at Borough Road College in the belief that the best candidates would be attracted to those colleges offering degree courses. A key factor in arriving at this decision was the improved financial position of the BFSS by 1925.

Fred Attenborough, therefore, arrived at an opportune moment in time to take advantage of this new optimism and to develop the work of the college. The much-increased expenditure and investment at Borough Road College was aimed at driving up and improving the standard of academic work. The new principal was cautiously optimistic in his reports about the intellectual calibre of the students and their ability to cope with the rigours of the three-year courses, although in 1929 he admitted that 'there was a minority who are not properly equipped to read for a degree'. In 1930 thirty degrees were obtained and fifteen degrees in 1931, with most graduates subsequently obtaining posts in grammar and other secondary schools.

During 1931 the worldwide economic crisis was taking hold and already threatening to halt the period of expansion and relative financial prosperity for Borough Road College and for the BFSS, which had coincided with the tenure of Fred Attenborough. Towards the end of 1931 a new challenge and opportunity arose for Mary and Fred and their young family to return to their East Midlands roots. Fred Attenborough was appointed principal of the then University College, Leicester. Just before this new turning point, however, the previous year, 1930, had been a very eventful year for the Clegg family.

CHAPTER FOURTEEN

1930 – TWO WEDDINGS AND TWO FUNERALS

On 12 March 1930 Mary's father, Samuel Clegg, died at home, aged just fifty-nine years. The cause of death, certified by their neighbour, Dr Latham, was 'angina pectoris', and the death was notified by Mary's younger sister, Barbara, who was still living at home shortly before her wedding. For much of his full and busy life Sam Clegg had suffered from poor health, his frequent bouts of illness as a pupil-teacher even giving rise to questions about his suitability for teaching. In 1920 he had to ask for special leave to take a recuperative break in Italy. Did Sam travel out to Italy with Mary when she went to Bologna, or possibly visit her for some time if she was already in the country? It seems likely we will never know the answer to this unless more diaries kept by Mary are discovered. By the mid-1920s the economic situation was badly affecting local industry in Long Eaton as elsewhere, and school numbers at the Long Eaton school were declining as more parents took their children out of school earlier than planned. In 1926, the year of the General Strike, the school was forced to reduce staff numbers by one to reflect reduced pupil numbers and the reduction of income from fee-paying students. However, at the end of the year the school was able to celebrate positive news when former pupil Harry Godwin was elected as a Fellow of Clare College, Cambridge. In July 1928 only twenty-three students sat the school entry examination and only fourteen passed. There were still 262 pupils, however, and the

*Portrait study of Sam Clegg
by Fred Attenborough*

school governors had been pressing Derbyshire County Council to build an extension to the original school. In January 1929 numbers were down to 247, but the council still approved the extension, with an anticipated start of work in 1930. In June 1929 Sam suffered two heart attacks and was absent for most of the summer term, and a further attack followed in November. Sam was still at work just two days before his death. He received the plans for the extension of the school on the day he died.

The funeral was reported in the local weekly newspaper the *Long Eaton Advertiser* on 21 March 1930:

> *A farmer's waggon rumbled along Tamworth Road, New Sawley, on Saturday afternoon, the horse ploughing its way without difficulty through the snow to the Baptist Church Sawley. It was in accordance with the wishes of the late Mr. Samuel Clegg that his remains were borne to their last resting-place in this simple but what some may regard as an unconventional manner. But the deceased gentleman was not a slave to convention, and a pledge which Mr. Amos Mills (a close friend of Mr. Clegg), gave many years ago, was thus honoured. The widespread esteem in which the late Mr. Clegg was held found expression at the little burial ground. In spite of the wintry elements there was a gathering representative of every section of the community.*

Family mourners included Sam's daughter, Margaret, son Alec and son-in-law Fred Attenborough. Mary presumably stayed at home in Isleworth on a bleak wintry day to look after the three young boys then aged six, three and one.

Tributes to Sam Clegg were legion. The *Long Eaton Advertiser* told its readers that Sam's death would:

leave a town the richer for his life and the sadder for his sudden and ill-timed death ... He believed in the fundamental goodness of human nature, in liberty, in gentleness, and in the silent but inevitable influence of cultivated surroundings, and he was profoundly convinced that materialism, vulgarity, cruelty and injustice could be banished from life by an educational system in which the acquisition and use of knowledge was motivated and directed by a love for the humanities. He was never happier than when he was teaching, and though his knowledge was wide and various – in the days of the Pupil-Teacher Centre he taught every subject in the curriculum single-handed – he loved best of all to teach English and Art and Music, and to lead his scholars into these 'realms of gold'.

Distinguished former pupil Sir Harry Godwin later wrote in his book *Cambridge and Clare* (1985):

Now, fifty years since his death, I still find it impossible to account for the breadth, imagination and incisiveness of his mind except as the product of a natural swift eruption of a genius for learning and the gift of perceiving how best to develop love of learning and culture in young people. A biologist thinks of hidden genes suddenly found in harmonious contiguity and suitable environment. Some suggestion of the same assemblage can be seen in the personality of his grandson, the much-respected biologist, David Attenborough.

Another of Sam's distinguished pupils, whose potential was identified and nurtured by Sam, was William Bullock, who later adopted his first wife's surname and became Dr William Gye. He went on to become a distinguished pathologist and cancer researcher, director of the Imperial Cancer Research Fund's laboratories at Mill Hill from 1934–49, and a Fellow of the Royal Society. According to Gye:

[Sam's] friendship was a delight. During a quarter of a century of intimacy, renewed again and again by gifts of beautiful books or refined by lovely letters, I have never known any base thought or uncharitable word to coarsen our communications ... He supported whole-heartedly

all movements for the liberation of the human spirit from the dullness and stupidity of convention and make believe; he worked unceasingly for the freedom of the masses of our people. No reverse could dampen his enthusiasm or diminish his faith in the ultimate triumph of truth and beauty.

Sam had made a will on 15 March 1927. Probate was granted by the courts to:

Mary Attenborough (wife of Frederick Attenborough) of The Lodge Borough Road College Isleworth in the County of Middlesex and Margaret Clegg of Rye Hill Close aforesaid Spinster Daughter of the deceased two of the executors,

with power being reserved to grant probate to the other executor, Alexander Bradshaw Clegg, the youngest of the siblings. Under the terms of the will all Sam's property was granted:

unto my trustees Upon trust for my dear wife, Mary Clegg [senior].

In the event of his wife's death the estate was to be administered in such a way as to provide for:

the maintenance or benefit of my daughter Dorothy Clegg during her life

and then:

after the death of my said daughter Dorothy Clegg

the estate was to be divided between the surviving children. Dorothy, born in 1899, was the third daughter and had what we would today refer to as 'learning difficulties'. She would presumably, therefore, by implication require some form of supported living for the rest of her life, and Sam was determined to make future provision for the vulnerable Dorothy an absolute priority in his will, stating that:

*my trustees may if they think fit retain any house and furniture which
I may possess at my decease to provide a residence and home as they
think suitable for my said daughter Dorothy Clegg.*

During the summer of 1930 Mary's younger sisters, Margaret and Barbara
Clegg, were married respectively to Gilbert Peaker and Frank Barraclough.
Both Gilbert and Frank had been students training as teachers at Borough
Road College and were almost certainly introduced to the younger Clegg
sisters by Mary and Fred. Margaret and Gilbert Peaker were married at
Birmingham South Register Office on 31 July 1930 when Margaret was
thirty-three and Gilbert was twenty-eight. Margaret was living at the
time in Edgbaston and was described as a 'High School Teacher', while
Gilbert was living in Coventry and described as an 'Assistant Director of
Education'. Barbara and Frank Barraclough were married just six days later
on 6 August 1930 at Sawley Baptist Chapel when Barbara was twenty-
seven and Frank was twenty-nine. Mary Attenborough was one of the
witnesses. Barbara was still living at home with her recently widowed
mother at Rye Hill Close at the time of her marriage, and did not have a
'rank or profession'. Frank was described as an 'Assistant School Master'
and was living in Redland, Bristol.

Just seven months after the death of Sam Clegg, his widow Mary, who
had been ill for some time, died at home on 16 October 1930, also aged
fifty-nine. Mary Clegg senior was buried at Sawley Baptist Church next to
Sam. The *Long Eaton Advertiser* reported that:

*Many old Long Eaton associations are severed by the death ... of Mrs
Mary Clegg ... Of a retiring disposition, Mrs Clegg loved most of all
to attend to the needs of the family, but twenty years ago she took a
very active part in Long Eaton affairs, and before the erection of the
Secondary School she was frequently hostess at many little scholastic
gatherings.*

Family mourners included all of Mary and Sam's surviving children,
Alexander (Alec), Dorothy, and the three married sisters with their
husbands, Mary and Fred Attenborough, Margaret and Gilbert Peaker,
and Barbara and Frank Barraclough. Also present were Sam's sister,

Bernice Baxendale with her husband, William, and their daughter, Irene, first cousin to the Clegg siblings.

The events of 1930 would have been arguably more life-changing for Dorothy Clegg than for anyone else in the family. In the space of just seven months both her parents had died, and her two remaining sisters living at home had married. Assuming her sisters had moved away following their marriages Dorothy would have been suddenly left alone in the house. Sam Clegg's will had been very clear about his priority concern that Dorothy should be provided for financially for the remainder of her life, and it would not have been possible for Dorothy to remain alone at Rye Hill Close without support. In his book *About Our Schools* (1980), Dorothy's younger brother, Alec, by then Sir Alec Clegg, described his broad experience in education, including what we would now call special needs education, and made reference to his own personal family experience with sister, Dorothy, who:

never developed intellectually beyond the age of six or seven.

At the time of her death on 4 April 1966, at the age of sixty-seven, Dorothy was living with her cousin, Irene Baxendale, at Wylne, Lang Lane, West Kirby on the Wirral in Cheshire. Irene was just three years younger than Dorothy and had never married. In the 1911 Census, when Irene was just eight years old, and living with her parents at 5 Lingdale Road, West Kirby, also living with the family along with two domestic staff was Margaret Clegg senior, one of Sam Clegg's sisters, then aged thirty-three, and described as a 'Governess' to Irene. Margaret, known as 'Peg', was an aunt to both Irene and Dorothy. She never married, later became a teacher in her native Derbyshire, and died in 1959, aged eighty-one, in Allestree, Derby. In 1930, when both her parents died, Dorothy was thirty-one and her cousin Irene was twenty-eight. It is likely, therefore that Irene's parents, Bernice and William Baxendale, sister and brother-in-law of Sam Clegg, had agreed at some stage soon after the death of Mary Clegg senior to accommodate and support their niece, Dorothy, in an arrangement that may have been mutually beneficial for both single female cousins and would have been supported financially as necessary by the executors of Sam's will. It is possible that the arrangement had been drawn up by the family even before Mary Clegg senior's death. Precisely when Dorothy moved in with the Baxendales is not clear, but in all probability the move took place very soon after her mother's death.

Dorothy's aunt, Bernice Baxendale, died in 1940, aged sixty-seven. William survived his wife by twenty-one years and died at the age of ninety in 1961. Dorothy Clegg died in April 1966, aged sixty-seven, from broncho-pneumonia and Parkinsonism. She had probably lived with the Baxendales, who fulfilled Sam's wishes of long-term care for Dorothy, for about thirty-five years, and her death left her cousin, Irene, alone in the large house in West Kirby on the Wirral. Irene herself passed away some ten years after Dorothy, aged seventy-three, in 1976.

It seems that the Clegg family eventually let Rye Hill Close to tenants after Dorothy was settled with the Baxendales in Cheshire, although precisely when it was first let is not certain. An interesting advertisement in the *Long Eaton Advertiser* on 2 April 1937 announced a sale by public auction of various items seized:

> *under distraint for rent re: A.C.E. Sinclair of Rye Hill Close, 194, Tamworth Road, Long Eaton.*

The auction was to be held on 6 April 1937 at the premises of Newton & Sons and involved:

> *a quantity of household furniture and effects including: Maple bedroom suite, Oak dining table, Oak sideboard, Oak side table, sundry stair carpet, carpet felts, household crockery and utensils etc.*

Possibly the unfortunate tenant had become a victim of the long-term effects of the Depression of the 1930s, and before the days of housing benefit there was no 'safety net' for tenants, who fell on hard times and simply could not pay the rent. Although by 1937 the British economy was beginning to recover from the worst years of the Depression the effects of unemployment in some heavily industrialised areas of the Midlands and Northern England were still profound.

The electoral register for the New Sawley ward, Long Eaton, in 1939 shows that Rye Hill Close was let to Reginald and Anne Thompson, although when they took on the tenancy or left the house is not known. We do know, however, from the *Long Eaton Advertiser*, that in June 1941 Reginald Thompson was one of a number of local residents who had been:

> *neglectful in the matter of taking out – or renewing – licences for their dogs.*

He was fined 7s.6d. for his indiscretion!

We know from a letter sent to Mary's sister, Margaret, on 30 April 1982 by Mr W.L. Fletcher that, from April 1943, Rye Hill Close was occupied by Mr and Mrs Fletcher, who subsequently bought the house from the Clegg–Attenborough family in 1959. In the same letter Mr Fletcher mentions that:

> *we were visited some years ago by your brother, Sir Alec Clegg and your nephew Richard Attenborough.*

He goes on to explain:

> *The reason the name of Rye Hill Close is not used is that Tamworth Road is a long road and the Post Office discourage the use of house names, and prefer numbers to assist sorting and delivery problems.*

I can confirm that the present owner is proud to include the house name 'Rye Hill Close' in her postal address!

CHAPTER FIFTEEN

FREDERICK ATTENBOROUGH'S
ESTRANGEMENT FROM HIS FAMILY

In early 1932, just as Mary and Fred were embarking on their new life in Leicester (to be explored in the following section), the death was announced of Fred's older sister, Laura Attenborough, at the age of forty-seven. The story of Laura and Fred has been mentioned earlier in the text. On 13 February 1932 the *South Notts. Echo* reported that:

> *Miss Laura Attenborough, daughter of the late Mr. and Mrs. F.A. Attenborough of 'The Roach', 2, Derby Road, Stapleford, has died at the Womens Hospital, Peel Street, Nottingham, after a long and patiently borne illness. Identified with the Stapleford Methodists, Miss Attenborough was formerly a member of the Nottingham Road Church choir. The Rev. W.P. Porter conducted the service at St. Paul's Methodist Church prior to the interment at the Stapleford Cemetery. The mourners were: Mr. and Miss Attenborough [Fred and oldest sister Ada?], Mr. John Attenborough, Miss Maud Attenborough (brothers and sisters); Mrs. Marjorie Attenborough (sister-in-law); Miss Corden, Misses A. and L. Brown, Miss Burgess.*

Fred's youngest sister, Maud, died on 8 March 1965, aged seventy-five, and his oldest sibling, Ada, passed away on Christmas Day 1983, just short of her hundred and first birthday, surviving Fred by almost eleven years. None of the three Attenborough sisters married.

Fred's mother, Mary Attenborough senior, had died in 1917, aged sixty-four, while he was at Emmanuel College, Cambridge, and his father, Frederick Augustus, died in 1924, aged seventy-four, while Mary and Fred were newly married and still in Cambridge.

There is no evidence as to whether or not Fred attended his parents' funerals and no recollection within the family of any later reconciliation between Fred and his family.

| *Eastcombe Baptist Chapel, near Stroud, Gloucs, 2020*

| *Sawley Baptist Chapel, 2019*

Interior of Sawley Baptist Chapel, 2019

Westbourne Park Baptist Chapel, London, c.1910,
where Mary and Frederick Attenborough were married in 1922

Rye Hill Close, Sawley (centre) with the former doctor's house (left), 2020

John Bradshaw's house, Sawley (see also fig.2, the wedding day photo),
Rye Hill Close left, 2020

The doctor's house at the junction of Bradshaw Street
and Tamworth Road, Sawley, 2020

Inside Rye Hill Close, barley-twist original oak balusters on staircase,
looking down to reception hall, 2019

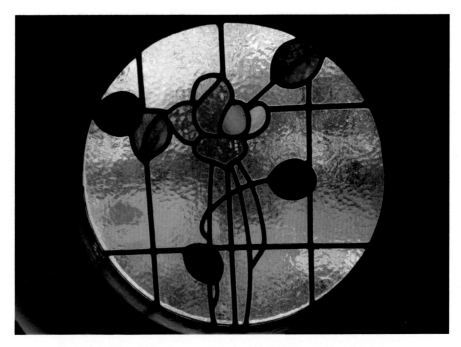

Coloured leaded glass panel after the 'rose' style of Charles Rennie Mackintosh,
Ground-floor front elevation, Rye Hill Close, c.1906, 2020

Coloured leaded glass panel facing the main entrance porch,
Rye Hill Close, c.1906, 2020

Coloured leaded glass panel side elevation in the Oak Room,
Rye Hill Close, c.1906, 2020

The 'Oak Room' at Rye Hill Close, with original fire surround,
mahogany wall panelling and mahogany ceiling beams, 2020

Blue Plaque to Sir Alec Clegg in Wakefield, Yorkshire
(note date of death should be 1986 not 1984)

The first home of Mary and Fred Attenborough,
from 1922-25, at 45 Tenison Road, Cambridge, 2020

SECTION FOUR

THE LEICESTER YEARS 1932–51

CHAPTER SIXTEEN

THE MOVE TO LEICESTER, 1932,
NEW OPPORTUNITIES, NEW CHALLENGES

In the autumn of 1931, as the economic downturn was threatening to undermine the progress made under his tenure at Borough Road College, Frederick Attenborough was appointed to the post of principal at University College, Leicester.

The post had become vacant in August 1931 when the first principal of the university college, Dr Robert F. Rattray, had resigned to move to Cambridge where he took up the post as pastor of the Unitarian Memorial Chapel. Rattray, a Glaswegian, was educated at Glasgow University, Oxford and Harvard, as well as in Germany, before moving to Leicester in 1917 to become pastor of the Unitarian Great Meeting. He was a strong advocate of adult education and joined the Leicester Literary and Philosophical Society (also known as the Lit & Phil), established in 1835, which in turn was promoting, along with other organisations, a scheme to establish a university in Leicester.

The Lit & Phil had been 'agitating' for the strengthening of higher education in the city for the past fifty years, aware that Leicester needed to keep up with its Midlands competitors. The campaign can be traced in detail through the 'Transactions' and the 'Minutes' of the Lit & Phil, and in October 1912, in the presidential address of a respected local doctor, Astley Clarke, he threw down the gauntlet and declared:

I look forward to the time when Leicester will not be content without some University College in its midst, where the various branches of knowledge will have a fitting home, and the Institution may be part of Leicester's daily life.

The Lit & Phil endorsed this idea wholeheartedly, and although the outbreak of war paused progress for a while, the *Leicester Daily Post*, on 14 November 1917, argued that the most fitting war memorial for Leicester and Leicestershire after the end of the conflict should be the establishment of a university college. After a major funding campaign and the generous gift of a site of thirty-seven acres by local textile manufacturer, Thomas Fielding Johnson, the new university college, under its original name of the Leicester, Leicestershire and Rutland College, opened its doors and accepted its first handful of students on 4 October 1921. In early 1921 Dr Rattray had been approached to become the first principal of the planned college and in May 1921 he was duly appointed to the post. Uniquely the institution had been founded as a war memorial, and the Latin motto of the institution, *Ut vitam habeant* ('That they shall have life'), reflects this concept perfectly.

After the resignation of Rattray in August 1931 the first attempt to appoint a new principal was thwarted when the preferred candidate withdrew his initial acceptance of the position. The re-advertisement of the post attracted twenty-six applicants, including some from the first round. The Academic Committee, having taken advice:

from men eminent in the University world,

reported that:

they cannot emphasise too strongly that the first consideration in the appointment of a new Principal should be that he be an eminent scholar, and a man of University experience and ideas, and that anything that might stand in the way of securing such a man should be viewed with great care,

and:

they are of opinion that great care should be exercised in seeing that the future policy and development of the College should be on such lines as to maintain its University status, and that no measures should be taken that might militate against its being recognised by the University Grants Committee for a grant at some future date.

In his letter of application Fred Attenborough set out the ways he believed he met what we would nowadays call the 'person specification' and ended his letter with the sentence:

Perhaps I ought to add that I am 44 years old, and that I have a wife and three sons.

Until relatively recently, history has been slow to acknowledge and respect the achievements of women, so it is interesting to read in a testimonial in support of Fred's application dated 20 August 1931 from F.F. Potter, then director of education for Cheshire and chairman of the Committee of the Borough Road College, that:

It remains only to be added that he is fortunate in his wife, who shares his vision and ably assists him in all his undertakings. Her charming tact and courtesy have established her firmly as the graceful and reliable leader in the social life of a large educational institution.

Welcome to Leicester both Fred *and* Mary!

On 19 November 1931 an extraordinary general meeting of the court of governors unanimously passed the resolution:

THAT Frederick L. Attenborough, Esq., M.A., Principal of Borough Road Training College, be, and is

Mary Attenborough, photographed by Frederick Attenborough, (undated) hereby appointed Principal of the University College, Leicester, at a salary of £1,400 (One thousand four hundred pounds) per annum, with residence (free of rent, rates and taxes) in College House, and with superannuation allowance in accordance with the scale of the Federated Superannuation System for Universities.

The family duly moved into College House during the Christmas holidays. The university college had agreed, in conjunction with the Attenboroughs, to carry out some alterations and work to the property for the incoming residents. The architect's estimated cost for structural alterations was £475 and for internal and external painting and decorating £150. In the event, according to a report of the Buildings and Sites Committee, the lowest tender for the structural alterations was £590, possibly reflecting the scarcity of suitable contractors as the economic situation was worsening. The committee report, however, noted that:

In view of the urgency of this work and with the approval of the Chairman of the College Council, your Committee have given instructions for this work to be put in hand. Your Committee has left the question of painting and decorating in the hands of Mr Attenborough and propose allowing him the sum of £150 for this work.

One wonders whether it was 'in the hands of' Mr or *Mrs* Attenborough. According to both Richard and David Attenborough, Mary was very much the practical partner in household and family matters.

College House is a large, three-storey Victorian building with tall chimneys, a slate roof and large bay windows. During the nineteenth century what is now the main administrative building of the University of Leicester was actually Leicestershire and Rutland County Asylum, built in 1837 and subsequently extended and enlarged over the next sixty years on a site off what was then Occupation Road, later Victoria Road and now University Road. In 1872 College House was built on the edge of the main site as a residence for the medical superintendent of the asylum. The grounds of the asylum extended over twenty acres. In 1908 the patients of the asylum were transferred to a new purpose-built asylum known as Carlton Hayes in Narborough, just outside Leicester. For the next six years

College House, Leicester, back left, 1920s. Victoria Park to the left.
The Charles Wilson Library is now on the site of the buildings to the right.

Fielding Johnson Building, University College, Leicester, 1932.
Principal's study to the right of the main entrance

the site was empty, but within a few weeks of the outbreak of the First World War the former asylum buildings were requisitioned and altered for use as a field hospital as the first casualties began to arrive from the Western Front, and in 1915 it became known as the 5th Northern General Hospital. The British Army evacuated the buildings in 1919, and the site plus thirty-seven acres of adjacent land were acquired for £40,000, the equivalent of about £1.8 million today, by Thomas Fielding Johnson, a retired local textile manufacturer. He in turn gifted the land to the Borough of Leicester for the proposed university college. College House then came back into use as the new residence for the first principal, Dr Rattray, in 1921. Nowadays it sits on the edge of the university campus, opposite Victoria Park, no longer with grounds of its own and dwarfed by much larger modern buildings erected over the last half-century. It is used as offices for the university.

When Fred and Mary moved into College House it had a reasonable garden area. Sir David Attenborough described the house in a letter to me as being:

> surrounded by a great deal of open ground presumably to allow for the future expansion of the College. There was a large paddock (in which there was at one time a horse). My father used this paddock to grow vegetables and soft fruit and to keep a pig and chickens.

The paddock was originally pasture and was dug up early in the Second World War in order to grow food crops for the family. By 1941 several acres at the western end of Victoria Park itself in front of College House had also been transformed into temporary allotments as part of the Dig for Britain campaign.

In a later letter Sir David recalled:

> A cobbled yard and what were originally stables. They still had mangers and hayracks in them, and one served as a garage for the family car. Opposite the gates there was an outhouse where my mother had a gigantic washing machine which she used weekly, clouds of steam belching from the door.

When Fred commenced his duties in January 1932 his task had been clearly set out: to build on the achievements of the first decade of the university

| *Fielding Johnson Building, College Library, 1920s*

college and ultimately move the institution towards full university status, when amongst other things, it could award its own degrees. Until that time degrees awarded would continue to be University of London external degrees, in the same way that Mary gained her degree at University College Nottingham.

CHAPTER SEVENTEEN

SETTLING IN SOCIALLY IN LEICESTER

Despite her educational achievements Mary had never had an independent career of her own. Since her marriage to Fred in 1922 she had in effect committed to supporting her husband in his roles, firstly as a Fellow of Emmanuel College, Cambridge, for three years, and then as principal at Borough Road College for the next six years. The importance of this supporting role in its own right should not be underestimated, and it is hinted at in the previously mentioned testimonial from F.F. Potter at Borough Road College when he referred to Mary as:

> the graceful and reliable leader in the social life of a large educational institution.

As at Cambridge, academic wives at Leicester were probably expected to help with organising aspects of the institution's social life, and Mary certainly helped to organise student social dances and the annual College Ball, usually held at the Grand Hotel or the Bell Hotel. In reality when Mary and Fred arrived in Leicester there were very few academic wives until student and therefore staff numbers started to increase, so it is reasonable to assume that the lion's share of social organisation probably fell to Mary, a role she no doubt assumed with maximum efficiency and minimum fuss.

Mary's second role during the past nine years of course had been to bear and nurture her three sons. When the family arrived in Leicester, Richard,

David and John were aged eight, five and three. They were still very young, of course, but just easing past the 'high dependency' age. Mary had a 'high octane' personality, as we have seen in the Sorbonne diary, for example, reaching out, absorbing and analysing everything and everyone she came across. In fact in so many ways she was, unsurprisingly, a model Samuel Clegg pupil. When she married, supported Fred and started a family her energy levels, of necessity, moved up to the next level. She also had so much to give, and, while she was obviously using her resources to the full in her two new roles described above, the impression remained that sooner or later there would be a release of even more energy in the most positive and creative sense. Within five years of moving to Leicester, as political events in Europe began to take an ominous turn for the worse, opportunities arose unwittingly for Mary to act decisively. She would identify first one and then another 'cause', which she would embrace with total commitment, passion and humanity, literally helping to save young lives in the process. History defines Frederick Attenborough as the head of the most senior academic institution in Leicester for twenty years during a crucial period of its history. Mary Attenborough, by contrast, barely warrants a mention, apart from acknowledgment as 'the wife of Frederick'. At a time when the University of Leicester celebrates the official centenary of its founding, the achievements and importance of Mary Attenborough in her own right should be not only at the forefront of those celebrations but also cemented in the history of the city and the nation.

Before Mary became involved in international causes, however, both Mary and Fred wanted to establish their new position in the life of Leicester. They did this by considering how they could best contribute to the local community. At the same time Fred's immediate priority was to steer the university college through the perilous waters of the 1930s, and later the Second World War, so that it was in a healthy position to take advantage of the better times ahead to expand and gain full university status. A photograph from 1932 taken shortly after the new principal took charge shows a college staff which numbered fourteen, excluding Fred. Only one woman, Ethel Miles Thomas, head of botany, features in the photograph. Despite the small number of staff and heavy workload, the chemistry department under Dr Hunter had started to attract some of the first external research grants to the university college. The increasing need to expand the facilities available was not immediately matched by the funding to do so, and the university college still relied heavily on its many regular supporters and their annual subscriptions. Student fees were also raised. It would be another three decades before the state paid student tuition fees and began to pay grants to university students. Student numbers at the college remained below 160, and less than half of those were full-time degree students. In March 1933 Fred Attenborough made an eloquent appeal, through the pages of the *Leicester Evening Mail*, to the city of Leicester to support its university college:

> *It remains to place the University College second to none among the provincial institutions of a similar kind. To stimulate its development would be rendering a national service, and Leicester would be conspicuous among those communities which care not only about commercial success, but about those things of the mind and spirit which are the distinctive marks of an educated and cultured people.*

This was an interesting and pointed appeal to a city which survived the economic battering of the 1930s better than most because it was not reliant on one main primary industry but prided itself on its broader industrial and commercial base. Nevertheless, the enforced lack of real growth of the university college during the 1930s, common to most of the provincial universities at the time, was a major challenge for the new principal and the college council.

Shortly after taking up his duties as principal Fred Attenborough joined Leicester Rotary Club. Whilst at Borough Road College Fred had been a member of Hounslow Rotary Club. The Rotary movement was born in Chicago in 1905. The Leicester branch had been founded in 1916 and was the thirteenth club in Great Britain and the 340th in the world, part of a rapidly spreading movement. The original concept was to form a local club where like-minded men could get to know each other and apply their energy and talents to improving their own vocations and serving their fellow human beings. The aim was to meet regularly in each other's place of business in rotation, hence the name. The Education Committee of the Leicester Rotary Club was a keen promoter of the idea of a university for the city and received enthusiastic support from the wider membership.

The first principal of the college, Dr Rattray, and the first secretary, W.G. Gibbs, were both Leicester Rotarians, and the link between the club and the university college, and later the university, was to be perpetuated. Fred Attenborough joined the club soon after his appointment.

One of Fred's later roles in civic life was that of external advisor to the City Education Committee. We have an insight into the nature of both the Education Committee and also Fred's own personality from a letter he wrote on 3 April 1940 to Edward Welbourne, senior tutor of his old Cambridge college, Emmanuel, requesting a reference for one of the college's former research fellows, who had applied for the post of Director of Education for the City of Leicester:

> I imagine that his relatively small experience may be made much of by certain members of the Committee. I myself set very little store by mere length of experience and R ... has had some of course in Essex. ... If he is as good as he seems to be on paper, he might be an outstanding success and do excellent work for us in the city. We are anxious to avoid appointing, if possible, one of those rigid administrators who are so common among Directors ... We have suffered very badly from an overdose of rigid administration which has put everybody into a strait jacket and left them the minimum of initiative.

The forthcoming reference is not recorded, but in the event the prospective candidate was unsuccessful in his application.

Both Mary and Fred had a great interest in music. Fred was a fine baritone singer, and Sir David remarked that his father's knowledge of German probably came initially from his love of Schubert's *Lieder*! Both Mary and Fred were accomplished pianists and Sir David also followed suit. He recalls playing Beethoven, particularly his Second Symphony, with Mary 'four hands'. Music had been one of the foundation subjects of the early college, and shortly after it opened, a department of music was established in the charge of a sole part-time lecturer, Malcolm Sargent (later Sir Malcolm Sargent). Around the same time in 1922 Sargent founded the Leicester Symphony Orchestra, based at the De Montfort Hall, very close to the college, also on the northern side of Victoria Park. Although Malcolm Sargent had moved on by the time Fred was appointed at Leicester he became acquainted with the Attenboroughs, perhaps through retaining certain links with his old department. When working in Leicester or conducting visiting orchestras at De Montfort Hall Malcolm Sargent would visit Mary and Fred at College House and sometimes join them for a musical *soirée*.

Another venerable local institution with close links to the university college was the Leicester Literary and Philosophical Society, which had been instrumental in the establishment of the original Leicester, Leicestershire and Rutland College, as we have seen above. Fred Attenborough became a member when he arrived in Leicester, and he was elected as the society's president in May 1939. When the society's base, the New Walk Museum, was requisitioned for war purposes, the main activities of the society were suspended. Presidency of the Lit & Phil normally changes hands every year, but in the unique prevailing circumstances Fred remained president throughout the Second World War years, handing over to his successor, George Tarratt, at the beginning of the 1946/47 season. Fred's links with the museum remained strong throughout his time in the city. He was for a number of years a non-councillor member of the city council's Museums and Libraries Committee both in his own right and as a voice of the Lit & Phil. Family links with the Lit & Phil continue to this day. Lord Richard Attenborough was president in 1999/2000 and Sir David Attenborough is an honorary life vice-president of the society. In addition, proposals for the inauguration of an 'F.L. Attenborough Lecture' as part of the Lit & Phil's annual cycle of winter season lectures have been agreed, and the first such lecture 'Do the Arts have any Role in Education?', was delivered on 22 March 2021 by Fred's grandson, Michael Attenborough.

It is my sincere hope that one day the memory of Mary Attenborough also may be marked in some way by either the university or the city council, or indeed both, in recognition of her contribution to the social, cultural and humanitarian life and reputation of the city.

Full female suffrage on the same terms as men had only been achieved in 1928, just four years before Mary and Fred moved to Leicester. During the following decade Mary was at the forefront of launching new organisations locally, as well as joining local branches of national groups, which promoted the woman's point of view and the right to be heard and taken seriously on the same terms as men. She became actively involved with two movements, which had some parallels and links with the Rotary club but with more targeted aims and aspirations around women's issues. Soroptimist International (SI) was founded in California in 1921. The aim is in the name, *soror* being the Latin for 'sister' and *optima* meaning 'best', hence a movement seeking the best for women. The current promotion of the organisation, which is still thriving, describes SI as:

> *a global volunteer movement with a network of around 72,000 club members in 121 countries … advocating for human rights and gender equality … on grassroots projects that help women and girls achieve their individual and collective potential, realise aspirations and have an equal voice in communities worldwide.*

During 1933 members of Soroptimist International Birmingham proposed forming a club in Leicester. Contact was made with Miss D.R. Smith, headmistress of Collegiate School for Girls in Leicester, and she formed a small subcommittee with Mary Attenborough and Miss F.M. Hughes, matron of Leicester Royal Infirmary and an international figure in the nursing profession at the time. The swift outcome was an inaugural charter dinner for the new Leicester branch held on 17 March 1934 when the guest speaker was Harold Nicholson, who twenty months later became National Labour MP for Leicester West from 1935–45. Mary remained on the local SI committee until the family left Leicester in 1951. Other founder members included Mrs E. Bond, wife of a local surgeon, who was the first woman magistrate on the city bench, and Miss Dora Warner, also later a magistrate and president of Soroptimist International. It is worth mentioning here that Mary herself later became a magistrate in Leicester during the Second World War. This will be discussed in detail in a later chapter as she continued as a magistrate after Fred retired and the couple moved away from Leicester. The membership and welfare officer of SI Leicester, Patricia Mansfield, explained to me in November 2019:

> *It was when our club was raising funds for the* Richard Attenborough Centre for Disability and the Arts *that we made contact with Richard, who said his mother always spoke warmly of her time as a Soroptimist. Because of this he brought the premiere of* Chaplin, *his latest film, to*

Leicester, and Soroptimists gave out leaflets about the Centre and we did a bucket collection as people were leaving which raised an excellent amount towards the project.

An insight into the Soroptimist movement may be gained from the *Leicester Evening Mail* edition of Saturday 21 March 1936. Reporting on the second commemoration dinner of the Leicester branch, held at the Grand Hotel the previous evening and attended by both Mary and Fred Attenborough, the account quotes the main speaker, Miss Elizabeth Hawes, then secretary of the National Union of Soroptimist Clubs of Great Britain and Ireland:

Most associations are made up of people, men, women or both, of like ideas or aspirations, who have been drawn together by some grievance or interest common to all. Soroptimism is somehow different. In each club one finds women, whom one would expect to differ rather than agree, so varied are their activities and interests, but it is this variety and lack of uniformity which constitutes its charm.

Importantly Miss Hawes went on to say that it was the desire of each local branch of SI to render service in its own community and immediate surroundings.

The *Evening Mail* continued:

Mr F.L. Attenborough, who proposed the toast of the Soroptimist movement, praised the Leicester branch for the valuable assistance to the Leicester Rotary Club with regard to the families who have been brought to the city from the distressed areas. 'I think there is a political and social philosophy spreading over Europe stressing the importance of the State and minimising the value of the individual. The Rotary and Soroptimist movements are based on an individualistic philosophy and composed of individuals transmitting and spreading the gospel of Rotary and Soroptimism.'

We know from newspaper articles and from Mary's household accounts (of which more later) that she was, soon after her arrival in Leicester, a member of the Leicester branch of the National Council of Women (NCW). The origins of the NCW date back to 1895 when the National Union of Women Workers was formed to draw attention to the poor working conditions faced by many women workers. Within a few years the organisation began its campaign for 'Equal pay for Equal work' and was particularly concerned with the position of women in the armed forces. In 1918 it became known as the National Council of Women of Great Britain. In the decades following the Second World War the NCW was particularly active in working to remove discrimination against women in all spheres and in encouraging women to play a full role in society. This work continues today, increasingly as part of an international network of organisations with similar aims. Mary would most certainly have supported the aspirations of the movement, although we know little about her active role within the group. There was a Leicester branch of the NCW by the 1930s if not before, and in fact this branch closed only very recently due to dwindling support, although the East Midlands regional group is still active. We do know from the minutes of the local branch executive committee that in 1948 Mary offered the use of Knighton Hall, Leicester, where the Attenboroughs were living at the time (see later chapters), for a fundraising 'bring and buy sale' to be held at the hall and that the sale was held there on 17 September 1948. By a cross-reference to Mary's household accounts books we have a small insight into the preparations for this event. On 14 September Mary bought cleaning items:

12 tins polish £1, 6 packets of swabs x3 at 2/3d each 19/-, wire scourers 2/3d, total £2.1.3d

Clearly Mary was having a thorough spring-clean at Knighton Hall before the sale!

In 1934 Mary was one of the founder members of a new group known as Leicester Women's Luncheon Club, who regularly invited eminent guest speakers for lunchtime talks. Mary was the first chairman of the club, and she delivered her opening speech at the inaugural luncheon of the club at the Grand Hotel, Leicester, on 10 April 1934, just three weeks after the launch of the Leicester Soroptimists branch. The occasion was recorded by the *Leicester Evening Mail* the following day. Mary said she had been asked many times why yet another club was being formed in Leicester when there were already so many. She explained:

> *The difference is that in order to belong to one of the other clubs you either have to be a professional woman, a business woman, the wife of a member who belongs to a club, a bridge-playing woman, or have some other qualifications, but to belong to this club you only have to be a woman. Many live in a little world of their own. We have to if we are good housewives. The aim of the club is friendliness, and we hope that once a month by having a meal prepared for us and meeting in this way we may be able to get out of the routine for an hour or two.*

According to the newspaper, Mary said that 'having come into the city as an outsider two years ago, she had found none of the barriers of which she had been told, and she was now proud to call herself a Leicester woman'. Mary concluded her speech:

> *We have been told that we must break down international barriers, and I think that the best way to do this is to begin in our own city and break down the barriers among ourselves.*

At a meeting of the Luncheon Club on 13 November 1934, to which male partners were also invited, Mary Attenborough, speaking in her capacity as chairman, was keen to emphasise in both light-hearted and serious fashion the need for women to begin to exercise their new democratic rights in terms of intellectual and cultural independence. The *Leicester Evening Mail* once again reported the following day:

> *Mrs Attenborough (chairman) said at the various ladies' evenings and lunches to which wives were invited by their husbands' organisations she has always been impressed by the mantle of eloquence that fell on the chairman when he has mentioned the word 'ladies'. But when the speech ended she came to earth like Cinderella with a bump. 'As a sex we are not as used to paying compliments as the men are but maybe we are more truthful.' In describing the Luncheon Club Mrs Attenborough*

said 'This is not a hot bed of sedition but just a gathering of women who come together to chatter, to eat and to listen to eminent women and to eminent men – other than our own husbands!'

The theme of welcome in a strange city was again taken up by Mary when she was invited to open a bazaar at the Girls Social Guild in February 1936. This was reported by the *Leicester Evening Mail* on 28 February 1936. She referred to the fact that young women were coming from 'distressed areas' into Leicester, which was weathering the storm of the Depression better than many cities:

> *Mary Attenborough pointed out that, although these girls might leave after a comparatively few attendances, either through having made friends outside the club or through other interests, she felt that, even so, the club was very valuable to them when they first came to the city. The girls were probably extremely lonely, and the club gave them a warm welcome. She did not think that the clubs need worry if they did not always retain the membership of a number of girls, they could rest assured they had bridged the gap.*

For Mary Attenborough the concept of welcoming strangers to the city was not merely abstract idealism. We shall see in the following chapters how she put this into practice in the most proactive and pragmatic fashion. In doing so she not only enriched but literally saved young lives.

During the interwar years women were starting to demand more control over their own lives and bodies, and one aspect of this was increased focus on better medical care during pregnancy, where public attitudes still needed a nudge in the right direction. This was the theme of a talk to the Luncheon Club on 12 March 1935, just before its first anniversary, presided by Mary Attenborough. The topic explored by Dr T.W. Allen was: *The Present Situation Regarding Maternal Mortality*. The *Evening Mail* quoted from his talk:

> *Ante-natal supervision is a relatively and tremendously important part of any maternity service. It is most important that the general public should demand and accept this service from either a doctor or midwife*

or should attend one of the established ante-natal clinics of which there are a thousand in this country. It is a matter of much concern that the large amount of public money spent on these clinics has not brought obvious results in some areas. Public education can and will bring about an improvement in this respect.

As Mary's own family became more independent she became increasingly interested in and involved with issues of women's independence, as witnessed by her later involvement with the Marriage Guidance Council and also with the matrimonial courts as a magistrate. This will be discussed in later chapters.

The various new and established women's groups in the city frequently came together for joint meetings and discussions in the 1930s and often had cross-memberships. On 1 May 1934 eight different groups came together to organise a meeting at the Edward Wood Hall (now the Fraser Noble Hall) near the university college in Leicester. The groups listed by the *Leicester Evening Mail* were:

The Leicester and county branches of the Federation of University Women, the National Council of Women, the National British Women's Temperance Association, the Y.W.C.A., the Free Church Women's Guild, the Congregational Women's Guild, the Railway Women's Guild and the Soroptimist Club.

The guest speaker on that occasion was Vera Brittain, then aged forty. She had just recently (1933) published *Testament of Youth*, the first volume of what would eventually become an autobiographical trilogy. The newspaper recalled how, in her recent book, Vera Brittain had referred to Leicester:

… in a most dramatic fashion. Miss Brittain was then at Oxford and was anxious to meet her fiancé before she returned [from her family home in Staffordshire]. It was a question as to whether she would meet him at Leicester or London, and finally it was decided that she would meet him in the lounge of the Grand Hotel in Leicester. She had to meet him this way, as her parents knew nothing about it.

Mary Attenborough, who presided at the meeting, had earlier welcomed Vera Brittain at Leicester's Midland Railway Station, just a quarter of a mile from the venue. The topic of the speech was 'Peace and Security'. Miss Brittain had noticed in talking to youth groups recently, half a generation since the end of the First World War, that there was a decline in cynicism and a strong desire to fight for peace.

She said that the cause of peace could best be served by parents and teachers in instilling into the minds of children, not the horrors of actual warfare, but the aftermath of suffering and privation which sweep the world as a result of war.

The speech by Vera Brittain seems to have inspired further co-operation between the various women's groups, with the formation shortly afterwards of the Leicester Women's Peace Committee, which then lobbied the Prime Minister and local MPs. At the request of the Peace Committee the Leicester branch of the League of Nations Union, of which Fred Attenborough was a prominent member, arranged a series of discussion meetings. On 16 October 1934 the speaker at one of these meetings was Miss K.D. Courtney, a member of the National Executive of the League of Nations Union, talking about 'Arms and the International Situation'. The chairman of the meeting was Fred Attenborough, and the *Evening Mail* reported the chairman's comments to the effect that:

… sixteen years after the end of the Great War it was ironical that a peace meeting was being held. But everyone was conscious that unless there was an alteration in international policy armaments would be piled up in every country. Economically the present international policy was crippling Europe; politically it was leading to the extinction of democracy by the substitution of tyrannical Government; and ethically it was leading to a state of degeneration which had been apparent during the recent months with the assassinations and upheaval in Europe. 'The only way to have peace is to seek peace and not to prepare for war', Mr Attenborough urged.

Prophetic words, and they confirm how, during the 1930s, both Mary and Fred Attenborough were perceptive students of the international situation and proactively involved in addressing it. Quite how proactive Mary in particular would be during the following decade could not be imagined at that point in time.

The Luncheon Club's links with Rotary were mentioned in the *Leicester Mercury* in Rita Wakefield's daily column 'A Woman's Diary' on 27 January 1939 in a light-hearted and slightly tongue-in-cheek report on a ladies' evening event:

> *Since the Rotary Club of Leicester held its first ladies' evening several women's organisations have taken root in the city. Among them is the Leicester Women's Luncheon Club, founded chiefly by Rotarians' wives, and the Leicester Club of Soroptimism, in the starting of which the Rotary Club took a brotherly interest. Husbands' day is a red letter one in the calendar of the Luncheon Club, when speaker and menu are chosen with special care. The Soroptimists, also, have given sisterly support to Rotary projects.*
>
> *But even though the time-honoured excuse for the annual ladies' evening – that it was some compensation for stay-at-home wives who faced the remains of Sunday's joint on Mondays, while their husbands lunched together – has worn a little thin, the event has lost none of its popularity.*
>
> *Thus once more last night, at the Grand Hotel, Leicester, Rotarians entertained their womenfolk with all their customary gallantry, and the enthusiasm of both hosts and guests showed that the occasion had retained its glamour. The visitors were received at the head of the staircase leading to the King's Hall by Rotarian F.L. Attenborough, president of the Leicester Club, and Mrs Attenborough. ... After dinner the visitors, who included the Lord Mayor and Mayoress (Alderman and Mrs T.J. Gooding), were welcomed by Rotarian Attenborough.*
>
> *To Rotarian Kenneth Holmes, Principal of the Leicester College of Art, was entrusted the delicate task of toasting 'The Ladies'. In a humorous speech Mr Holmes professed himself a hundred per cent feminist, as a small boy, he had seen a Suffragette belabouring a policeman with her umbrella. He hastened to add that he was converted through admiration and not fear. With deft and masterly strokes Mr Holmes sketched the wayward way of feminine fashions, and observed*

with masculine cynicism how the hat which appeared to be merely a bit of lining might cost more than a whole hat.

Mrs Harry Martin replied for the ladies, and proved well able to take advantage of the privilege of having the last word. Her husband was toastmaster, and she admitted that, when she was asked to speak, she found the thought of him 'craving silence' on her behalf quite irresistible. Referring to the cavalcade of fashions which Mr Holmes had quoted as showing the fickleness of feminine taste, Mrs Martin reminded him that most of the designers were men. Their perpetrations, she claimed, were worn by women in patience to please men. … Mrs Attenborough looked very well in a striking black and white ensemble. Her white chiffon dress had an accordion pleated hem and the décolletage was outlined with mother of pearl bead trimming. She wore a narrow black sequin trimmed neck band and black gloves. A white shawl, patterned with black and white chenille, with a black velvet border, completed her ensemble and she wore a single white flower in her hair.

Two months later, Mary and Fred were back at the same venue for the Fifth Commemoration Dinner of the Leicester Soroptimists. The *Leicester Mercury* once again followed events in Rita Wakefield's column. The speaker at the event, a Mrs John Crosskey, referred to:

Idealism, moral courage, perseverance, friendliness, the ability to treat people as individuals, faith in the fundamental decency and reasonableness of human nature, conscientiousness and a passion for detail. These qualities, it was claimed … had contributed to the success of women in public life. The speaker was Mrs John Crosskey, a Birmingham visitor with a record for social work, who toasted the Soroptimist movement. Women, claimed Mrs Crosskey, had a pretty good record considering the short time they had had the power of the vote … They had changed the very stuff of politics. They thought of Acts of Parliament in the terms of those whose lives would be affected by such legislation. Women worked with selflessness and without an eye on the honours list.

The toast was replied to by another Birmingham visitor, Miss H.L.M. Gibbs, a barrister and National President of Soroptimists'

Clubs. She briefly summarised the objects of Soroptimism, which are to encourage and foster high standards in professional and business life, to promote the spirit of service and friendship, to encourage civic movements for the betterment of general social conditions, and to encourage the spirit of friendship among representative women of different nations. In briefly summarising the various activities of the Soroptimists' Clubs, Miss Gibbs stressed the fact that these represented work done by busy women in their spare time.

It is easy to recognise most of the qualities listed above in Mary and to see why she was well-placed to promote and spearhead new movements which would give a voice to women, who could now expect their voice to be heard on equal terms. Certainly 'moral courage, perseverance ... the ability to treat people as individuals' were qualities displayed in abundance by Mary when the contorted politics of 1930s Europe caused opposing ideologies to explode in savagery in an unexpected corner of the continent.

CHAPTER EIGHTEEN

MARY AND THE BASQUE REFUGEE CHILDREN, 1937–39

On Tuesday 6 July 1937 the *Leicester Mercury* reported that, earlier that same day:

> *A huge crowd of Leicester people waited outside the Leicester Great Central Station to welcome the Basque children refugees, who are to stay at Evington Hall.*

Shortly after their arrival:

> *Members of the committee, including Mrs F Attenborough, and members of the Leicestershire A.A.* [Automobile Association] *waited for them and took them to Evington in their cars. The children were accompanied by several helpers, some of whom could not speak a word of English.*

This was a group of fifty children out of the 3,826 who had arrived on 23 May 1937 at Southampton on board the steamship *Habana* from Bilbao in northern Spain. It was the largest single influx of unaccompanied young refugees ever to arrive in Britain, in a mass evacuation known as the *Expedición a Inglaterra*. They were refugees of the Spanish Civil War, which by then had been wreaking havoc in their homeland for a year.

| *Basque refugee children disembarking from the Habana, Southampton, 23 May 1937*

By the spring of 1937, after a first winter of the civil war, approximately half of Spain was in the hands of the rebel Nationalist forces led by General Franco. The industrial and mining belt in the north of Spain, including the Asturias and the Basque provinces, was staunchly loyal to the democratically elected Republican government but was now isolated and cut off from the rest of Republican Spain. Franco vowed to terminate the war quickly and by whatever means he had at his disposal. These means included a *Luftwaffe* detachment of Hitler's Condor Legion, which was serving with the Nationalist forces. For Hitler, Spain's internal fratricide presented an opportunity to test and hone his aerial weaponry in support of sympathetic Fascist allies, a rehearsal for the wider European conflict just thirty months later. On Monday, 26 April 1937 fighter planes and bombers attacked the market town of Guernica, the ancient seat of government and therefore of enormous symbolic significance for Basque culture and the aspirations of the nation for independence. The intention of the attack was to undermine morale by using aerial power for the first time in history to systematically kill and terrorise a civilian population and destroy their homes. After four hours of saturation bombing and aerial machine-gunning the town was razed to the ground, left in flames and an unknown number of civilians was killed. Events in Guernica raised a new level of consciousness around the world, not only about the conflict in Spain itself, but also about the indiscriminate effects and the impact of modern warfare on civilian populations.

As refugees swelled the population of major urban centres such as Bilbao, the autonomous Basque government appealed for other countries to relieve the pressure by taking in young refugees. In Britain the National Joint Committee for Spanish Relief (NJCSR) had been established at the end of 1936 to co-ordinate the activities of a multitude of voluntary relief agencies in Spain. As public pressure to act increased, the NJCSR set up a Basque Children's Committee. The chair of the committee, Conservative MP for Kinross, the Duchess of Atholl, eventually managed to persuade a reluctant Prime Minister Stanley Baldwin to allow up to 4,000 young refugees into Britain on the strict condition that the British government would not take any financial responsibility for the children. This would be the responsibility of the Basque Children's Committee, which would have to guarantee at least ten shillings per week for the care and education of each child.

A site for a tented reception camp for the refugees was identified at Swaythling Lane Farm, North Stoneham, near Eastleigh, Southampton. A local committee enlisted many volunteers from the community, and the site was prepared in two weeks. A ship, the *Habana*, which normally carried around 800 passengers, left Bilbao on 21 May 1937 carrying 3,826 children, accompanied by ninety-six *maestras* (female teachers), 118 *señoritas* (young women who had volunteered to accompany the children), fifteen Catholic priests, two English doctors and five nurses. The ship arrived in Southampton on 23 May, welcomed by thousands of people lining the quayside. The passengers were ferried on a fleet of buses to the camp at North Stoneham.

The intention was to disperse the young refugees in smaller groups around the country as soon as practically possible. Local committees were hastily set up all over the country, and temporary refuges were found and prepared to receive the refugees, and it was suggested that a minimum of forty to fifty children per centre was a desirable number. Finance was to be raised locally to support as many of the children as possible, with recourse to the National Basque Children's Committee for funds if necessary. The local refuges became known as 'colonies', in the sense of the Spanish word *colonia*, or *colonia escolar*, a summer camp for schoolchildren. In all around a hundred colonies were established across the country, including one in Leicester.

CHAPTER NINETEEN

MARY LEADS LEICESTER'S RESPONSE
TO THE BASQUE REFUGEE EMERGENCY

Mary Attenborough was at the forefront of the local response in Leicester. Mary had witnessed first-hand what it meant to be a refugee, forced to flee your homeland by an invasion of enemy forces, when her father took onto his teaching staff two young Belgian refugees at the Long Eaton school in 1914. No doubt this experience was in her mind when the sudden urgent need arose to accommodate and care for a large group of refugee children unaccompanied by their parents. An invaluable source of information about the response in Leicester at this time is the pages of the local daily newspaper, the *Leicester Mercury*, covering a story which at the time caught the imagination and sympathy of many local communities across the country but was then largely forgotten two years later when the population at large had wider preoccupations, including the very real threat of the invasion of Britain itself.

Ten days after the *Habana* docked in Southampton the *Leicester Mercury* reported that:

> *Fifty Spanish refugee children will be arriving in Leicester within a fortnight or three weeks' time, according to present plans, and the committee responsible for their reception and care has still to settle upon suitable quarters for them. The chairman of the committee is Councillor C.R. Keene and the secretary Mrs. Attenborough.*

By 5 June 1937 it was confirmed that:

> the 50 Basque children who are coming to Leicester will be housed
> at Evington Hall. This was settled at a meeting of members of the
> committee last evening, and the children will arrive by the end of the
> month. The Hall, which will be rented, is a big brick mansion with
> considerable park ground, and buildings that can be adapted as play
> houses.

Evington Hall is a large, former country mansion nowadays within the
boundaries of the city of Leicester, and in 1937 it had been empty for about
seven years. The local committee, together with a host of volunteers, had
around three weeks to clean, repair, furnish and prepare the hall for use as
a hostel and teaching base for fifty children, with ages ranging from seven
to fifteen, who did not speak English and many not even Spanish, except in
some cases as a second language. They were separated from their families,
who in turn were fearful about their own lives and futures. The task facing
the local committee required strong leadership and organisation.

Cometh the hour, cometh the woman. We learn from the *Leicester
Mercury* that the local committee was:

> representative of all religions and social activities in the city. The Lord
> Mayor (Councillor A.H. Swain) is president, the Bishop of Leicester
> chairman, and Mrs. Attenborough of University College House, the
> Secretary. The Rev. Glan Morgan is the chairman of the executive
> committee, and there is an appeals committee, of which the Deputy
> Lord Mayor, Councillor Richard Hallam, is chairman and Councillor
> Charles Keene secretary.

There is little doubt, however, that the driving force behind this massive
local effort was Mary Attenborough, who now had a new focus outside
of home and the university college and channelled her superabundant
energy into addressing a humanitarian crisis created in a foreign land.
Following a public appeal to raise £1,000 for the initial outlay on repairs
and refurbishment, Mary, as secretary, was the conduit for other offers of
help including gifts in kind, subscriptions and voluntary assistance. David

Attenborough, who was eleven years old at the time, recalled to me his mother's involvement in preparing Evington Hall:

> My clearest memories of this are of seeing my mother on her hands and knees scrubbing the floors of this disused house to make it ready for them. The children, when they eventually arrived, seemed very exotic to my eyes with their black hair and dark complexions, and did not of course speak much English. I accompanied my mother on some of her regular visits and got to know some of the children slightly as their English improved.

Richard Attenborough also had vivid memories of Evington Hall and was a regular visitor there either with Mary or independently. In his autobiographical memoir, *Entirely Up to You, Darling*, co-authored with Diana Hawkins, published in 2008, he looked back seventy years in reflective and whimsical fashion:

> As I approached my fourteenth birthday ... I fell totally under the spell of a Spanish beauty called Rosa. I can still see my first love now, waiting for me in the sunshine at Evington Hall. She can't have been more than fifteen; a small, perfectly proportioned, olive-skinned girl who always wore a rose tucked into her pitch-black hair. And for a few months she was my one and only for evermore. Had she but asked, I would have gladly laid down my life for her. The youngest of the Basque refugees were traumatised and very homesick. Rosa helped with the little ones and took it all in her stride. At every opportunity I would cycle up to the Hall to spend hours holding her hand and gazing into those dark brown eyes.
>
> We stayed in touch after they went home. In the 1960s I was invited ... to the San Sebastian Film Festival. My friends from Evington, having read in the local press that I was coming, wrote to say they'd like to meet me. I saw all of them – except Rosa. There was no quarrel, no dramatic bust-up. After Britain shamefully recognised Franco's regime in 1938 she had returned to her parents. And first love – always remembered, never consummated – had simply withered away like the flowers she wore in her hair.

During the summer of 1937 the *Mercury* carried regular reports from Evington Hall as the young refugees gradually settled in and continued to arouse interest and sympathy from local people – occasionally too much interest of the wrong sort:

> According to the matron, Miss McPhee, visitors sat on the railings surrounding the grounds after they were kept out by the police and plied the children with cigarettes. 'It is most undesirable that the children should be spoiled like this', said Miss McPhee. 'Of course we know that some of the older boys like to smoke occasionally, but we do not want them smoking a lot.'

At the end of July the newspaper gave a brief update:

> Business as usual at Evington Hall although 14 older boys are away, 10 with the Scouts, 4 more with Dr Ellis in Devon. Miss McPhee said she was rather glad on the whole that so many boys are to be away for a fortnight. 'It will give me a chance to get the house cleaned up. There isn't much hope with 14 nearly grown-up boys all over the place.' The children enjoy going to Leicester to the shops. They do not like walking much. Most are town-bred and are much more at home in the busy streets of the city than on a country walk. Some have received letters from their mothers, who had fled to France.

As the Spanish Civil War entered its second year with no end in sight the realisation dawned that most of the refugees may be in Britain for the long haul and that the colonies would need to extend their provision until it was safe for the children to return to their homeland. After six months at Evington Hall the Leicester committee published a report on the first six months. Mary Attenborough was the author of the report and, amongst other matters, she expressed serious concerns about the safety of children returning to Spain just yet:

> The £25 weekly for our 50 children provides for their food, and that of the six adults on the staff, for the matron's salary, the wages of the cook and part-time man, for heat and light, postage on the

children's letters to Spain, some clothes and incidental expenses, and bus fares (which, now that the boys go to school, cost at least £1 a week). Many of those who have adopted a child by promising to subscribe 10s. weekly, have chosen a special child, and have taken a personal interest in him. Such a relationship is particularly valuable to these children, who have been suddenly cut off from their family and country; it gives them back confidence in themselves, and we should be glad if more of our subscribers would come to Evington to choose a child.

We learn from Mary that seven children have gone back to Spain, but others will not return until their parents are living in better conditions:

Either both parents are refugees, living in appalling conditions, or the mother is a refugee and the father a prisoner in Franco territory. We cannot send these children back yet, and undo all that we did when they were rescued from Bilbao.

Mary's concerns were echoed by the Duchess of Atholl MP, chair of the National Committee for Basque Children, who attended a fundraising event organised by the Leicester Committee in February 1938 at the Edward Wood Hall in Leicester. As a member of the national committee Mary would by then have known the Duchess personally. Mary travelled about once a month to meetings of the national committee in London, tirelessly devoting her energies to the cause at both local and national level. The Duchess explained:

that those who said that the children were rescued from imaginary dangers either did not know the facts or did not want to know them… When the children first arrived in this country, the impression made by the experiences they had gone through was seen by the way they would hoard bits of bread and butter, or secrete bits of clothing.

In May 1938 the *Mercury* referred to the impending first anniversary of the arrival of the Basque refugees in England. Mary explained that there were now forty-five children left at Evington Hall, who would remain there until the end of the civil war. Their parents were either not traced, or were prisoners or were themselves refugees:

> *She [Mary Attenborough] has heard from most of the children who recently went back to Spain in Franco territory. The reports are not encouraging, for many of the boys who were here doing so well in school are now running the streets, there being no school for them to attend. This is a real shock to those who, in Leicester, had put such hard work into making these children happy here and their days useful.*

After May 1938 there was no more reporting in the local press from Evington Hall. Instead, through the spring and summer of 1938, we see an intense debate about the pros and cons of repatriation for the refugee children, expressed through the correspondence pages of the *Leicester Mercury*. When the Basque children had arrived in England in May 1937 it was against a backdrop of extensive and daily reporting on the war in Spain, not only in the national press, but also locally. The British public was therefore fairly well-informed at the time about the context for the evacuation of the Basque refugees. By the middle of 1938, however, it seemed clear that Franco's Nationalist rebels would be the eventual 'victors' in Spain even though the conflict only formally ceased almost a year later. Events in Central Europe were now dominating the news.

The situation of the Basque refugees was subsumed in the public consciousness as Britain faced its own external threats. As the conflict in Spain extended into a second and a third year the events at Guernica became more distant in the public memory. When the public remembered the refugees there was more often now a sense of impatience that the Basque refugees should return home as their own conflict had been 'resolved', and Britain should focus instead on the mounting threat to its own existence and identity. In reality of course the situation in Spain was far from resolved by Franco's 'victory'. On 26 May 1938 the *Mercury* published a letter from a group known as the Spanish Children's Repatriation Committee based in London. The letter sought to counter the image of returned refugee children 'running the streets'. The letter claimed that the new Spanish Nationalist government had made education:

a very special feature in the reconstruction of Spain … and the number of schools already constructed in war time is considerable.

The letter goes on to say that readers need have no concerns about the treatment of children:

returned to their own country and people, as they should be at the earliest possible moment. Any of them who have lost their parents, or whose parents cannot for the time being be traced will be well and carefully looked after by the social welfare organisations of National Spain. These centres have been personally inspected by three members of this committee, who can vouch for their humanity, efficiency and the good food supplied therein, all children being treated with impartiality, quite irrespective of the political colour or acts of their parents.

This letter produced a swift response from Mary Attenborough, in her role as Secretary of the Leicester Committee for the Basque Children:

[The Repatriation Committee] *has not helped to repatriate any of the 1,800 children that have been sent back to their parents by the Basque Children's Committee. … We know that at least three of our families in Bilbao and one in San Sebastian are not able to attend school. In one case the aunt of a child still at Evington wrote saying how thankful she was that her niece was receiving regular lessons since her little friend who lived in the same street in Bilbao and who had been repatriated to her parents had to 'run the streets'. … We now have 45 children at Evington whose parents are either prisoners or refugees. Sir Arnold Wilson's Committee has previously suggested that these children, too, should be sent back en masse to Bilbao, there to be cared for in institutions – where, no doubt, they would be taught that their parents are traitors and the cause for which they are fighting is wicked.*

Addressing directly those who had supported the cause in Leicestershire, Mary concluded passionately:

We should be failing in our duty to the children, and to their parents who confided them to our care, if we adopted the course urged by these gentlemen, and I cannot believe that charitable people in Leicester would agree for one moment that we should do so. Our desire is to be able to keep our Leicester children until they can return to their parents, but at the end of June our funds will be exhausted, and if we are not to fail in our task we must beg all our friends to help generously once again.

The Spanish Children's Repatriation Committee members continued their 'dialogue' with Mary through the correspondence pages of the *Mercury*. On 20 July 1938 the Repatriation Committee, still single-minded in its view, wrote in a further letter:

We can without hesitation, affirm that all children, whether their parents can be traced or not, and whatever the politics of parents or relatives, will be cared for by the social welfare centres of Nationalist Spain with the utmost kindness; there is, in fact, no reason why all the Basque children now in this country should not be sent back to the Basque region of Spain.

On 2 August 1938, in her final word on the matter, Mary makes her most impassioned statement yet in a letter:

I had not intended intervening again ... but I have had so many messages and telephone calls regarding the letter in your issue of July 20th that I feel obliged to request again the courtesy of your columns. ... If we were to write to the refugee mother of one of our families at Evington and say that we had decided to send her children back to Bilbao into the hands of those same people who are holding her husband prisoner, it would not be much comfort to her to be assured that, in the words of your correspondent, her children will be treated 'with the utmost kindness'. It is difficult for her to realise that the same authority who is still bombing open towns and villages with unparalleled barbarity can be relied upon to treat her children 'with the utmost kindness'. ... If we can send back children to parents with homes to receive them, then we think that they should go, whether the parents are in Nationalist or Government Spain – but we will not deliver the children up to their parents' enemies.

After close scrutiny of the situation at Evington Hall for the last fourteen months, followed by the 'repatriation debate' through its letters pages, the *Leicester Mercury* carried no further reports about the Basque children between August 1938 and March 1939, when it reported that Evington Hall was to become a convent school. The lease was about to expire and the owners had agreed a sale of the property. The cost of conversion work would run into many thousands of pounds. Before that, however, the minutes of the National Basque Children's Committee record that at the meeting in London on 8 November 1938:

A formal note had been received from Mrs Attenborough informing the Committee that Evington Hall must be closed next Easter, and the Leicester Committee could not obtain alternative accommodation. It was agreed to use the Leicester Home to its fullest capacity as long as it remained open, as the children there enjoy many advantages not available elsewhere.

Three months later in February 1939 the minutes record that:

Mrs Attenborough reported that when Evington Hall closed, the House Committee would continue its work for the purpose of keeping in touch with the children who were in private houses in the district. Mrs Attenborough thought her Committee would be very willing to cover the whole of the Midland area for the Central Committee if this were necessary.

Evidence suggests that the sale of Evington Hall was completed on schedule around Easter 1939, and it must be assumed that the Leicester committee relinquished its lease on the property sometime between April and July 1939 when the 'colony' ceased to exist. How many refugees remained by that time is not known. Presumably the remaining children were repatriated, transferred to other colonies or found new homes, and possibly employment, within the host community in Leicester or elsewhere.

It is not clear what happened individually to the Basque teachers, *señoritas* and priests, who originally accompanied the children to Leicester, and who faced serious personal risks if they returned to Nationalist Spain. Nationally many of the Basque carers of the children chose to remain in Britain, even at risk of long-term separation from their families back home. In some cases ideological differences with their families were never resolved, such is the nature of civil war. Many were able to use and develop their skills to make new lives, raise families and forge new careers in Britain. A significant minority of the older child-refugees themselves also remained in Britain and forged successful careers, often as teachers.

In 2015 Sir David Attenborough recalled to me an incident in 2010 when he attended a festival in Santiago de Compostela and:

found myself sitting next to a man of about my own age who said he had come from a hundred miles or so away to the east in order to meet me, since he had been one of the boys at Evington – and he wished to say thank-you. He remembered the whole episode very well and was anxious to say how grateful they had all been. Apparently after the children returned to Spain many of them kept in touch.

After two years of intense effort by Mary it is not clear exactly when and how her involvement with the Basque refugees finished. Mary and her family would very soon be deeply affected by incidents in another part of Europe, which would shape their family life for the next seven years.

CHAPTER TWENTY

LIFE IN THE FAST LANE!

As if to demonstrate that Mary had inexhaustible energy and was unwilling or unable to slow down, a short news item hidden away near the bottom of page four in the *Leicester Mercury* issue of Thursday 8 June 1939, has what now seems a slightly amusing and tongue-in-cheek air about it, as the newspaper reports how Mary Attenborough received a fine for speeding:

> *Mrs. Mary Attenborough, of College House, University Road, Leicester, was fined £1 and had her licence endorsed at Leicester Police Court today, for exceeding the speed limit in Lutterworth Road. It was stated that when Mrs. Attenborough was told her speed – 43 miles an hour – she replied, 'I had no idea it was that'. When he asked if the defendant had a speedometer, and was told that she had, the Chairman remarked, 'They seem to be quite useless, these machines for recording speed'.*

CHAPTER TWENTY-ONE
WAR WITH GERMANY LOOMS AGAIN

In April 1939, at the Grand Hotel in Leicester, a joint meeting of the Leicester Women's Luncheon Club and the Leicester Soroptimists, attended by Mary, welcomed guest speaker, Vicki Baum, musician and writer. At the time Vicki was fifty-one, and she talked to the audience about her life and philosophy. She had moved to America in 1932, shortly before Hitler came to power, and settled there. From the security of America she was later to witness the banning and burning of her books in Germany. Born into a Jewish family in Vienna she had a difficult childhood and eventually made her way to Germany where she spent the First World War years and experienced privation, near-starvation, the birth of a baby in primitive conditions and eventually revolution in late 1918. After four years of war a mutiny in the German navy triggered widespread civil unrest, which led to the abdication of Kaiser Wilhelm II and the proclamation of a republic. The *Leicester Mercury's* 'A Woman's Diary' feature carried a report about the meeting and quoted Vicki. She described wheeling her young baby in the pram through streets which exploded in gunfire:

Perhaps I shall shock you when I say we welcomed the revolution. ... It stopped the war; it set us free; it came like a thunderstorm at the end of a hot day. The trouble was that there was not enough of a revolution; too many of the wrong elements remained in power, and so Germany drifted back into militarism.

Prophetic words, and four months later the Attenborough family was to witness and experience first-hand the results of the 'wrong elements' remaining in power in Germany. In the middle of August 1939 Irene Bejach, aged thirteen, and her sister, Helga-Maria Bejach (hereafter referred to as Helga Bejach), arrived in Leicester on Helga's twelfth birthday, after a three-day journey by train and boat on one of the *Kindertransports* (literally Children Transports) from Berlin. The plan was for the girls to stay with the Attenborough family at College House for a few weeks until they could continue on their way to New York, where they had an uncle who had agreed to provide temporary sanctuary for his brother's two youngest daughters until they could be joined by their father and older sister.

Less than three weeks after the girls' arrival in Leicester, Prime Minister Neville Chamberlain announced that Britain was at war with Hitler's Germany. Transatlantic shipping for civilians was no longer safe with U-boat attacks on Allied shipping. Irene and Helga thus stayed on with the Attenboroughs for the rest of their formative teenage years until they finally obtained a passage to America in October 1946. A 'few weeks' turned into seven years and two months as the girls were cared for by Mary and Fred Attenborough, *in loco parentis*, according to David Attenborough. They became the 'adopted sisters' of brothers Richard, David and John as the five teenage children all grew up together in wartime Leicester.

CHAPTER TWENTY-TWO

THE BEJACH FAMILY

By 1939 Berlin was the second largest city in Europe with a population of 4.3 million. Jews had lived in Berlin since the end of the thirteenth century, apart from a gap between 1573 and 1671, when they had been expelled from the city. From 1812 to 1910 the Jewish population increased greatly from 3,300 to 142,000. The rapid rise was the result of a mass influx from provincial towns in Germany, from what is now modern Poland, and from other countries of Eastern Europe. A high percentage of the Berlin Jewish population was therefore made up of *Ostjuden* ('Jews from the east') and by the 1930s Jews were prominent in many aspects of the city's economic, intellectual and cultural life.

During the 1920s and early 1930s, even before Hitler came to power, the atmosphere of daily life was becoming increasingly intimidating and menacing for Jews in Berlin. The National Socialist Party was disseminating anti-Semitic propaganda and attacking the Jewish press in the city. In 1931 and 1932 there was a spate of physical attacks on Jewish university students and academics in the city.

Soon after Hitler was appointed Reich Chancellor in January 1933 the process of *Arisierung* ('Aryanisation') of some Jewish-owned enterprises began. However, until *Kristallnacht* ('Night of Broken Glass'), or *Pogromnacht*, as it is often now called in Germany, on 9 and 10 November 1938, many Jewish businesses continued to operate both locally and internationally. It was mainly salaried public employees who felt the initial effects of Nazi policy in Berlin.

From 1933 there was a steady increase of Jewish emigration from all over Germany. By September 1939 the community in Berlin had reduced by about half to 83,000. In Germany as a whole, however, the Jewish population had reduced by around two-thirds in the same period. It has been suggested that the Jewish community in Berlin may have felt more secure, in the relative anonymity of the capital city, than the rest of the Jewish population. A member of the Berlin Jewish Council, Sigmund Weltlinger, recalled:

> *I did not leave because in my life I have seldom gone out of my way to avoid danger, because I was deeply rooted in Germany – I had grown up in the sphere of German culture and found no obstacles. I had friendships with all and did not believe that there was any threat to me personally for my body and life.*

Irene and Helga Bejach were born in the Berlin of these volatile interwar years in January 1926 and August 1927 respectively. Their father, Dr Curt Bejach, was at the time *Stadtarzt* or Medical Officer for Health in the Berlin administrative district of Kreuzberg. Curt had been born of Jewish parents, who were not practising religious Jews. Like many Jewish families in Germany they understood the practical benefits of 'assimilation' in a society and culture where anti-Semitism was never far below the surface. Their mother, Hedwig, a nurse, was born in 1895 into a Protestant family in the town of Brieg, on the River Oder, in what was at the time the German-Prussian province of Schlesien (Silesia).

Curt was born on 20 December 1890 in Jena, a university town in central Germany, the third of seven sons of Max Bejach, a dentist, and Helene Berliner, who had married in 1887. The family moved to Berlin in 1892, first to *Potsdamerstraße*, and then in 1894 to *Claudiusstraße* in the old *Hansaviertel* (Hansa Quarter), where Curt grew up. The *Hansaviertel* was described as a '*ruhiges, gutbürgerliches Wohnviertel*' ('a peaceful, prosperous bourgeois quarter') where no factories or warehouses were permitted, and where professionals, businessmen, actors and artists made their home, many of them Jewish. Curt studied at the local *Friedrichs-Gymnasium* – grammar school – and half of his fellow pupils who took the higher school exams (*Abitur*) went on to become doctors.

Curt's father, Max, died unexpectedly in 1905, aged forty-three, leaving his widow with seven sons and one daughter, aged between two and sixteen years old at the time. Curt studied medicine and dental health between 1910 and 1915 in Berlin, Munich and Königsberg. By 1912 it seems he had joined the Social Democratic Party (SPD). As the First World War interrupted his studies Curt volunteered for service and was a doctor in Königsberg, now the Russian enclave of Kaliningrad on the Baltic coast between Poland and Lithuania. Early in the war he met his future wife, Hedwig Ottow, who was working as a Red Cross nursing sister on the Eastern Front. Hedwig was born on 3 April 1895, the daughter of a Prussian soldier, Max Ottow, and Margarete. By 1900 Max had been promoted to the rank of major.

Curt passed his exams as a dentist in 1919 and married Hedwig on 29 October 1920. It seems that Hedwig's family at first disapproved of their daughter marrying a Jewish dentist as it was fully expected that Hedwig would marry into the Prussian military. Curt obtained his first post-war position as a *Stadtarzt* (literally 'Town Doctor', or Medical Officer for Health) in the small town of Nowawes, near Potsdam, where he remained in post from 1919 to 1921.

In 1921 Curt was appointed to the position of *Stadtarzt* for Kreuzberg, a district of Berlin with major social problems and poverty and correspondingly high social expenditure. The role of the *Stadtarzt* was to decide the public health priorities for the district and control the resources to implement these aims. Many of the newly appointed *Stadtarzt* postholders were Jewish doctors. A comparison of the names of postholders in 1937 shows that only three remained in post out of the twenty appointed in 1933.

Curt was particularly concerned with public health issues, such as the contributory social causes of tuberculosis. He was also an early advocate of birth control. In April 1925 the Kreuzberg authorities established the *Gesundheitshaus am Urban*, a concept of the Mayor Martin Kahle, *Stadtarzt* Curt Bejach and the local public health committee. This was a one-stop health centre on a large scale where all aspects of public health, preventative healthcare, school healthcare and sexual healthcare came together in one large centre. It was heralded as a new, progressive and unique undertaking, not just for Berlin but also for Germany as a whole.

All three of Curt and Hedwig's daughters were born in the 1920s while Curt was in post in Berlin-Kreuzberg. Jutta was born in November 1921, Irene in January 1926 and Helga-Maria in August 1927. In April 1931 Hedwig died of tuberculosis, at the age of thirty-six. Helga was not yet four years old at this time, and although she recalled that her mother was 'tall and good-looking', she did not have much memory of her mother, who was always busy with work and 'not around much'. Jutta recalled that after their mother's death the girls 'did not want Dad to re-marry'.

After the death of the girls' mother Curt continued living in their house near Potsdam and employed a number of *Kinderfräulein*, or nannies, described later by Helga as 'surrogate mothers', to look after the children, and a cook. Later a brother of Hedwig, Dr Eugen Ottow, also moved in with the family. All three sisters attended a state primary school. Jutta and Irene then went to the *Dorothea Lyzeum*, a girls' high school, in the nearby town of Nowawes, while Helga attended a *Lyzeum* closer to home.

After the National Socialists came to power in 1933 circumstances changed rapidly for Curt and his family. On 11 March 1933 members of the SA (*Sturmabteilung* – 'storm detachment') occupied the *Gesundheitshaus am Urban*. Shortly afterwards forty-three Jewish doctors were dismissed from their posts under the new *Gesetz zur Wiederherstellung des Berufsbeamtentums* ('Law for the Restoration of the Professional Civil Service'), introduced on 7 April 1933. Curt was eventually dismissed from his post on 21 August 1933. In the twisted language and ideology of National Socialism, Curt Bejach's three daughters were 'classified' as Jewish, albeit *Mischlinge*, i.e. of mixed heritage. Curt himself was supposedly 'protected' initially because of his *Mischehe* or ('mixed marriage') and the fact that he was now the father of three motherless daughters. The term *Mischling*, literally meaning 'hybrid, crossbreed, mongrel', was used in a derogatory sense during the Third Reich to denote people who were deemed to have only partial Aryan heritage. Ironically it has been estimated that up to 160,000 soldiers who served in the German armed forces during the Second World War were one-quarter, one-half or even fully Jewish.

Helga recalled that after her paternal grandmother died in 1932, when Hitler was on the threshold of power, there was talk within the family about possible emigration, although she was only five at the time and would not have understood the full context. Later she could remember a general consensus within the family that Hitler:

was a maniac who was not going to last.

The girls allowed themselves to be baptised around this time in the hope of achieving a little extra protection. In March 1936 the family's villa was forcefully repossessed and sold:

at an unfair price to Nazi sympathisers.

Curt and his daughters returned to live in an apartment in the old family home at *Claudiusstraße 15* in the *Hansaviertel* district of Berlin.

On 30 September 1938 Curt Bejach and other Jewish doctors had their professional registration removed. They were now officially only 'Krankenbehandler', or 'nursing attendants'. They were only permitted to care for and receive their income from Jewish patients. Curt had very few private Jewish patients; most of his patients were the elderly and the poor in Kreuzberg.

As the situation deteriorated significantly after *Kristallnacht* in November 1938 Curt began to consider how he could save his daughters by sending them out of the country to safety. He was still surprised and shocked that as an 'assimilated' Jew he was facing this dilemma. Curt's eldest sibling, Hans-Egon Bejach, born in 1889, had been a school dentist in Berlin-Neukölln. In early 1939 he had managed to emigrate to New York, where he was working as a doctor. Hans had tried to persuade Curt to register for emigration, but Curt at first resisted the notion that in order to enter the United States he may have to be prepared initially to undertake more 'menial' work. He delayed filling in the necessary paperwork. By the time he came to terms with this idea it was already too late. Helga said in a newspaper interview in 1983:

That was like him. He was so busy with his work.

CHAPTER TWENTY-THREE

THE KINDERTRANSPORT RESCUE MISSION, 1938–39

Curt's immediate plan was to move his daughters out of Germany to safety, with the longer-term aim and hope that his brother, Hans-Egon Bejach, already in New York, could provide a home for them in the event of an enforced family separation, until Curt could join them.

In the immediate aftermath of *Kristallnacht*, in an echo of the Basque refugee crisis eighteen months earlier, the British government eventually agreed to waive certain immigration requirements to allow the entry into Britain of unaccompanied children up to the age of seventeen. No official limit on permitted numbers was ever publicly announced. However, the eventual planned target number of the agencies working to organise the arrangements was for up to 15,000 unaccompanied children to enter Britain in this way. The various agencies initially operated under a non-denominational organisation, known as the Refugee Children's Movement (RCM). The RCM promised to find homes for all the children, including hostels as well as family homes. There was no insistence that prospective homes for Jewish children should be Jewish homes. The British government agreed that, in order to speed up the immigration process, travel documents would be issued on a group, rather than individual, basis.

Meanwhile Fred Attenborough had academic interests in certain German universities, and became well aware of the deteriorating situation for Jewish academics in Germany during the late 1930s. He chaired a committee to bring Jewish academics to Britain. Some of these came to Leicester. Sir David explained:

> Such refugees were only allowed into this country if they had jobs here. So the University College offered distinguished scientists in Germany posts as laboratory assistants which they held until such time as they could get something more suitable in Britain, or were able to continue on their journey to the United States, as I believe several did.

Places were also facilitated for refugee students in certain circumstances.

A network of organisers was established in Germany to identify those children in greatest need or danger, and on 2 December 1938 the first *Kindertransport* arrived in the port of Harwich with 196 children from Berlin. Most groups travelled to England from Dutch ports after long train journeys from locations in Germany, Austria, Czechoslovakia and Poland. In the event almost 9,400 children arrived in Britain on the *Kindertransports* before the outbreak of war.

Mary and Fred had employed a number of young refugees as domestic staff at College House. One such was Ingeborg Gessler. Sir David recalled to me:

> I remember Inge very well. She was a bouncy and cheerful woman around twenty when she arrived and one of several who lived with us in College House helping my parents round the house and with entertaining.

Ingeborg's son, Daniel Herlinger, who now lives in Santa Barbara, California, has given me permission to quote from his letter written to Sir David in April 2020. Daniel's mother came from the town of Schönbeck in what is now the region of Mecklenburg-Vorpommern in north-eastern Germany, close to the Baltic coast and the Polish border:

> My grandparents from Schönbeck, Germany, sent my mother, Ingeborg Gessler, to England after 1938 for her safekeeping. She was taken in by your parents, Frederick and Mary, with a few other girls ostensibly as 'domestics'. She often spoke fondly of the graciousness of your family,

noting that your father was the Dean of the College in Leicester, and that 'Richie picked her up at the train station when she arrived.' While in Leicester she met my father, Rudolf, who was in the Czech army under British command. After the war they moved to Czechoslovakia, where I was born in 1946. Then to London and immigrated to the United States in 1949. … I have a warm spot for your family. In some sense I feel I wouldn't be here if it were not for them.

Ingeborg and Rudolf had married in Leicester before moving to Czechoslovakia after the war. Daniel's letter with reference to his own family background illustrates perfectly how so many individuals were:

strewn around by the four winds,

to quote another *Kindertransport* survivor, Ruth David, as a result of the chaotic and devastating processes of war.

Another of the young European refugees to live with and work for the Attenborough family was a highly educated young Jewish woman, whose name is now lost. She had worked as a housekeeper for Dr Curt Bejach. She begged Mary and Fred to provide a temporary home for Helga and Irene, and they agreed to do so. While Curt anxiously awaited the permits for Helga and Irene to leave Berlin on one of the *Kindertransports* Mary and Fred arranged with a widowed friend, Mrs Hancock, who lived in Letchworth Road in the Western Park area of Leicester with her son and daughter, to take Helga initially while Irene would join the Attenboroughs at College House.

On 10 August 1939 Helga and Irene went to the station in Berlin with their father and elder sister, Jutta, who was by now eighteen and as such too old to travel on a *Kindertransport*. Jutta may have been able to secure a job in Britain as a 'maid', but Curt was not happy about this prospect, so she stayed behind in Berlin. At the station, according to Helga:

there were about 50–100 Jewish children, I can't remember the exact number. I think we were the only Mischlings on the train.

They said goodbye to their father and sister and the train travelled to the Hook of Holland. Although they had lived through *Kristallnacht* in Berlin

| *Helga (left) and Irene Bejach in Berlin, shortly before leaving for England, 1939*

the girls had nevertheless been shielded from the worst horrors of Nazi intimidation. They did not fully appreciate the danger of their situation in Germany, and as they boarded the ship there was a sense of adventure about the journey and the future awaiting them. All three sisters and their father believed that they would be reunited within a year or so, therefore the magnitude of the departure was not felt at the time.

Many of the children would have quite recently witnessed first-hand threats and assaults on lives and property on *Kristallnacht*. They may have experienced discrimination, disruption and exclusion in the education system. When they left their homes to join the *Kindertransports* some may even have sensed that they may never see their families again. Despite their sense of adventure Helga and Irene, at the ages of eleven and thirteen, would nevertheless have had some comprehension of the political and cultural climate, which made their journey necessary, and would have understood their father's desperation to send them to a place of safety.

CHAPTER TWENTY-FOUR

HELGA AND IRENE SETTLE IN LEICESTER

Helga and Irene landed in England at the port of Harwich on 11 August 1939, Helga's twelfth birthday. They were met at Liverpool Street station in London, by a 'social worker', presumably from the Refugee Children's Movement, who accompanied them on the two-hour train journey to Leicester where they were met at the station by Mary Attenborough. Mary and Fred Attenborough had agreed to give a home to the daughters of Curt Bejach until they could continue their journey to their uncle in New York. Irene was to live with the Attenborough family in College House, whilst Helga initially went to stay with Mrs Hancock, although she was still ultimately in the guardianship of the Attenboroughs. Almost as soon as the girls arrived at College House Mary must have realised that another war was imminent, and she may already have been anticipating and planning in her own mind for a much longer stay for her two young charges.

Just seventeen days after Irene and Helga's arrival Britain was at war with Germany, and the girls could not complete their journey to America. Mrs Hancock said she would not be able to continue looking after Helga for much longer, not only because of the cost involved, but also, according to David Attenborough, because:

Helga at this stage was understandably very unsettled.

Mrs Hancock was a widow but had a son and a daughter, Clifford and Peggy, both slightly older than Helga. Although to a twelve-year-old, Mrs Hancock seemed 'stern' and 'old-fashioned', Helga always acknowledged that the family was very kind to her. After a few months with Mrs Hancock Helga joined her sister, Irene, to live at College House. When Irene and Helga first arrived in August 1939 it was not a complete surprise to Richard, David and John that their parents would 'foster' vulnerable children. Mary and Fred would often take one or two boys, who had never seen the sea, with them on annual family holidays to Wales. Richard recalled:

> There were always other children in the house who were in some way disadvantaged. Fred and Mary were constantly looking for ways to address the problems of poverty, injustice and cruelty.

The brothers were already well aware, through their interaction with the Basque children, of the personal tragedies inflicted by war. When it became clear that the girls' onward journey to New York would have to be postponed indefinitely Mary and Fred explained to the boys that:

> it was their wish to take the girls permanently into the family and to treat them as their daughters. They would become a family of seven as opposed to five and they would all be treated alike.

Richard Attenborough conceded that this sudden change to family life caused tensions:

> but we felt excited rather than compromised.

He also later wrote that the arrival of Helga and Irene:

> brought into our ordered, middle-class household an awareness of a wider and more dangerous world. It was their presence which allowed [Fred and Mary] to show us in an immediate and practical fashion that actions do indeed speak louder than words.

We can look back now and see the war as a major historical event, which started in September 1939 and ended, in Europe at least, in May 1945. It is difficult for me to imagine the state of mind of my own parents and grandparents at the time, who had no idea how long the conflict and disruption might last and, in the first years of the conflict, had recurring nightmares about the very real prospect of invasion. It speaks volumes for the selfless and pragmatic approach of Mary and Fred Attenborough that they accepted so readily the de facto fostering arrangement of two German teenage refugees with no clear end or plan in sight. This does not mean, however, that they had no concerns or anticipated no frictions after their decision, but their humanity overcame or subsumed these concerns as they and their young family quickly adapted to the 'new normal'.

In relation to the living arrangements at College House, David explained to me that both Helga and Irene:

> at some time or other certainly slept on the very top floor which I imagine, in the Superintendent's day, accommodated domestic staff. My brothers and I shared a playroom on the ground floor at the back on the right-hand side; and the basement/cellar certainly was in use – as an air-raid shelter. It was strengthened with large wooden timbers supporting its ceiling and I can remember sitting down there listening to the sound of what we were convinced was German bombers overhead. ('You can tell they are jerries,' we used to say sagely to one another, 'because the sound of their engines wavers.') Pure invention, I suspect.

Fortunately both Mary and Fred had some knowledge of German. Mary learnt and studied the language, as we have seen, at both the Sorbonne and also at University College, Nottingham, although she chose not to 'major' in the language. Fred also spoke a little German, although Sir David commented to me that much of his father's knowledge of German:

> I suspect came from singing Schubert Lieder!

After the summer break, and just a month after arriving in a strange country with virtually no knowledge of the language, the girls entered the nearby Wyggeston Girls' Grammar School in Lancaster Road, Leicester, the sister school to the Wyggeston Boys' Grammar School attended by all three

Attenborough boys. Both schools were and still are within a five-minute walk of College House. Helga's daughter, Beverly, says that her mother was 'hyperactive' at school, and she thought the school uniforms were 'hideous', but she acknowledged that this meant there was no competition among the girls for clothes. Helga and Irene were always aware of their half-Jewish heritage, but they had grown up in a non-religious environment. At College House no religious rituals were observed, but the Attenboroughs employed Jewish domestic staff from time to time, and these young women were allowed a room and space to celebrate key events in the Jewish calendar such as *Pesach* (Passover). Irene and Helga were allowed to observe these rituals, although they did not participate.

Helga found Leicester 'exciting' and found a strong role model in Mary. She said of life at College House with the Attenboroughs:

> *They were a most extraordinary family, really brilliant. As well as being intellectual Auntie Mary was wonderful at looking after the house,*

Aerial photo Leicester looking south-west, 1930s. Wyggeston Girls School (centre), De Montfort Hall (top left), Pavilion (far top left), War Memorial (top centre) with Victoria Park, and College House (far top right corner)

good at everything. Uncle Fred was stricter. Two gongs would sound at mealtimes, one to wash your hands and one to be at the table and we all toed the line. They were so supportive of my passion for ballet ... David and Irene were the same age and they fought but he was very nice to me. He would bring me books on ballet from the library. We were really so lucky.

Richard Attenborough admitted that sharing the family home with Helga and Irene in wartime Leicester strongly influenced the future themes of his artistic work and his portrayal of human rights issues in particular:

Instead of hearing of the horror of racial prejudice, anti-Semitism and brutality in theory we heard it first-hand.

Once in Leicester Helga and Irene had few discussions about their former life in Germany, and they were 'not particularly overjoyed' even when they received mail from Germany. This may have been in part a kind of defence mechanism to suppress their anxieties. Helga admitted that new interests and activities at school, particularly dance, helped her to look forward and not to the past. She said that dance absorbed her and 'became my salvation'.

Both sisters left Wyggeston after three years on 28 July 1942, Irene aged sixteen and Helga aged fourteen. Helga had presumably expressed a wish to leave the school at the same time as her older sister. The earliest state school leaving age at the time was indeed fourteen, but Mary and Fred, and presumably Helga herself, were no doubt keen to channel Helga's energies into pursuing some form of continuing education and perfecting her acquaintance with the English language, particularly as the longer-term aim was for the sisters to travel on to relatives in America.

Helga Bejach practising ballet, grounds of College House, 1942

Acting *in loco parentis,* and having no idea at that stage how much longer the war would continue and therefore how long the girls would have to wait for onward travel to New York, Mary and Fred had very difficult decisions to make in respect of continuing education and development for two girls with very different personalities. How they dealt with this dilemma will be explained later, largely in Mary's own words.

CHAPTER TWENTY-FIVE

THE EFFECTS OF WAR IN LEICESTER

When war broke out just three weeks after the arrival of Helga and Irene in Leicester they found themselves living in a new country, indefinitely, staying with strangers, with only rudimentary knowledge of English at that stage, knowing that their father and elder sister were now trapped in 'enemy territory'. They were also now old enough to understand the implications of their Jewish background for their family still in Germany. They seem to have quickly made new acquaintances, many of them Jewish, some made perhaps at school and some perhaps introduced to them by Mary and Fred. In Leicester the Orthodox Synagogue, consecrated in September 1898, is still in Highfield Street, about half a mile from College House. There had been a small influx of Jewish refugees into the city from Central Europe throughout the 1930s which augmented the existing core community. The European arrivals were only a part of the sudden growth of the Leicester Jewish community during the 1940s. More significant was the influx from other large cities in Britain, such as London and Manchester, as they sought a 'safer' refuge from bombing. A number of immigrants from London in particular chose Leicester as a destination because it was an important European centre of hosiery, textiles and fashion. One refugee from London amusingly quotes the removals man who moved her family to Leicester as saying:

You'll find a better class of Jewish people in Leicester than in the East End.

Events in Europe had different effects on Jewish refugees who had fled to Leicester. For some their traditional identities were strengthened, others were quick to adapt to the Anglo-Jewish way of life, while some broke their Jewish ties completely.

College House looks out across the seventy acres of Victoria Park towards Clarendon Park, Knighton and Stoneygate in Leicester, suburbs already well established by the turn of the twentieth century and largely inhabited by middle-class professionals, artists and businessmen. Many physical features of this area around Victoria Park today would have been familiar to Irene and Helga in the 1940s. The southern side of Victoria Park Road, facing College House across the park, with its large Edwardian villas, would be recognisable, as would the busy local shopping centre in nearby Queens Road. The Arch of Remembrance, designed by Sir Edwyn Lutyens, and the De Montfort Hall concert venue, which celebrated its one hundredth birthday in 2013, would have been very familiar sights to Irene and Helga, who mentions in her diary several visits to the hall for dances and concerts. This iconic venue has regularly hosted local, national and international classical orchestras, as well as the likes of Ella Fitzgerald, Frank Sinatra, The Beatles and The Rolling Stones. David Attenborough was a member of a local Scout group, whose members acted as programme sellers at the hall and were then allowed to watch the concerts for free. He told me that, as a consequence:

by the age of 12 or 14 I knew all the Beethoven and Brahms symphonies.

As a major industrial city Leicester was always a likely target for German bombing raids, but it did not suffer the same level of damage and fatalities as neighbouring Coventry, or ports like Plymouth and Southampton. Irene and Helga, however, could not have failed to notice various activities on their own doorstep, which would have reminded them of the ongoing threat and danger. For example, a large aircraft searchlight was installed close to De Montfort Hall.

On 14 November 1940 Coventry was targeted in a major raid by the *Luftwaffe*. The glow in the sky from the destructive fires twenty-four miles away could be seen clearly to the south-west of Leicester. The city of Leicester was also hit that night by bombers en route to Coventry. The area worst hit was Highfields, just half a mile away from College House to the east of Victoria Park. Around 550 houses were destroyed, over 4,000 were damaged and over eighty industrial premises were either demolished or disabled. Most of the 108 fatalities and 200 injuries were sustained in Highfields, and the Orthodox Synagogue itself was badly damaged by bombs which fell on the other side of the road.

On Wednesday 20 November 1940, another raid of much smaller proportions came even closer to home for Irene and Helga. The *Leicester Mercury*, reporting on Thursday 21 November, in the anonymous style required by wartime censorship, noted:

A Midland town that had suffered in the bombing of Tuesday-Wednesday night stood in preparedness last night and for many hours suffered intermittent bombing. The raid was by no means as severe as in the previous night, but casualties were caused ... A German plane dropped a flare to light up its target, and then a large bomb fell in a park. The blast from this bomb caused a great deal of damage in houses surrounding the area.

In fact two parachute landmines were dropped by a Heinkel bomber, which had flown in from Belgium. The first destroyed a factory in St Saviours Road, Highfields, which was producing parts for RAF Spitfire fighter planes, and the second damaged beyond repair the large pavilion in Victoria Park, which had been erected in 1876. Sir David recalled that:

A tramp was sleeping [there] that night. He emerged from the ruins a bit shaken but uninjured. However, the bomb did make a satisfyingly large crater from which us kids were thrilled to collect little bits of twisted metal.

David and his friends collected various items from the site:

The prize of my collection was a bit of the rope that had attached the parachute to the landmine – which is how we kids knew it wasn't a normal bomb.

Later intelligence reports revealed that the intended target of the second landmine was in fact a secret radio transmitter, which was housed in the nearby university college, so the family in College House may have had a very lucky escape on the 20 November 1940.

By the middle of 1940 many people in Britain were convinced that it was only a matter of time before the country was invaded. Ironically, just three years after desperate parents in the Basque country in Spain were countenancing sending young children out of the country for safety, and only twelve months after the *Kindertransports* had similarly rescued nearly 10,000 children from almost certain death in Nazi-occupied Europe, plans were now being made for British parents to apply for their own children to be evacuated, not only from threatened urban areas to quieter rural locations but also out of the country completely. One wonders whether Irene and Helga were aware of a meeting at their school, attended by almost a thousand parents to discuss this very subject, reported in the *Leicester Mercury* on 10 July 1940, and if so their reaction to it. Mary and Fred would certainly have known of the event, held under the auspices of the Children's Overseas Reception Board (CORB), an agency sponsored by the British government. The proposed destinations were Canada, Australia, New Zealand and South Africa with some also going to the United States. In all over 211,000 children had been registered by their parents for the scheme before it was abandoned after a few weeks as being logistically impossible to achieve without unacceptable risks to life during passage. It is also estimated that around 14,000 British children had been evacuated overseas by private arrangement by the end of 1941. Parents who sent their children overseas during the war faced criticism in some quarters for the many risks they were taking.

CHAPTER TWENTY-SIX

NEWS FROM GERMANY

When Helga and Irene left Germany on the eve of the outbreak of war their sister, Jutta, was almost eighteen and as such was too old to be rescued by the *Kindertransport*. Jutta had wanted to study medicine in Berlin but was now barred from doing so on account of her Jewish heritage under the *Rassengesetze*, or 'race laws'. She worked in an office for a while and then as a *Zwangsarbeiterin*, or 'forced labourer', in a parachute factory.

A letter to Helga dated 3 June 1941 from her father, Curt, in Berlin, explains that Jutta will be returning home at the end of June after four and a half months away. Curt makes the effort to remain upbeat in the letter to his youngest daughter, and says that they are now starting to make preparations for their *Ausreise* ('emigration'). They were apparently on a waiting list for a US visa. He writes that, with luck, they might all be reunited by the end of the year. Twelve months later, in June 1942, Curt Bejach was sent as forced labour for three months to work in his downgraded capacity as a *Behandler*, or 'medical assistant', at Waldlager Britz, a camp in north-eastern Brandenburg, which housed prisoners of war and foreign forced labour workers, mostly Polish Jews. One of the survivors recalled thirty years later that the prisoners did not acknowledge the term *Behandler* but referred to Curt instead as the *jüdischer Arzt*, the 'Jewish doctor'.

Shortly after Curt returned to Berlin, on the night of 22–23 November 1943, most of the old *Hansaviertel* was destroyed in Allied bombing raids, including the Bejach family home at *Claudiusstraße 15*. Fortunately neither Curt nor Jutta were there at the time, but they quickly had to make emergency housing arrangements. Curt moved into the home of a colleague, Dr Georg Braun, in Berlin-Charlottenburg, whilst Jutta stayed with a friend from school in a Berlin suburb. Jutta continued to see her father during this time. On 18 December 1943 a message was sent from Jutta via the German Red Cross to Irene in Leicester. The message was sent on behalf of both Jutta and Curt, saying they were both well and wishing Irene a happy birthday. The message was not received until 25 January 1944, three weeks after her birthday. Irene replied on 7 March 1944, by which time she would not have known that her father was no longer in Berlin.

In December 1943 a Nazi party circular authorised local security police to deport Jewish spouses of formerly protected mixed marriages if those marriages had been ended by divorce or death. Very soon afterwards, on 10 January 1944, Curt Bejach was deported by train with 351 fellow prisoners on the 99 *Alterstransport* from the goods station in Moabit, Berlin, to Theresienstadt, where he was forced to continue working in a medical capacity as long as his strength held up. This was the fate of many deported Jewish doctors. Theresienstadt (Czech name Terezin) had been built as a fortress township by the Habsburg Emperor Joseph II. During the Nazi period it was referred to as a 'ghetto', and the Nazis used it as a transit camp mainly for Auschwitz.

On 17 July 1944 Curt sent a typed letter from Theresienstadt to Jutta saying that he was still receiving correspondence intermittently, and he had received the card celebrating and depicting Jutta's recent marriage. Jutta, now aged twenty-two, had married Axel Grosser, like herself half-Jewish, earlier in 1944. Jutta recalled that they took their marriage vows on a copy of the Bible, unlike many young German couples at the time, who swore their vows on a copy of Hitler's *Mein Kampf*.

A letter in English dated 8 May 1945 from Jutta and Axel to Irene and Helga explains that they are now living near Hamburg. Jutta says that they have not heard news of their father since October 1944, but:

at all events we will try to come out of Germany.

She asks her sisters to pass on her new address to their Uncle Hans in New York and sends:

cordial regards to you and Attenboroughs.

Jutta says she hopes to be able to pass the letter to a British or American soldier, who will send it on to Leicester. In the event it would be another five years before Jutta and Axel finally left Germany and Jutta was reunited with her sisters after a ten-year separation.

After eight months at Theresienstadt Curt Bejach was deported on a transport with around 1,500 other prisoners on 29 September 1944 to Auschwitz, where it is believed he was murdered on 31 October 1944. Irene and Helga would not learn their father's fate for certain until well after the end of the war.

CHAPTER TWENTY-SEVEN

NEW YORK, NEW LIFE, HELGA AND
IRENE EMIGRATE TO AMERICA, 1946

Following the cessation of hostilities, firstly in Europe in May 1945, and later in the year in Asia and the Pacific, it was possible to believe that the final stage of the long journey of Irene and Helga, emigration to America, may soon become a reality. Their Uncle Hans in New York made enquiries in September with the RCM about the possibility of onward travel but was told that it was impossible to predict when they may sail as the shipping situation was only just beginning to return to normal. A regional representative of the RCM had, however, met Irene and Helga in Leicester and assured Hans that the girls are:

a success in every respect.

He also said that the girls in turn have:

every reason to be thankful to Mr and Mrs Attenborough for all the care and excellent education they have provided for the girls.

It would be over a year before Helga and Irene, who had arrived in Leicester as girls of twelve and thirteen, finally sailed on the SS *Aquitania* from Southampton on 27 October 1946 and were 'admitted permanent' at New York on 2 November 1946, as young women aged nineteen and twenty.

Irene was described in the ship's manifest as 'short-hand typist' and Helga as 'student'. Their nationality or country of origin was listed as '(Germany) Stateless'. Their last permanent address was listed simply as 'England, Leicester'.

New York at the end of the war was a very different place to the city which had entered the war four years earlier, and this was to a large extent due to the war itself, which propelled the city out of the Depression of the 1930s into a new era of unparalleled prosperity. In her book *Manhattan 45* Jan Morris describes the scene and atmosphere just fifteen months before Helga and Irene sailed into Manhattan, as the *Queen Mary* approached, bringing back the first large contingent of American troops after the end of the war in Europe:

> ... *ahead of them waited the towers of the city ... glittering in the afternoon sun ... they stood there metal-clad, steel-ribbed, glass-shrouded, colossal and romantic – everything that America seemed to represent in a world of loss and ruin.*

This then was the new world facing Irene and Helga as they disembarked in New York on 2 November 1946. Irene and Helga's destination in New York was the home of their uncle, Hans-Egon Bejach, the oldest of the Bejach brothers, and his wife, Frieda. Hans had managed to emigrate from Germany in 1939, and he was practising as a doctor in Lower Manhattan.

Irene soon found work in New York using the secretarial skills she had learnt at college in Leicester. She had a brief marriage, which ended with a divorce, and there were no children from this marriage. In 1960, aged thirty-four, she married Sam Goudsmit, who was fifty-eight at the time, a major figure in American physics. Irene and Sam met when they were both working at the Brookhaven National Laboratory on Long Island. Both Irene and Helga had maintained contact with all the Attenborough family, and the bond with their English 'family' was very strong, even to the extent that Sam flew from America to England to ask Fred Attenborough for Irene's hand in marriage. Sam died of a heart attack on 4 December 1978 in Nevada. In America Irene did not pursue any formal further education or degree course, but she was, according to her niece, Beverly:

smart as a whip, and could hold her own with all of her husband Sam's colleagues (who you can imagine were quite intellectual).

Irene passed away on 25 May 1994, aged sixty-eight, with no children from either marriage. Beverly said she was:

probably one of the kindest and most generous people that I have known. When she died quite suddenly in 1994 I felt a huge void as did our family.

Helga found work as a telephone operator in New York. She also picked up once again her interest in dancing and attended a number of dance classes and courses. Helga met her future husband, Herman Waldman, a clinical psychologist, on a 'blind date' at an ice-skating rink in Bear Mountain Park on the west bank of the Hudson River in 1952. Helga continued to pursue her passion for dance, encouraged by Herman. After teaching modern dance at the Rockland Center for the Arts in West Nyack, New York, for many years, she became the center's director of dance education. She also continued her pursuit of formal further education and obtained a BA from the Rodger Williams University when she was in her forties and later a masters in occupational therapy and recreation from Lehman College in the Bronx in her fifties.

After retirement Helga and Herman moved permanently to live in Florida in 1989. Helga passed away in 2005 and was survived by Herman, who died in September 2016, aged ninety-three. She was also survived by two daughters, Beverly Waldman Rich and Hilary Waldman, and six grandchildren. Both Beverly and Hilary assisted me enormously when I undertook initial research into the story of their mother and their aunt. I now consider both very good friends, and, with the kind permission of the University of Leicester, I have been able to show both Beverly and Hilary and their families on separate occasions around College House, where their mother and aunt spent so much of their formative years, sheltered and guided by Mary and Fred. Bev and Hilary have maintained close contact with the Attenborough family and usually visit them when in England.

Irene and Helga's older sister, Jutta, who had survived the war years inside Germany, eventually emigrated to America with her husband, Axel,

| *The Bejach sisters re-united in New York, 1950. Left to right, Irene, Jutta and Helga*

in 1949, when she was almost twenty-eight, ten years after she had said goodbye to her sisters as they departed for England. Jutta and Axel had one son, Rene, born in New York City. They divorced in 1967. Jutta worked for a medical textbook company, Grune and Stratton, in New York, and became the company's vice-president for medical books and operations when she was in her fifties. At the time of writing Jutta still lives in New York State, now approaching her one hundredth birthday.

In the words of another *Kindertransport* survivor, a very good friend of mine, Ruth David, when writing of her own siblings, who found themselves in three different continents:

> *We have been strewn around by the winds, made new homes, created new families. That is the pattern of human evolution. We would have preferred a different route.*

CHAPTER TWENTY-EIGHT

THE DISCOVERY OF NEW PAPERS
IN THE UNITED STATES, 2019

In mid-2019, shortly before a visit to England by Helga's daughter, Beverly, and her family, Beverly and her sister Hilary had been sorting through and trying to order the possessions of their father, Herman Waldman, who had died three years earlier. They came across various documents and papers, which they thought might interest me in my various research projects as they related to the Attenborough family and to the time when their mother and aunt were living in Leicester. When we met once again in Leicester on 4 July 2019 Beverly explained that one of the items they had found was a three-year diary kept by Helga which covered her final years spent in England, 1944 to 1946. The diary was approximately A5 in size, one page per calendar day, so there were three entries per page, one for 1944, 1945 and 1946. The space for entries was, therefore, limited and really only sufficient for brief notes and memoranda, in total contrast to Mary's Sorbonne diary, where she could allow as much daily diary space as she wished for her micro-detailed recollections of people, places and events in Paris. The equivalent level of detail for Helga's three-year coverage would have required almost one million words!

Another interesting document they found was a letter of 2,500 words written by Mary Attenborough to Uncle Hans-Egon Bejach (Uncle Hans) in New York in October 1946. The purpose of the letter, which also had a short introduction by Fred Attenborough, was to summarise the educational achievements and progress in the broadest sense, the character development and a personal view of the future prospects and possible career choices of the two young women who were about to embark on a new life with their uncle and aunt in America some eighteen months after the end of the war in Europe. Although the document's purpose is as a letter of introduction for the sisters to their own blood relatives, whom they had not seen for over seven years, it also inevitably tells us much about the character and personality of Mary, who had the main responsibility of caring for, nurturing and guiding Helga and Irene through the most difficult transitional period of their lives from young teenagers to young women.

Both the diary and the letter are very special primary sources from a research point of view as they offer additional insights into the life of Mary and the Attenborough family during the wartime years in Leicester. Both documents taken together offer two sides of the same coin, particularly as they relate to Helga, as they show the viewpoints of both the child and the carer on the same subjects and time period.

Beverly initially suggested that this 'treasure trove' of papers should come to me for safekeeping and also to assist my ongoing research, but after further discussion we agreed that the most secure and appropriate location to preserve the papers, given the links to the Attenborough family and the university, would be the library of the University of Leicester. After further liaison with Simon Dixon, Head of Archives and Special Collections, the papers were received by the university from Helga's family in the autumn of 2019 for safekeeping on a long-term loan basis, where they will continue to be a valued resource for ongoing research.

CHAPTER TWENTY-NINE

HELGA'S LEICESTER DIARY, 1944–46

Helga's diary starts on New Year's Day 1944 when she was sixteen years old, very different from the girl who was eleven when she left Berlin in such traumatic circumstances and 'celebrated' her twelfth birthday on the day she arrived in Leicester. Both Helga and sister Irene were of the generation of German Jewish children who in many cases effectively lost their school years, due in the first instance to harassment and anti-Semitic bullying and the closure of primary schools, and then to the disruption of enforced flight and uncertain futures during their secondary school years. In the case of Helga and Irene their schooling was reasonably 'normal' and planned until the point when they left Berlin and then reasonably stable once they arrived in Leicester. For Mary and Fred Attenborough the challenges and the responsibilities were enormous and unenviable. Almost overnight they were expected to become 'foster parents' to two adolescent girls who had been 'shepherded' from Berlin in haste after hurried farewells to their elder sister and father with no clue as to when, where or if they would ever be reunited. At the time the future as such was not uppermost in their minds. Helga recalled many years later:

> *The trip to England was an adventure for me at the time. It was all new and an exciting thing to do. I remember I was very happy. How could we as children fully comprehend?*

For Mary and Fred, however, it was considerably more than an 'adventure' as they had to quickly review and revise their living arrangements at College House. With three boys of their own to consider, they also had to revise budgets to cater for five active and hungry teenagers, and they had to sort out educational plans for the two girls with no idea about long-term planning needs or the potential length of the conflict in Europe and the disruption this would cause. This aspect, as we shall see later, is very much the key subject of Mary's letter to Uncle Hans in October 1946 as she tries to explain in a single letter the decisions they had to make and continually reappraise *in loco parentis* in respect of the girls' broader education and future career prospects. The extent of the influence on Mary of her own father's radical and comprehensive approach to education will be assessed and judged by history, but I would argue that it was significant. Mary's approach to the position now facing the family seems to have been typically pragmatic and no-nonsense. David Attenborough recalled:

> *My parents then explained to me and my two brothers that we now had two sisters, who would be staying with us until the war was over. And so they did.*

Helga later recalled:

> *Looking back, I do feel Irene and I were exceptionally lucky.*

When she started writing the three-year diary, however, Helga did not ostensibly appreciate just how fortunate they were. The opening entry for 1 January 1944 was inauspicious and blunt:

> *New Year. Life boring as usual.*

Not an unusual reaction from a sixteen-year-old, perhaps, and hardly surprising given the circumstances in which she and her sister were living. Helga's life up to that point had been anything but normal. For Helga and Irene life was continually in flux. Their hopes of a departure for America were being constantly dashed by the continuation of the conflict and, even after the cessation of hostilities, they were thwarted by what they saw as bureaucratic delays. Irene seems to have been personally in touch with the relevant agencies and family relatives, including cousins in the United States, more than Helga, and when their expectations of onward travel were repeatedly pushed back Irene's moods of depression were then often picked up by her younger sister.

By 1944 Helga was completely wrapped up in her new passion for dancing, which dominated thoughts about her future direction in life and also acted as a kind of defence blanket against the harsher realities of their situation, which included underlying anxieties about their loved ones in Germany. Helga later said that dance absorbed her and became her salvation. Although Helga's diary entries frequently and openly express her boredom, frustration and introspection they are never negative about their generous hosts. They are often light-hearted, self-mocking and amusing. Although Helga's diary as a seventeen-year-old in Leicester is completely different in style from Mary's diary as a seventeen-year-old in Paris it is similar in one respect as an important and fascinating snapshot in time and hence a significant contribution to the social history of a city and a family. It is also written with a level of competence and confidence in English which does not suggest in any way being the writer's second language and indicates that the written and spoken language had been mastered by Helga in a relatively short space of time. Compared with some of their fellow refugees they had the enormous advantage of living in an environment which naturally nurtured and encouraged that competence of understanding and education in the broadest sense, albeit unconsciously. Richard Attenborough's son, Michael, told me that even after many years living in America, Helga's heavy mid-European accent was still very evident, and she would be teased about it in the most affectionate way.

Helga always referred to Mary as 'Auntie', 'Aunty' or 'Mrs. A.'. Fred was referred to as 'Uncle' or 'Mr. A.', but, as he was less involved in the day-to-day household, there are far fewer references to Fred. As she grew into a young woman Helga's relationship with Mary seems to have been part 'daughter–mother' and part 'sister–elder sister'. Helga records regular shopping trips into Leicester where they would buy clothes together, and also, as they must have shared similar clothes sizes at the time, Mary would often lend her own outfits to Helga for special occasions. On 8 January 1945 Helga:

> *Went to meet Mrs. A. in town in afternoon. Bought sweet green dress at Adderley's and stockings.*

Adderley's was a large and popular store in Gallowtree Gate in the heart of Leicester city centre and seems to have been a frequent clothes shopping destination for Mary and Helga. On New Year's Day 1946 Helga:

> *tried on Auntie's red evening dress for 21st party,*

and a week later, on 9 January:

> *Audrey's 21st party. My first evening dress do. Aunty lent me her lovely red flowered chiffon frock. All the family said I looked very nice.*

In 1945 on 17 May:

> *Aunty got all her evening frocks out. College dinner tonight. I love looking at fancy clothes.*

The realities of wartime living, shortages and a tight budget are illustrated by an amusing entry on 10 January 1945:

> *Broke a cup. Have to face Mrs. A. in the morning.*

There are several references to 'housework', never a popular occupation, and no doubt well-organised on a rota by Mary. On 18 April 1945:

> *Was moody in morning. Housework is so boring.*

Helga does not record whether the boys did their share of housework! On a different plane Helga also records a number of conversations, discussions and debates held within the family. Shortly before VE Day, on 20 April 1945, she notes:

Had terrific conversation about politics with John, Mrs. A. and Irene.
Good fun.

Another responsibility, which would have fallen mainly on Mary, might come under the heading of 'moral protection'. A note in the diary on 12 December 1944 concerns a name, which has not previously appeared in the diary:

Mr R. came while I was out. Mrs A. talked to him but won't let me go
out. She sent him away.

From 1943 Helga was spending several weeks each year at the relocated Ginner-Mawer School of Dance and Drama in Cornwall, which she absolutely relished. It seems these terms were at least in part funded by the generous benefaction of Mr Percy Gee. On 7 September 1944 Helga noted:

Mr Gee rang up the other night. I can go to Cornwall. I am so happy.

Percy Gee was a founder member of the university college, chairman of the college council and generous benefactor of the university college from the outset, personally financing the institution during the financial crises of the 1930s. There are indications that he also helped to sponsor Helga and Irene when they first came over on the *Kindertransport*. However, his sponsorship was not limitless, and presumably the funding for Helga's dancing courses was shared with the Attenboroughs, who themselves were on a tight budget. The dilemma facing Mary and Fred regarding the best longer-term training routes for the girls is illustrated in June 1945 when it was clear that an early sailing for New York was out of the question and Helga desperately wanted to go back to the Ginner-Mawer School for another term in the September. On 24 June:

Aunty and Uncle are back [from holiday], *bought me lovely ballet*
painting by Dégas, La Repetition.

By the next day, however:

am most depressed. Aunty is not too keen on paying for next term.

Three days later:

Another talk about future, no training for me, not enough money, everything uncertain. Was most depressed. Dick talked to us.

The emotional roller-coaster continued over the next few weeks leading up to Helga's eighteenth birthday. On 6 July she wrote:

I hope to get a job soon, am fed up with wasting time at home

Two weeks later:

Am going to be called up in August [when Helga would turn eighteen], *will probably have to do munitions work.*

A week later and Helga is definitely feeling very sorry for herself:

Aunty and Uncle went this morning [on holiday], *house seems quiet and lonely. Already things are going wrong. Boiler burst, not enough rations,* Hilda [one of the staff] *grumpy etc.*

Three days before her eighteenth birthday Helga expresses feelings many people could empathise with:

Wished I could be 17 a bit longer. Don't want to get older.

After a short holiday in Wales in mid-August with Mrs Hancock's daughter, Peggy, Helga's mood was lifted a little, and she was pleased when:

Aunty told me how very much she liked my hair long with the wave.

The frustration and continuing uncertainty were bound to affect Mary and Fred as well as the girls, particularly as the war was over, yet the way forward still seemed no clearer. Helga gives a hint of this in an entry on 21

September 1945 after Mary had received a letter from a Mr Bohmer of the Refugee Children's Committee explaining that the shipping situation to the US was no better:

> Aunty's a bit cross, he seems to think we've got all the money in the world.

By early October Helga was set to return to Ginner-Mawer for the term, a relief for all no doubt. On 3 October, in preparation for the term:

> Aunty bought me a smashing new brown coat, shoes, knickers, scarf.

Irene, however, suffering from tonsillitis at the time, was 'still feeling rotten'.

On 27 December 1945 Helga wrote:

> One more Xmas over. I hope the New Year will really this time fulfil my dreams.

The very next day Mary had to undertake the worst possible task for any parent or surrogate parent. Helga's diary entry reads:

> Aunty gave us a sad letter from Bohmer and a Prague Committee about Vati [Daddy]. She had had it some time. Vati was sent to Auschwitz and has not returned, the only hope is the Russians. I can't believe the worst!

In a later newspaper interview in 1983 Helga said that Mary and Fred were appalled at her apparent coldness in her reaction to this news:

> What's the matter with you? they asked. They couldn't understand why I wasn't showing more emotion. But I didn't want to go through the unhappiness. I didn't want to have to think about it. I didn't want to.

In the diary we see many affectionate short notes about other members of the family, particularly the three brothers, and also Margaret, 'Aunty Maggie',

Mary's closest sister in age, who was living at the time in South London, and whose only child, Jane, had spent much of the early war years with the Attenborough family and household in Leicester as an evacuee. Margaret, unlike Mary, did not have immediate responsibilities towards the girls, so Helga's relationship with her could be much freer and more relaxed in many ways. As the pressure eased in the later years of the war Helga and Irene also spent the occasional short holiday with Aunty Maggie and Uncle Gilbert in London. In early June 1944 Helga spent a few days with them in Wimbledon:

> Aunty M. met me at Marylebone Station. We did some shopping and then had tea and went out to Wimbledon. Aunty has a lovely modern house. It's terribly clean.

The following day:

> Helped Aunty in the house, did a bit of shopping. Love it here, Aunty is awfully sweet. I like her very much. She cooks lovely dishes. There is a happy atmosphere. It is awfully cosy here.

In mid-February 1945 Irene travelled from Leicester and Helga from Cornwall to meet up in London, where they had to visit 'the Embassy' and other agencies for ID papers presumably in conjunction with their eventual onward travel, which would not happen for another twenty months. They had booked in lodgings near Russell Square for a couple of nights while they sorted out their business. They stayed the first night there, but Helga notes:

> The boarding house was filthy. Met Aunty M. and she took both of us to Wimbledon. Stayed there.

Next day they travelled back to Leicester and Cornwall respectively, and Helga notes:

> Aunty was awfully sweet to me.

Just a few weeks later on 28 March, Margaret and Jane stopped off in Leicester overnight as they were travelling to Wales:

Hectic day. Aunty Mag and Jane were going to Wales today when their case was stolen, in charge of a porter. Aunty had nearly all her belongings in it, new clothes, everything, poor thing, she was so upset. She always has bad luck. We went to police and ran round town for new clothes.

In the circumstances of wartime rationing and clothes coupons this incident would have been more than a passing nuisance, and in order to help Margaret replace the clothes no doubt a hasty pooling of coupons took place within College House! In late July 1945 when Mary and Fred went on holiday for a couple of weeks Maggie and Jane stayed at College House for a while:

We have a grand time with Aunty M., have long interesting conversations, she's a darling. I do like Aunty, she's perfect company, so sweet, kind, amusing and broad-minded.

In the diary Helga picks up and uses the family names for the boys. For instance Richard is invariably 'Dick' and David is often 'Dave'. On 31 March 1945 Helga was the one to answer the telephone when some good news arrived for David:

Dave has won £60 scholarship to Clare, Cambridge, jolly good. I answered the telephone. Everyone was in very good mood. Had ginger ale to drink his health.

David was recorded by Helga in several roles: chaperone, guide, educator, friend and occasional tormenter! On 7 June 1945 Helga and Irene went with the family to a formal event and concert in the college, where:

The Master of Christ's, Cambridge gave a speech. It was marvellous. Uncle also made a good speech. Later Dave took us round College.

On 4 July 1945, after picking fruit in the garden on a warm day, Helga:

had a long talk with Dave about ghosts, telepathy. I am thoroughly scared and ready to imagine anything. It's horrible.

A few weeks later, at the end of July:

> *David took me to London Philharmonic concert* [at the De Montfort Hall]. *Lovely programme. Dave was charming and very polite.*

Just one week later, 7 August 1945, we see an amusing comment on life with the Attenborough men:

> *Dave and Uncle have gone to London, thank goodness, house is cleaner now.*

In the months following the end of the war the atmosphere in towns and cities was uneasy at times as serving men gradually returned home. On 12 December 1945, when David was home from his first term at Cambridge, Helga notes:

> *Went to MD Club. David came too. It is risky going out at night now, deserters about and people have been attacked.*

Just four days later, as Helga was practising dance routines at home she noted:

> *Danced around in Modern Dance dresses. Great fun, Dave made rude remarks.*

While in Leicester, Helga, like many people in the war years, was a regular cinema-goer, typically two or three times a week. It was a form of escapism. In June 1944 she notes:

> *Went to flix, saw Andy Hardy's 'Blond Trouble'. Mickey Rooney is awfully like Dick.*

The house was seemingly lively, noisy and bustling when Richard was visiting for a few days. On Christmas Day 1944 Helga noted:

> *Everyone has been awfully jolly, jokes and laughter all the time. Dick and Sheila* [Sim] *will marry soon. They are very much in love, one can tell.*

The couple married exactly four weeks later in Kensington, and their marriage of sixty-nine years was only broken when Richard died in 2014. Helga and Irene were with Richard, Sheila and Mary in London on 26 October 1946, their very last day in England:

Saw Dick and Sheila, got lovely flapjack. Lunch at Chelsea. Goodbye to Darling Aunty Mary was awful, was in floods.

CHAPTER THIRTY

MARY'S LETTER TO AMERICA, OCTOBER 1946

The long letter dated 22 October 1946 to Uncle Hans in New York, written mostly by Mary, with a salutation and introduction by Fred, was intended to explain to Hans how, *in loco parentis*, Mary and Fred had tried to make the best judgements they could in order to equip Helga and Irene for future careers and life choices as young women in the United States. They had to make those judgements within a constantly shifting time frame and taking into account the respective personalities, strengths and weaknesses of the girls. In some instances we see the 'other side of the coin' in the letter, and both Helga's diary and Mary's letter taken together are wonderful sources of information, and, directly and indirectly, they give insights into the person Mary was.

In Fred's short introduction to the letter he acknowledges with good-natured irony that Mary will do a far better job than he in comprehensively detailing the girls' progress and development whilst in their care during the war:

> *My wife is sitting opposite to me writing what seems to me to be not a letter but a life history of your two nieces. There will be no need for me to add anything by way of information since my wife will have told you everything you want to know.*

However, he goes on to say that he hopes Hans:

will approve of what we have done. We believe they should be able to earn their own living and become useful and happy young women, able to make for themselves interesting and successful careers. … They are naturally excited at the prospect of joining you in New York. I envy them the chance of seeing a city and a country I have always wanted to visit. Someday we may be able to get over.

According to Sir David, Mary and Fred never did manage to get to New York.

Finally Fred expresses his hopes for the future:

It's an unhappy Europe at the moment and though the outlook isn't over bright I still think we may have enough common sense and human decency to get the world on its feet again and walk decently along together.

Mary's opening sentences in her letter, in the form of a self-deprecating apology, indicate how busy and fully occupied she still was, even though her two eldest sons were now away, Richard married and David at Cambridge, at least in term time. She had of course been helping Helga and Irene to get ready for their emigration, not just by packing, buying clothes, etc., but also trying to keep their natural impatience, frustration and excitement in check. She was also as busy as ever with local organisations and community activities in Leicester, which, like all major cities in the immediate post-war world, was examining its own identity and trying to plot the most appropriate route into the future. The University College Leicester now found itself immediately launched into an exciting new era within days of VE Day, and Fred's role in ensuring that the college was best placed to take advantage of the new opportunities over the next phase of its development consumed his time and energy at a period when his own health was beginning to suffer. Mary's task in supporting Fred in his career whilst holding the household together, as well as no doubt taking the lead role in arranging the move to Knighton Hall over the next few months (see later chapter), would be crucial for the next phase of their lives.

The tone of Mary's opening gambit in the letter to Hans can thus be seen in this context with the benefit of hindsight:

I hope the receipt of a letter in my handwriting will not give you too much of a shock. If you were one of my own relations you would at once say to yourself – 'This means at least a birth, a death or a marriage in the family' – those being the only occasions on which my relations expect to hear from me. And indeed this occasion is about as important, for this letter announces the imminent departure of Irene and Helga to join their own people – after all these long years of war.

The major changes in the family and household circumstances after the war, coinciding ironically with the move to much more spacious and adequate accommodation after fourteen years at College House, were explained by Mary to Hans with characteristic pragmatism, even if with a hint of nostalgia:

This parting is a big break both for the girls and us; they have become so much part of our family. We shall feel quite lost without them especially as of all our big family of six children – the three boys, Irene and Helga and my little niece, only John is still at home. We do hope that you will be pleased with the two young women who have developed from the little nieces you knew, and that you will never be sorry that they have spent seven of the most important years of their lives in England.

Mary is focussed on the future not the past. The 'little niece' referred to in the letter is Jane, only child of Mary's closest sister, Margaret, and her husband, Gilbert Peaker. They were living in South London through the war, and Jane spent the most dangerous periods of the war years as an evacuee staying at College House in the care of the Attenboroughs. Jane herself explained to me that she effectively 'swapped with Richard' during the war. Richard spent most of the war years either away in London studying at the Royal Academy of Dramatic Art (RADA) or serving in the Royal Air Force. To Jane, born in 1936, the other young people in the household must have seemed very much like older sisters and brothers.

Mary goes on to explain how the personalities and characters of Helga and Irene were so different when they arrived in their care:

Their characters were formed when they came to us, but we have tried to see to it that the habits and ways of thinking that girls learn in their teens should not be such as you would disapprove of. They are so different – these two children as I expect you know. Indeed you will soon recognise their own essential characteristics – Helga so friendly and vivacious and easy to live with – Irene a much more nervous girl, inclined to be egocentric and less adjustable than Helga. Neither has given us any trouble. They are really good children with nice interests. I'm sure you will find them loving and grateful.

She thanks Hans for the regular letters and parcels for the girls, which served as a reminder that they had a caring and loving family ready to receive them in New York:

It is difficult for young girls (who after all are always a little selfish) to realise how much you have sacrificed for them – but we have tried to point this out to them especially when Irene has been impatient at the endless delays which they have had to endure. We have tried to make them see that they are only two out of thousands of young people most of whom have been less fortunate than they, and that however long they had to wait, they always had your home to look forward to.

Mary and Fred had very difficult decisions to make during the war about the most appropriate education and training routes for both girls. Decisions had to be made to take account of the different personalities of the girls, and the totally unknown time frame for longer-term planning would have been a major headache. As 'foster parents', however, Mary and Fred could not and did not shy away from these decisions, which they would have taken in consultation with Helga and Irene. Talking about Irene, Mary tells Hans that:

She is ambitious and works best when she has to fight against competition. Had we known that she was to be with us all those years I think we should have sent her to college as she would have liked to go. But at that time she expected to be joining you in a year and so we thought she could not finish any course. I must confess that there was

also the fact that I dreaded exams for her. She lost weight over [exams]
and was altogether so much better after it that I think we decided rightly
in not encouraging an academic career.

Mary had considered information sent by Hans regarding a number of
potential careers for Irene in America, and as preparation for those,
without restricting Irene's options too much, it was agreed that Irene would
complete a shorthand typing course at:

the best Commercial College in Leicester. As things turned out it was
just as well she had done this and had obtained a job with the Women's
Land Army. Had she been at college and doing an ordinary business
job she would have been taken away and directed to munitions once she
reached calling-up age.

In the case of Helga the decisions were complicated and influenced to some
extent because Helga, unlike her sister, as far as we know, had a single clear
passion in life. In her own mind Helga could not see a future career path,
which did not in some way involve dancing. Her overwhelming 'obsession'
with dance and the adverse moods, which followed any apparent setbacks
to this vision in her mind, are very clear in the diary. This must have been
quite difficult for Mary to deal with as she explained to Hans:

I think we should have been inclined to discount her enthusiasm for
dancing as just a child's fascination for a glamorous career had she not
always been so very serious about it. Even at the age of twelve or thirteen
she was interested enough not only to want to dance but to know about
the history of dancing and to read every book she could lay hands on. It
was this that gave us the idea of allowing her to have dancing lessons.

Mary and Fred decided to seek expert advice about Helga's true potential
before she left school. Fred wrote to Ninette de Valois at the Sadler's Wells
Ballet, who offered to test and assess Helga in London:

We explained to Helga at the time that unless M. de Valois (or her
ballet mistress) strongly advised it, she must give up the idea of being a

dancer. At the end of the month, as you also know, the ballet mistress was most frank with us and gave us her reasons for believing that Helga would never get to the top of the tree as a dancer (too big and too old were two reasons) but that she had most marked ability in character-dancing and would probably make a very good teacher of dancing. So we decided to let her continue with occasional dancing lessons on condition that she settled down seriously to work for her School Certificate (the school leaving exam).

Having explained to Helga that she should effectively banish all dreams of a stage career as a dancer Mary and Fred steered her to thoughts of dance teaching:

We consulted the heads of the two big high schools here [Wyggeston Girls and probably Collegiate School for Girls] *and they both advised us to let Helga train with the Ginner-Mawer School – or some school like that – as the modern trend in education is more and more to encourage young people to express themselves by dance and mime and acting – there are not nearly enough teachers to do the work.*

Mary decided to consult her brother, Alec Clegg, who by then, in his early thirties, was already director of education for the West Riding of Yorkshire. He endorsed the advice Mary had been given locally when he told her that:

he cannot get enough people for such posts in his schools or as youth organisers in the village colleges etc.

Helga duly spent several rather disconnected terms at the Ginner-Mawer School, which had been relocated from London to Cornwall for the duration of the war, but this illustrated again how difficult it was for Mary and Fred to make planned long-term decisions for the girls:

If Helga had been able to complete her third year here and take her teacher's diploma she would have been sure of a very well paid job and we do hope that she will be able to do something of the same kind in America and so be happy and successful in her work. But we have impressed on her that she may at first have to do quite different work in order to earn money until she has saved enough to complete her training. We have always hoped that both girls would be able to stand on their own feet when they got to America, knowing how great are your responsibilities towards other members of your family.

Mary expresses personal comments about the sadness of loss for Helga and Irene during the war but also a clear sense of a brighter future now the conflict is over:

I suppose there is little hope now for the girls' father. Irene and Helga speak of him with great love. They have very happy memories of their childhood. Since we have not been able to meet their father, as we always hoped we might – we look forward to seeing you both one day. I think it is more likely that you will be coming to England rather than that we shall be in New York. It will be an exciting trip when you do come for the girls will have so many friends to take you to see. As they will tell you we expect to be moving into a beautiful old Hall next spring so you must all come and stay with us sometime.

Mary closes the letter with a mention of the perfect gift from America for many women in Britain during the war:

Before I close, may we thank you over and over again for all the generous gifts you have sent us – for the lovely silk stockings I am wearing (a real luxury in war-time England) – for the songbook both the girls gave Dave and which he has enjoyed so much – in fact for all these things we should have thanked you for long ago.

CHAPTER THIRTY-ONE

MARY'S TIES WITH SAWLEY AND
LONG EATON ARE LOOSENED

Following the deaths of both her parents in 1930, Mary's family home, Rye Hill Close (194 Tamworth Road, New Sawley), had been retained and let by the family, presumably in part to fund the ongoing care and support of Dorothy, as required under the terms of Sam Clegg's will.

The semi-detached house built at right angles to Rye Hill Close as a doctor's house and surgery (196 Tamworth Road) had also been retained under the terms of John Bradshaw's earlier will, to be sold at a future date if and when the family thought fit. After 1930 William Innes Baxendale, Sam Clegg's brother-in-law, Mary Attenborough's uncle, was the sole surviving executor of the will of John Bradshaw, Mary's grandfather. In 1934 William Baxendale rationalised matters by appointing Mary Attenborough and Alec Clegg as new joint trustees, along with himself, of Bradshaw's will. By the end of the war the doctor's house was occupied by Dr Philip Henry Hay-Heddle and his wife Frances Emma. Hay-Heddle was only the third doctor to live and work in the house since John Bradshaw had it built in around 1906. After the war the trustees decided to realise capital by selling the house. By a conveyance dated 13 May 1946 the property and associated land was sold to the sitting tenants, the Hay-Heddles:

at the price of One thousand six hundred and twenty two pounds eighteen shillings.

The Hay-Heddles seem to have lived in the house until around 1973, to be succeeded by a Dr Wheatley. The property finally stopped being used as a doctor's house and surgery around 1978, four doctors and seventy-two years after the house was built and opened for this service to the local community by John Bradshaw. 196 Tamworth Road, designed by Sam Clegg and built in the Arts and Crafts style in purple brick with a slate roof, is also included in Nikolaus Pevsner's survey of the buildings of Sawley and Long Eaton.

The house also adjacent to Mary's childhood home on the other side, 192 Tamworth Road, built by Bradshaw for himself and his family when he moved back to Sawley had also been sold probably in the 1940s. Mary's ties with Sawley and Long Eaton were loosening, but the family still owned Rye Hill Close for the time being.

By a strange twist of irony Nikolaus Pevsner, who later picked out Rye Hill Close and the adjacent doctor's house for mention in the Derbyshire volume (1953) of his monumental survey of buildings of architectural interest, *The Buildings of England*, had written to Fred Attenborough in October 1939 enquiring about employment prospects at the University College Leicester. Pevsner, then aged thirty-seven, had left his native Germany and fled to England in 1933 when he lost his post as a lecturer at Göttingen University as a result of Hitler's *Rassengesetze* ('race laws') – his father was Russian–Jewish. He first settled in Hampstead but struggled to find permanent work during the 1930s. He had perhaps written to Fred in the knowledge of Fred's links with, and assistance to, German Jewish academics since the rise of Hitler. On 12 October 1939 Fred Attenborough replied to Pevsner:

> *I am very sorry to hear of the upset which the War has caused to your mode of life, and I am more sorry still because I fear I cannot help you. Probably you do not realise that we have no Department in any of the Fine Arts in this College, nor are we connected in any way with the business interests of the City. I need hardly say that I would help you if I could and I will bear you in mind, but I fear my chances of being any use to you are exceedingly slender. I will mention your name to the Principal of the College of Art and if he can make any suggestion I will pass it on to you. With kind regards etc.*

Later Pevsner went on to establish a notable career and reputation in his adopted country when he became the first professor of art history at Birkbeck College, London, and he also lectured at Cambridge University for thirty years, whilst continuing to work on *The Buildings of England* series. Whilst at Birkbeck College Pevsner collaborated with Fred Attenborough in the production of a small book, published by Penguin Books (1945), entitled *The Leaves of Southwell*, describing the carved masonry leaves which adorn the capitals of the columns of the Chapter House at Southwell Minster in Nottinghamshire. All the photographs for this study were taken by Fred Attenborough. Clearly Pevsner bore no grudges from his earlier unsuccessful enquiry regarding academic posts at Leicester!

CHAPTER THIRTY-TWO

MARY AND FREDERICK ATTENBOROUGH MOVE TO KNIGHTON HALL, AND A BRIGHT FUTURE FOR THE UNIVERSITY COLLEGE

The end of the war in Europe signalled the start of a very busy period for Mary and Fred, and one which would stretch the household budget to the limits. This may be one of the reasons why Mary's family had decided fairly soon after the war to release some capital by the sale of the doctor's house and surgery in New Sawley early in 1946.

Whilst eldest son, Richard, was now fully independent and beginning to establish his own career, David went up to Clare College, Cambridge, in 1945, and youngest son John was still at home and still attending Wyggeston Boys' Grammar School, which occupied part of the same 'campus' as the university college. Helga and Irene, of course, were still with the family, and after VE Day they would have to wait another eighteen months before they were able to join their family in New York. The continuing uncertainties would make financial planning and budgeting very difficult for Mary in particular, who throughout her married life was almost obsessively meticulous in recording and maintaining the family budgets and accounts, as we shall see later.

In 1947, less than a year after Helga and Irene had departed for the United States, Mary and Fred moved from College House to the much grander and more spacious Knighton Hall, about a mile away. This move was all part of much larger plans for the university college, which, immediately after the cessation of hostilities in Europe, would elevate University College Leicester to the next level in academic terms over the next twenty years. Fred, supported and instructed by the college council, would oversee the first phase of this rapid elevation, and, at the age of fifty-eight, he began an extremely busy schedule of work, which would eventually take its toll on his health.

Within weeks of VE Day Mr Percy Gee, on behalf of the university college, announced, as reported by the *Leicester Evening Mail* on 8 June 1945, that:

> *The College has been recognised by the University Grants Committee (UGC) as a university institution qualified to receive grants from the Treasury.*

This was a hugely significant step forward as it meant that there was now a major third stream of income for the university college in addition to student fees and local gifts, bequests and benefactions. In the post-war era this was likely to be a much more dependable source of income going forward, which would allow longer-term planning, investment and expansion. The Barlow Committee, reporting in 1946, concluded that the expansion of university education could not be achieved by the established universities alone, such as Cambridge, Oxford, London and Durham, the Scottish universities and the original red-brick universities, but should now also be spearheaded by the five university colleges as well, at Exeter, Hull, Leicester, Nottingham and Southampton. This was a clear message and stimulus to the college council to get moving. Just two years later by the academic year 1947/8 the UGC grant accounted for sixty-five per cent of University College Leicester's total income, and by 1955/6 it was up to seventy-five per cent. The first year's grant of £12,000 facilitated new staff appointments, including the first three professorships, with plans soon afterwards for four more. The UGC also awarded a capital grant of £6,000, which would stimulate the development of building expansion plans. Thoughts turned to how far the existing site could be developed and whether in fact the university college should move to a completely new site, even outside the city. There was a fairly quick decision to remain in the city, although this view was not unopposed. Negotiations with the city of Leicester to acquire more land adjacent to the site were successful, and other buildings and sites were gradually acquired. It was quickly realised that a major new requirement would be residential accommodation for the growing student body.

One significant acquisition soon after the war was Knighton Hall and its grounds, which became available in late 1946. Knighton was formerly a separate village some two miles from the city centre and about a mile from the university college. It was now completely absorbed within the city boundaries. At the heart of the old village was Knighton Hall and its extensive grounds. The hall was originally a manor house, the oldest part of the building is from the sixteenth century with the modern frontage being largely an eighteenth-century extension. The minutes of the College Executive Committee dated 14 June 1946 note that:

> *The Chairman [Percy Gee] reported that the trustees of Knighton Hall were prepared to consider an offer and that he, the Vice-Chairman Alderman Keane and the Principal had visited the house and the site and were very favourably impressed by it as a possible site for hostels. It was agreed that a valuation should be obtained from Andrew and Ashwell [estate agents] and that the College would like to proceed with the negotiations for the acquisition of the site.*

The committee also agreed in the meantime to seek the views of the 'Town Planning Committee'. At the college council meeting on 3 October 1946 Alderman Keane further explained, in a discussion about potential sites for halls of residence, some already on offer, that Knighton Hall is one of these:

> *at present occupied by Mrs Oram, and comprising seventeen acres of land, a very charming estate and in every way an admirable site for halls of residence. The property is relatively near to the College, and access thereto is easy.*

As part of the wider post-war thinking about the elevated status of the university college consideration was also being given, at least off the record, to whether the principal and his family, and potential future vice-chancellors, should occupy smarter accommodation as befitting a modern dynamic university. From a purely practical point of view it also made more sense for College House to be converted perhaps into a small hostel on the main campus, probably for female students.

However, at a meeting of the Buildings and Sites Committee on 20 December 1946 Mr Gee pointed out:

> that it should be decided as soon as possible whether Knighton Hall should be the future residence of the Principal of the College, and suggests that the Principal and Mrs Attenborough should visit the Hall as soon as possible to make an inspection. The Principal advises that he is making arrangements for such a visit.

Interestingly, in her diary Helga records on 20 October 1946, just a few days before the sailing to New York:

> Most exciting day, Aunty and Uncle and Nan went to the New Estate, Knighton Hall. We looked all round house and grounds. It is marvellous, four bathrooms, masses of bedrooms, a little palace with much history. Heavenly grounds.

There is now no way of knowing for sure, but there seems to be a very strong hint in that innocent journal entry that the idea of the hall as the future residence for Mary and Fred was by then, mid-October 1946, pretty much accepted and talked about discreetly as a fait accompli. Mary's letter to Uncle Hans, written two days after Helga's diary entry, also hints that the decision was as good as made.

Perhaps also in keeping with the new 'image' of the university college the Finance and General Purposes Committee in January 1946 had recommended acceptance of a quote obtained by Fred Attenborough for the purchase of a new principal's gown from Ede & Ravenscroft at a cost of £64 6s.3d. Wartime austerity was quickly banished! Whilst the future use of College House and Knighton Hall was being debated, the Executive Committee still found time in March 1947 to be magnanimous to young Germans, who found themselves unintentionally living in Leicester as a result of the war. On 4 March 1947 the Executive Committee considered:

a proposal from the Commandant of a German Prisoner-of-War Camp, that a limited number of selected prisoners who had been university students should be admitted to the full-time degree courses. The Principal reported that he had consulted the Students' Union, which had expressed its approval of the proposal and had promised the co-operation of the student body. The Committee decided to submit the proposal to the [college] Council for its sympathetic consideration.

University College Leicester was definitely looking to the future and not to the past.

Meanwhile Fred had written an interesting letter to Percy Gee on 22 February 1947, ostensibly to accelerate decisions about the future use of College House, but in the process accelerating a definitive resolution about the principal's own future accommodation. Having stated that College House could accommodate a dozen or so undergraduate students with minimal alteration Fred goes on:

If the obvious course is adopted alternative accommodation would have to be found for the Principal which should not involve him in increased running expenses since that would be tantamount to a reduction in his salary.

He then quotes a number of people, who had suggested that Knighton Hall:

would make an admirable residence for the Principal, and later the Vice-Chancellor, and I heartily agree with them as I think you do, but it would be more expensive to run than College House. It would seem only fair that the Council, if it wishes the Principal to live in Knighton Hall, should bear the extra cost and this is where any advocacy on my part of Knighton Hall as the Principal's residence may be misinterpreted and lay me open to unfair and unpleasant insinuations. In the circumstances I feel I must be entirely left out of any further discussions on the future of Knighton Hall so that if I should go there eventually I can truthfully say it would be at the express wish of the College Council and not as the result of my own soliciting. I should enjoy living at Knighton but I am

*quite satisfied where I am. On the other hand, College House would be
such a valuable adjunct to the Hostel that I should be willing to vacate
it if a suitable alternative could be found. Obviously a decision ought to
be made immediately.*

Finally, on 21 April 1947, with the vacant possession date and completion on
the acquisition of Knighton Hall set for 1 June, the Executive Committee:

*considered the best way of using the Hall. It was pointed out that the
incorporation of College House in the Women's Hall of Residence was
an essential part of the scheme. The Committee recommended to the
Council that the Principal should be asked to vacate College House
and to take up his residence of Knighton Hall, and that, subject to
the Principal agreeing to this course, he should be granted an expense
allowance of £100 a year towards the additional cost of maintenance
which he would thereby incur.*

On 6 June 1947 the registrar reported to the Finance and General
Purposes Committee that the purchase of Knighton Hall had now been
completed, and that a treasury grant of £20,000 in aid of the purchase had
been received. Two weeks later we learn that the anticipated cost of repairs,
redecoration and alterations:

*to make the property suitable for occupation by the Principal would be
£1,250.*

Mary and Fred Attenborough eventually moved into the hall sometime in
the summer of 1947 in time for the start of the new academic year.

As the university college, and later university, increased its student
numbers over the following decades, part of the grounds of Knighton
Hall facing onto Knighton Road was eventually developed for student
accommodation.

One of the first appointments to the new professorships created by
the post-war University College Leicester was that of Professor Arthur
Humphreys to the chair of English in 1947, around the time Mary and
Fred were moving into Knighton Hall. Arthur and Jean Humphreys had

been married in 1946, and at the time of Arthur's appointment the couple had to make a choice between moving to Leicester or to Bratislava, where Arthur, a graduate of Cambridge and Harvard, had been offered a post by the British Council. Arthur apparently asked his wife, Jean, to make the choice, and Jean said later that she:

had no hesitation in saying 'Leicester – it's nearer to Arran'.

Jean had been brought up at Drumadoon Farm on the Isle of Arran off the west coast of Scotland. In the event Arthur remained in post at Leicester for almost thirty years, retiring in 1976. Both David and Michael Attenborough remember the couple with affection. Arthur Humphreys had been president of the Leicester Literary and Philosophical Society in 1965/6. He died in 1988. Jean Humphreys, who herself later became a Distinguished Honorary Fellow of the university, recalled these times some sixty years later when she was appointed president of the Lit & Phil for the year 2009/10 and delivered her presidential address on 5 October 2009:

The kindness of the College community and Leicester friends and neighbours helped to get us made into a going concern. Mr Attenborough was the College Principal, and he and his wife made us most welcome. They had just moved into Knighton Hall, and their sons, who were my age, had left home to embark on their remarkable careers. Mrs Attenborough taught me a lot, from how to get the lumps out of gravy (I had never cooked) to the need to bash the stems of cut roses to make them last longer (she was a great gardener, and we at Drumadoon had no flower garden, as every inch of land was needed for the crops).

Jean died in August 2019 at the age of ninety-four. Sadly I had not started my detailed research for this book before Jean died, so I never had the opportunity to talk to her about her further recollections of the family.

According to David Attenborough his parents were very happy to make the move to Knighton Hall. David said that his father had a great sense of history; for example he had a great fondness and respect for the architecture and antiquity of Oxford and Cambridge, and he thought that Knighton Hall would approximate to an: 'Oxbridge Master's Lodge'. Mary was also pleased about the move, according to David, but he felt that subsequent principals and vice-chancellors may not have always shared his parents' enthusiasm for Knighton Hall, which still required much work to make it comfortable! Mary was fond of interior design (this resonates back to the Long Eaton secondary school, where Mary's father, Sam Clegg, had believed strongly in the benefits of aesthetically pleasing school environments) and saw Knighton Hall as an interesting new project for her imagination. David recalls one of the rooms, which had semicircular ends, and Mary was determined to find an appropriately elegant nineteenth-century chandelier to enhance the room and turn it into a reception room for when the principal met and entertained special visitors.

Whilst at Knighton Hall, as travel around the country became easier after the end of the war, Fred pursued his lifelong interest in photography, particularly in collaboration with his great friend and colleague at the university college, W.G. ('Bill') Hoskins. Hoskins' career at Leicester paralleled Fred's career in time. He had been appointed at the age of twenty-three as assistant lecturer in economics in the department of commerce in 1931, shortly before Fred's appointment as principal later the same year. He had been educated in his hometown at the University College of the South-West of England, the precursor of the University of Exeter. During the war Hoskins was one of a number of staff at Leicester released for 'work of national importance', their posts held open during their absence. He was seconded to the department of trade and was not released until 1946. As part of the gradual post-war expansion of University College Leicester following recognition and funding by the UGC a new department of local history (later English local history) was established in 1948. This new department, the first separate department of local history anywhere in England, was headed up by Hoskins, who was appointed reader in English local history.

In 1950 a book written by Hoskins:

With [all] *fifty-two photographs by F.L. Attenborough, Principal of University College Leicester*

entitled *The Heritage of Leicestershire*, was published by the City of

Leicester Publicity Department. When Hoskins later published his seminal work *The Making of the English Landscape* in 1955, which brought him national recognition, seventeen of the eighty-two plates were credited to Fred Attenborough, all part of a remarkable collaboration between the two friends over almost twenty years. Apparently local residents became accustomed to seeing Fred in the late 1940s emerging from Knighton Hall onto Chapel Lane or Knighton Road in his cream and brown Humber car, heading off with the non-driving Bill Hoskins for another photographic expedition in Leicester or the surrounding countryside!

In 1951 Hoskins left Leicester at the same time as Fred Attenborough retired, when he accepted a readership in Oxford. In 1965 he unexpectedly returned to Leicester to take the newly established Hatton chair of English local history. His second spell at Leicester was short-lived. Hoskins much preferred active research and writing over the administrative work of a head of department. In 1968 he resigned his post and retired back to his native Exeter at the age of sixty.

SECTION FIVE

THE RETIREMENT YEARS

CHAPTER THIRTY-THREE
THE RETIREMENT OF FREDERICK ATTENBOROUGH, 1951

O n 6 April 1951 the *Leicester Evening Mail* announced:

> *Mr. F.L. Attenborough to retire from College.*

The article went on to say:

> *Mr. F.L. Attenborough will retire in July after 19 years as Principal of Leicester University College, and he and Mrs. Attenborough hope to retire to the London area to be near two of the members of their family of three boys – film-star Richard Attenborough and second son, David. Thus will end an intimate association with Leicester, and a personal triumph at the University College, for a few months ago the Royal Charter was granted, taking the college one step nearer full university status.*

In 1950 the college obtained a Royal Charter of Incorporation, and as a result changed its name from 'University College Leicester' to 'The University College Leicester'. This change may seem cosmetic, but the more significant changes in the structure and constitution of the institution accompanying the change in status brought it into line with all the other English universities. The local press certainly saw the Royal Charter as a major step forward. The *Leicester Mercury* reported on 21 December 1950:

The petition for the Charter passed safely through the Privy Council, and was signed on December 4 – a date to be kept at the College in future years as 'Charter Day'. In its comparatively short life Leicester's University College has already earned for itself a sound reputation, but with the granting of the Royal Charter its prestige and dignity will be enhanced.

The article continues, quoting the principal:

We are naturally delighted to see the college recognised in this way. While this Charter does not convert the college to a full university under it the internal organisation will be identical with that of a modern university institution, the only difference being that the college has no power to grant degrees. Until full university status is granted the students will continue to read for the external degrees of London University.

In his book *The University of Leicester, A History, 1921–76*, Brian Burch writes:

The Charter was almost the last achievement of Mr. Attenborough, who retired as Principal in the summer of 1951 in poor health. In almost twenty years at the head of the College, he had steered it through the difficult pre-war years, the rigours of the War itself, and finally to what Professor Simmons [the first professor of history at Leicester] *characterises as the 'triumphant success' of the early post-war years. In this he had been ably assisted by Mrs. Attenborough, a respected J.P. who had been much involved in service to the College and the City, not least during the War when she had helped the many refugees who came to Leicester.*

On 5 April 1951, the day before the *Leicester Mail*'s announcement of his retirement, the college council had met. The minutes record:

The Chairman reported that, following conversations that he and the Vice-Chairman had had with the Principal, the Principal had agreed to retire on 31st July 1951 in order to assist the arrangements for the new chartered College to take over from the existing College. It was unanimously resolved: (a) That with effect from the 1ˢᵗ August 1951 Mr. F.L. Attenborough be granted a pension at the rate of £585 a year for life. (b) That the draft Deed of Covenant securing such a pension and framed with a view to receiving the approval of the Inland Revenue Authorities, as now produced, be approved and that it be submitted in draft for such official approval. (c) That immediately the approval of the Inland Revenue Authorities has been obtained the Deed be executed and the Seal of the College be affixed thereto.

Two months later on 7 June 1951 the college council confirmed that the Inland Revenue had approved the draft agreement with a minor amendment. The way was clear for Fred to retire at the end of July as planned. Two days later on 9 June 1951 the academic board met for the final time before surrendering its functions to the senate of the new college as part of the new arrangements brought about by the effect of the Royal Charter to come into force from the start of the new academic year. After referring to a dinner recently held 'in honour of the Principal and Mrs. Attenborough' Dr Bryan, vice-chairman, proposed that the academic board:

place on record its thanks to the Principal and its appreciation of his services as Chairman of the Board and as Principal of the College since 1932, and extend to him its very cordial good wishes for a long and happy life.

Meanwhile the college council was now looking ahead to the appointment of Fred's successor as principal and had appointed a 'Joint Committee on the Principalship' to drive matters forward. On 21 June the council accepted the Joint Committee's recommendation:

That having considered the salaries and allowances at present being paid to the Heads of other university institutions, felt that it would be necessary to offer a salary of not less than £2,750 a year, with an entertainment allowance of £500 a year and residence in Knighton Hall free of rent and rates.

A few days later, on 27 June, the Finance and General Purposes Committee authorised the chairman and vice-chairman of the college council:

> to purchase, at an agreed valuation, such fittings etc. belonging to the Principal at Knighton Hall as he did not wish to take away and were of use to the College.

In such mundane details, recorded in the cold official minutes of the college, we are reminded that, even at a time of major changes for Mary and Fred Attenborough, the life of the institution had to go on.

Finally, on 5 July 1951 the college council resolved to:

> place on record its appreciation of the services rendered to the College by Mr. F.L. Attenborough since his appointment as Principal in 1932, and offer its good wishes to him and Mrs. Attenborough for a long life and much happiness in his retirement. The Principal expressed his thanks.

CHAPTER THIRTY-FOUR

MARY'S HOUSEHOLD ACCOUNTS,
ANOTHER TREASURE TROVE

In the late summer of 2019, when David Attenborough's sister-in-law Janet Attenborough was looking through the boxes of stored material, which had already revealed the Sorbonne diary kept by Mary, she also came across a number of 'Household Accounts' books, which had been completed and retained by Mary for every year of her married life. Mary used standard accounts books printed and produced by Charles Letts & Co. Ltd. of London, in a format slightly larger than the modern A5 size. In these books Mary had recorded, with meticulous and almost obsessive detail, every penny of household spending for thirty-five years. The preprinted accounts books usually had between twenty-five and thirty standard lines of entries reflecting common broad headings of household spending, starting with food by several definitions, e.g. butcher and grocer, and then headings such as clothes, rent and rates, and always concluding with an entry for 'wages and extra help'.

Through the years the format of the accounts books varied slightly to reflect changes in society, but the overall content remained basically consistent. Whatever the time period families always had to eat and clothe themselves, and, if they were fortunate, eventually had the opportunities to treat themselves. The books are also a reminder of what everyday items cost in the times when, for example, my own parents were growing up. The standard line entries could be changed by hand to suit each family's circumstances, but the Letts format covered most standard options. Each double page spread covered a week, with daily columns, total columns and summary boxes, and, at the bottom of the first page, a blank space for notes. Mary made full use of the blank space for detailed notes in her small, tight handwriting to explain and analyse certain spending heads, and, although sometimes difficult if not impossible to read, it is these notes which transform otherwise dry accounts books into a social and family history treasure and an invaluable primary source. The notes are, inevitably, frequently mundane, but if looked at in conjunction with other known facts they often support those facts with added detail and also reveal some forgotten gems of family life. In many ways, because of the almost forensic detail they are like a running diary of family life as seen through its daily expenditure. Such is the detail that Janet even joked to David that she knew from the books exactly how much it cost his parents, to the penny, when David was at Cambridge!

The accounts for October 1931 to October 1932 cover the period when Mary and Fred moved from The Lodge at Borough Road College in Isleworth to take up residence in College House on the campus of University College, Leicester. The Attenboroughs seem to have had three maids at Isleworth, Betty, Violet and Nannie, and when they moved to Leicester all three initially moved with the family. Presumably paid by seniority, or by length of service, Betty was earning £50 per annum, Nannie £42 and Violet £40. In addition they obviously had inclusive benefits of living-in accommodation, food and fuel. Clearly all three women were valued by Mary and Fred, and in turn all three must have felt a strong sense of loyalty and were prepared to move house and city with the family.

In her accounts at this time Mary had separate lines for each family member, Fred, Mary, 'R', 'Dave' and 'JM', to record mostly clothes items but also such items as Cubs fees, football fees, etc. In the last week of October 1931 Richard, then aged eight, had a new pair of football boots costing 6s.11d. (35p), but for an Old Boys' Dinner celebration at Borough Road Mary and Fred had to pay 35s. (£1.75) for champagne! The entries for the third week of January 1932 show a hotel bill of £9 13s.3d, presumably for a few nights' stay in Leicester whilst the family prepared to move into College House. These are the kinds of fees the university college would normally perhaps reimburse for an incoming principal and his family, but in the difficult financial climate of 1932 maybe this was not the case. There is a curious entry in mid-February 1932, 'Unaccounted for during move £3 10s.2d.', presumably referring to miscellaneous costs, which Mary was simply too busy to itemise at the time. In August 1932 the family drove for a two- to three-week holiday in north-west Scotland, taking in hotels in Fort Augustus, Gairloch and Carbost on the Isle of Skye. This would have involved at least 1,200 miles of driving from Leicester, but the petrol spending seems to have been a mere £5 2s.2d! The following month it was back to school for the nine-year-old Richard, for whom a new pair of football shoes cost 4s.6d., and for the six-year-old David, with a new cap and trousers costing a total of 7s. or 35p.

By late 1936 the three domestic staff still included Nannie but she had now been joined by Molly and Olive. On 9 November Mary paid for Molly to attend a cookery course costing £1. One of Fred's great lifelong interests was photography, and according to David his father had a room in the main college building set up as a darkroom for photography processing. In early January 1937 Mary records a payment of 6s.6d. for:

electrical fittings for Fred's Photography Room

with a note saying:

this paid by College previously.

The implication was that the college had supported Fred's hobby financially up to a point as he was making a photographic record of college life. In August 1937 there are entries for a new carpet for the same room, £5 17s.1d. and photo frames, camera repairs and a lens costing together £2 11s.6d. The entries for October 1936 to October 1937 are illuminating in another way. As Mary records every single detail we can see not only the itemised spending on daily food essentials, but also a breakdown of costs such as 'wages and domestic help' in the running of a household to support the principal of the city's senior academic institution and three young sons entering or about to enter their teenage years. For Mary, who attended a range of social functions with Fred, spending £18 10s.4d. on clothes and cosmetics over the year (around £1,275 in 2020) may seem relatively modest, as was Fred's budget of £5 4s.1½d. (around £358 in 2020). However, this certainly seems to be 'cutting the coat according to the cloth', bearing in mind Fred's salary at the time, and emphasises again the sudden financial impact on the family when two years later they took in Helga and Irene, for the duration of the war years. It is interesting that the cost of wages for the domestic support staff was £108.18.1d. (£7,520 today), which amounted to nearly a quarter of Mary's total household spending of £482 17s.2½d. (around £33,320 in 2020).

By October 1939, a few weeks into the war, the main domestic staff were Inge and Ella, refugees of war themselves, as were most of the staff during these years. Inge was Ingeborg Gessler, well-remembered by David, and the subject of correspondence in April 2020 referred to previously. Their wages were still around £50 a year, or £4 4s.4d. per month, as itemised definitively by Mary. The accounts tell us that David, by contrast, had his pocket money increased in May 1940 to 6d. per week to coincide with his fourteenth birthday! In line with her own financial self-discipline Mary was obviously adamant that the boys would have a sense of the value of money from an early age. In February 1940 she notes that all the boys still owe her for money presumably lent to buy Christmas presents:

R. still owes for Xmas gifts 4/-, D. 3/-, J.M. 2/-.

By the third year of the war, 1942–3, commodities were harder to come by. Food rationing had been introduced in January 1940, and clothes rationing by coupons was introduced in June 1941. Subtle changes can be detected in household spending to reflect the restrictions. By this time also there were five teenage children at College House since the arrival of Helga and Irene from Berlin in 1939. New clothes and other items were bought when necessary, but there is an increasing trend towards a 'make do and mend' mentality. For example, in November 1942 Mary spends 4s.6d. on a new 'umbrella handle for Helga', and a few weeks later she has an 'umbrella re-covered 17/8d.'. There are more than usual references to costs for shoes being 'repaired' or 'mended', which was in any case not uncommon at a time when shoes were generally made to last longer. There are a couple of 'social history' references to the time. Firstly, a reminder that in the days before television and the BBC licence fee almost all households had what we would now call a radio, for which they paid, as Mary notes in early November 1942, a 'Wireless Licence 10/-'. Secondly, Christmas 'tips' for certain regular callers were far more commonplace than now, and Mary records 'Tips dustman and postman 5/-'.

Mary was also making regular charitable payments, for example, in February 1943 to: 'Soroptimist Welfare Fund 15/- and F.V.W. Refugee Fund 10/-', the modern equivalents of around £38 and £25, also 'Food relief 10/-' on 2 October 1943. At this time Mary was president of the Leicester Drama Society on two separate occasions as she was closely connected with the Little Theatre in Leicester, where Richard Attenborough was learning his trade on stage as a teenager before eventually progressing to RADA. In January 1943 Mary bought thirteen tickets for the Christmas show *Treasure Island* at the theatre, for a group of disadvantaged boys in the city. Mary involved herself with backstage and front of house activities at the Little Theatre in typically 'hands-on' fashion. Sir David is quite sure that Mary did not act in any of the productions. Many of the records of the theatre were sadly lost in a fire at the venue in the 1950s.

In August during the school summer holidays of 1943, occurred an otherwise unremarkable event, which by good fortune has been recorded in two coinciding documents and from two perspectives, those of mother and son. In that year David was aged seventeen and about to start his final year in the sixth form at Wyggeston Boys' Grammar School. In an undated letter, which, however, can be shown to be early August 1943, David was planning a short holiday in the Lake District, where he was hoping to do 'a lot of geology' before the start of the new school term. He wrote a short letter to his Uncle Gilbert, who was a serious climber and mountaineer, and who would be joining him for at least part of the holiday. Gilbert Peaker was the husband of Mary's closest sister, Margaret. David wrote to him:

I shall be at R.L.H. [The Robertson Lamb Hut, the first dedicated climbing hut in the Lake District, opened by The Wayfarers' Club in March 1930] *at 8 a.m. on Saturday 14* [August]. *I am not cycling to the Lakes after all, as Mother says I can only have about a week without getting a really square meal. I don't know what she imagines the Y.H.A.* [Youth Hostels Association] *to be like. Anyhow I'm training to Kendal, getting there about 2.0. Then I bike to somewhere in the vicinity of Shap, probably Wasdale Head Farm and get lodgings (I hope).*

In other words Mary wanted him back home after a week so she could be assured that he would not waste away, hence the faster travel by train instead of the plan to cycle all the way to the Lake District. Even future world explorers had to deal with fussy mothers at some stage on the way to achieving their goals! This episode is also confirmed through Mary's accounts books. On 29 July 1943 there is an entry: 'Dave. Tyre. 6/6', preparing the bike for the rigours of the Lake District, and another entry: 'Dave. Y.H.A. 17/6 (3/6 Membership plus 4 nights @ 3/6)'. Four days later, on 2 August we see two entries totalling £8 to cover: 'Dave. Ticket to Shap plus bike, 36/2 plus 5/3', the balance being for pocket money. A tiny window, from two different sources, into the trials of teenage life!

In 1947 the Attenboroughs had moved from College House to Knighton Hall. Ironically by the time they were 'upsizing' in terms of accommodation they had dramatically 'downsized' in terms of family still living at home. David was away at Cambridge, Richard was married and based in London, John had been called up for National Service before he later went up to Clare College, Cambridge, and Helga and Irene had left for New York at the end of 1946. Fred celebrated his sixtieth birthday in 1947 and would retire within four years, and the whole emphasis of the household accounts had shifted suddenly after the war from the exigencies of day-to-day spending on bringing up three children, plus an additional two teenagers for seven years. The household accounts book for October 1947 to October 1948 show how Mary and Fred were busy spending their own money to make Knighton Hall comfortable and gradually equipping it and establishing it as an appropriate residence and entertainment base for future principals and vice-chancellors of a rapidly expanding university. The level of spending in that first year at Knighton Hall accounts for the decision of the college, already recorded, when Fred later retired:

to purchase, at an agreed valuation, such fittings etc. belonging to the Principal at Knighton Hall as he did not wish to take away and were of use to the College.

CHAPTER THIRTY-FIVE

MARY AND FREDERICK ATTENBOROUGH
IN SURREY, 1951–61

After Fred retired from University College, Leicester, in the summer of 1951 the couple moved south to be closer to their now adult family. All three sons were then living in the Richmond area of south-west London. Mary and Fred moved to a large Edwardian house known as 'Four Elms' in Long Ditton, Surrey, between Kingston-upon-Thames and Esher. Both Mary and Fred had a liking for Edwardian style. Janet Attenborough, who, with her husband John, lived with Mary and Fred for a few years at Four Elms, affectionately described them to me as 'an Edwardian couple'. As a joint gift to mark both Fred's retirement and the new home his three sons, Richard, David and John, presented and equipped a photography darkroom to enable their father to continue his lifelong interest. However, as David recounts, at this point their father decided to give up his long-time hobby forthwith, and so the darkroom was never used! Instead Fred developed a new passion for gardening, and Mary also joined in this to a certain extent. Mary was still aged only fifty-five when she left Leicester, and she had no real sense of being 'retired' herself. She never stopped devoting her time and seemingly boundless energy to causes she felt worthy of her support, and she generally directed her energy to these causes with a passion.

Mary remained as busy as ever and stepped up her involvement with the Marriage Guidance Council (MGC). The MGC, nowadays known as Relate, had been established in 1938, and within the next few years Mary had become one of the founder members of the Leicester branch and one of its earliest counsellors. Later Mary would become a member of the National Committee of the MGC. Throughout her life Mary never did things by halves and this was the case with the MGC. In a letter written by Mary in May 1950 or 1951 to Helga and Irene in America she apologises for not writing earlier, and she is now writing from an annual conference and training course of the MGC where:

> *We've been doing 6–7 hours lectures – all very solid and condensed – so we've been worked pretty hard. However I've enjoyed it thoroughly …*
> *I go back to my neglected husband on Sunday.*

When she moved from Leicester Mary became involved with the London branch of the organisation and was also more conveniently placed to continue her work with the national committee, which met in London. Mostly Mary would travel into Central London for meetings by train and taxi, occasionally by car. Within the space of three weeks in January and February 1959, for example, we know from her daily accounts book that she attended two meetings of the London branch and one national committee meeting.

Although Mary remained constantly busy with her voluntary work after the couple moved to Surrey, Janet Attenborough told me that Mary seemed to have few close female friends. She does not recall, for example, any informal telephone conversations with female friends whilst she was living with her in-laws. During those 'retirement years' Janet felt that Mary yearned for the occasions when the whole family could get together for a family meal at weekends, but as her sons were so often busy with work commitments, often even out of the country, such occasions did not materialise as often as Mary might have hoped.

After the move to Surrey, Mary continued her work as a magistrate. In 1942, as if she were not busy enough already, Mary had been appointed as a magistrate in Leicester. On 2 January 1942 the *Leicester Evening Mail* explained that:

> *Five women are included in a list of 16 new Leicester magistrates whose appointments are announced today. … The appointments include: Mrs.*

Mary Attenborough, College House, Leicester, wife of the principal of the University College …

The first female magistrates in the country were appointed from 1920 following the passing of the Sex Discrimination (Removal) Act on 24 December 1919, eight years before women achieved full suffrage on the same terms as men in 1928. The passing of the 1919 Act was another step towards legally recognising women as full and active citizens in all walks of life. It may also have opened the way towards equal access to divorce and guardianship of children for women. The task of appointing female magistrates fell to local advisory committees, and some areas were quicker off the mark than others in appointing women to the bench. Leicester appointed the first two female magistrates in 1920.

Interestingly several of the earliest female magistrates in Leicester had links with the university college, none more directly than Mary Clara Rattray BA (1885–1963), wife of Fred Attenborough's predecessor, Dr Robert Fleming Rattray, the first principal of the college. Born Mary Clara Brooks, she was the daughter of a dental surgeon from Banbury, Oxfordshire, and both her parents eventually became magistrates. She was educated at Cheltenham Ladies' College and the University of London, married in 1915, and the couple moved to Leicester in 1917, when Rattray became pastor at the Great Meeting Hall in Bond Street, Leicester. The couple were both very active in the adult education movement and taught classes for the Workers' Education Association, which led directly to Rattray's appointment as the first principal of the new college in 1921. Mary Clara Rattray was appointed as a Justice of the Peace (JP) in 1924. When her husband resigned as principal in 1931 the couple moved to Cambridge, but it is likely that Mary Attenborough and Mary Rattray would have briefly known each other and possibly kept in touch. Both Marys also had connections with Leicester Drama Society (LDS), which was based at the Little Theatre. Mary Rattray was an accomplished actress and played many leading roles with the LDS, just a few years before Mary Attenborough's involvement with the society.

Another early female magistrate with connections to the university college was Elizabeth Rowley Frisby, born and raised in Leicester and appointed as a JP in 1927. She had been educated at Wyggeston Girls'

Grammar School and later at the London School of Economics. Elizabeth joined the Women's Social and Political Union (WSPU) in 1910 and soon became an active suffragette in Leicester and London, serving five days in Holloway Prison in 1911. She was involved in several militant actions in and around Leicester. She nevertheless received an MBE for her voluntary work during the First World War and strengthened her commitment to politics and civic duty after the war, becoming a Conservative councillor in 1927, the same year she was appointed as a JP, a novel case of 'poacher turned gamekeeper'. She became a life governor at the Leicester Royal Infirmary and also at the university college. In 1941 she became the first female Lord Mayor of Leicester and during the Second World War she opened up her home at Stackley House in Great Glen, just outside Leicester, for evacuees.

Mary would, therefore, have had a number of female role models connected with the university college when she was herself appointed to the bench in the middle of the war. The 'Minutes of Meetings of the Justices' in Leicester show that the first such meeting attended by Mary was on 4 March 1942. The chair of the meeting on that occasion was the above-mentioned Councillor Elizabeth Frisby, who was then nearing the end of her civic year as Leicester's first female lord mayor. It is quite possible that Elizabeth Frisby had proposed the appointment of Mary and 'initiated' her during her term of office as chair and lord mayor. We also know from a New Year's card in 1945 that Mary Attenborough and Elizabeth Frisby remained in touch, and their paths probably crossed at different times through Elizabeth's civic and social work in the city.

At the Meeting of the Justices on 28 October 1942 Mary was appointed to serve in the matrimonial courts for the next twelve months and this appointment was repeated every year until she left Leicester. In the matrimonial courts she was:

assigned to deal with Domestic proceedings.

There were twelve such magistrates assigned to the matrimonial courts, perhaps surprisingly usually four women and eight men, although this probably reflects the overall ratio even as late as 1950 of women to men in the pool of magistrates for the city. On 28 October 1946 Mary was also appointed to serve on a juvenile court panel for the next three years.

On this occasion seven of the eleven panel members were women. Mary's particular concerns with women's and young people's issues whilst serving as a magistrate should come as no surprise, and they certainly tie in with her work for the MGC.

Eleven years later, in the accounts book of 1958 to 1959, when Mary and Fred were living in Surrey, Mary was still recording daily spending with the same attention to detail. However, there were no longer dependent children to support; in fact the generations had rolled forward so that the couple were now grandparents. The accounts once again read almost like a secondary journal of family life, and twenty years on that has changed considerably. Now they did not have so many mouths to feed or growing children to clothe and educate they were able to spend more on treats for themselves such as short day trips, or gifts to the family. In April 1958 Mary bought two shirts for Fred at 27s.6d. each, not just ordinary shirts but 'Finsbury "non-iron" shirts'. Although an American chemist, Dr Ruth Benento, is credited with 'discovering' the technology behind this new type of material in the 1950s, non-iron shirts were not widely available until the 1970s and 1980s, so Fred was trailblazing the new fashion some twenty years before its time! On 12 June 1958 Mary travelled by train to Derby. She spent a total of £3 3s.3d. on fares and taxis, including a supplement of 9s.7d. for first class on the train. This may have been a visit to solicitors in Derby to discuss and initiate the process leading to the eventual sale of the Clegg family home, Rye Hill Close, the following year. In the summer of 1958 Mary records expenses in connection with day trips to places such as Greenwich, London Airport and Ash Vale in Surrey. The family car was by now a new Ford Anglia, for which Mary records the cost of a second service on 13 September 1958 of £2 16s.6d. Fred's retirement interest in gardening is also well-recorded.

In mid-October 1958 there is an interesting entry:

Given to Mag [her sister Margaret] *for Dorothy's Xmas and birthday gifts £1.10.0d. (towards television).*

By now Dorothy, aged fifty-nine, had been living with her unmarried cousin, Irene Baxendale, and her by then widowed Uncle William, aged eighty-seven, in West Kirby on the Wirral in Cheshire for almost thirty years. The new television for Dorothy was presumably a joint gift from her siblings. At the time Margaret and her husband, Gilbert, were living less than a mile from Dorothy, also in West Kirby, and presumably they saw Dorothy and the Baxendales on a regular basis. By Christmas 1958 Mary and Fred's first grandson, Michael, was aged eight, and one of their Christmas gifts to him was a copy of the ever-popular *Swallows and Amazons* by Arthur Ransome, first published in 1930.

CHAPTER THIRTY-SIX

CONNECTIONS WITH SAWLEY AND LONG EATON SEVERED WITH THE SALE OF RYE HILL CLOSE

By 1959 Sam Clegg's children had made the decision to sell the former family home, where they had all grown up, been educated and spent their formative years. Rye Hill Close, whose postal address by then was 194 Tamworth Road, was the Cleggs' last remaining physical link with Sawley and Long Eaton. All the siblings were now living and working outside the East Midlands, including Dorothy, who was still being cared for and supported by her cousin on the Wirral. In September 1959 Sam Clegg's last surviving sibling, Margaret, known as Aunt Peg, died aged eighty-one. She had lived for many years with her younger sister, Isabella (Bell), also unmarried, who had predeceased her in 1950, in a house in Allestree, Derby, about thirteen miles from New Sawley. Both sisters were spinsters. It must have seemed very much like the end of an era with three generations of the Clegg family now suddenly gone from south Derbyshire, and an appropriate time for many reasons to sell the last of the three properties built over a period of almost thirty years by Mary's maternal grandfather, John Bradshaw, on the plot of land bounded by the railway embankment, Tamworth Road and Bradshaw Street in New Sawley.

In 1959 Rye Hill Close was occupied by Mr and Mrs Fletcher, who had lived there since April 1943. The conveyance shows that on 9 March 1959:

Mary Attenborough of 'Four Elms' Cockrow Hill Long Ditton in the County of Surrey the wife of Frederick Levi Attenborough and Margaret Peaker of 11 Marine Park West Kirby in the County of Chester the wife of Gilbert Fawcett Peaker

sold Rye Hill Close to the sitting tenant, William Leslie Fletcher, who paid the sum of £1,750 for the house and garden area. Solicitors acting in the sale were, appropriately, J. and W.H. Sale & Son of Derby! A separate conveyance of the same date also transferred:

All that piece or parcel of land situate near to Tamworth Road and Bradshaw Street at Long Eaton in the County of Derby containing an area of Two thousand and seven square yards or thereabouts

to the Fletchers for £500. This was the land immediately adjacent to the back garden of Rye Hill Close, forming an extended garden and orchard plot right up to the railway embankment just before it enters Long Eaton Station. When the Fletchers subsequently sold Rye Hill Close to the current owner in May 1996 this piece of land was again sold off separately for development.

Rye Hill Close is unique and an ongoing testament to Sam Clegg's love of beautiful and graceful surroundings. The current owner of Rye Hill Close is only the third owner since the house was built almost a hundred and twenty-five years ago. Although the Fletchers lived in the house for over fifty years in total as tenants and owners they did not undertake any major alterations to the property, either to the structure or the fittings. As they had lived in the house for the first sixteen years as tenants, by the time they bought the property they may have passed the stage where they might have wished to make significant alterations for a family who had now grown up. This probably contributed to the preservation of the property. When the current owner acquired the house it was a hundred years old, and she appreciated the unique qualities and history of the property and has lovingly preserved those qualities whilst making it a comfortable family home. Having grown up in Sandiacre, just four miles from New Sawley, and being keenly interested in local history, she fully appreciated the significance of the connection to Samuel Clegg, who had contributed so much to the educational and cultural life of Sawley and Long Eaton. By a fortunate chain of events, therefore, Rye Hill Close retains the key architectural features, which drew the attention of Nikolaus Pevsner, and it also retains many of the original internal features, which Mary and her siblings would instantly recognise to this day. According to a letter written on 30 April 1982 by Mr Fletcher to Mary's sister, Margaret, Richard Attenborough and his uncle, Alec Clegg, did in fact visit the house in the 1970s or early 1980s, so Alec would have revisited his childhood home for the first time in around fifty years.

If Mary or any of her siblings were to walk into the house today they would instantly recognise it as their family home of over a hundred years ago.

The entrance hall, designed to make an impact statement about the quality of the house, retains the original oak entrance door, parquet flooring and oak skirting boards. All the doors leading off the hall have original oak doors and frames facing into the hall itself, but they were made double-sided. The doors to the rear dining room and the kitchen have softwood on the other side, but the door to the large front drawing room ('the Oak Room') has mahogany on the room face. Another door into the drawing room, from the kitchen, also has mahogany facing. The hall retains the original oak ceiling beams. The pantry off the kitchen has an original quarry-tiled floor not even set in cement. It is three deep steps down from kitchen level and so is effectively a semi-cellar, with a constant cooler temperature for storage. It retains a stone thrawl with a brick-arched storage space beneath, and a second quarry-tiled thrawl. The dining room retains the original polished pine floor, fire surround, skirting boards and coving.

The Oak Room is in many ways the 'showpiece' of the house. It is very spacious, 7 by 4.5 metres, with a high ceiling approximately 3.5 metres high but quite dark, partly on account of its south-east-facing aspect, but mainly on account of its original oak floor, mahogany-faced doors and mahogany wall panelling and fire surround and fancy-shaped mahogany ceiling beams. There is a hidden cupboard for the coal scuttle built into the wall panelling to the right of the fireplace, and the bell for the telephone is original. The original Tudor rose wall lights have been converted to plug-in wall lamps. To the left of the fireplace is a very attractive, high-quality stained-glass leaded window, mainly in red, green and beige.

Panels of coloured glass with popular Arts and Crafts motifs are found in several main windows of the house, including the Oak Room, but very early photographs (c.1905) of the front elevation of the house indicate that these were not in the original Oak Room window. It has been suggested that the square top small lights of coloured leaded glass may have replaced the plain originals when the adjacent doctor's house, number 196, was built around ten years after Rye Hill Close. It would have been logical to carry out any minor alterations to Rye Hill Close when builders were working next door. This was a period when the Arts and Crafts style was still current, and the new glass is in the very popular 'rose' style of Charles Rennie Mackintosh. It is a feature picked out by Pevsner nearly fifty years later, who perhaps assumed all the coloured glass was original in keeping with the date and overall style of the house. The rose theme is also continued in the windows of the small front cloakroom, also added on around the time the doctor's house was built.

Some items of furniture noted in early photographs of the house have now found their way to subsequent generations of the Clegg family, much to the chagrin of the current owner!

The staircase to the first floor has an oak banister with barley-twist balusters and is original, as are the oak skirting and pine landing. The bathroom retains original fittings such as the bath, washbasin and toilet. All four bedrooms have original softwood doors, floors and skirtings. The front bedroom over the Oak Room and under the Dutch gable is four steps up from the landing to accommodate the height of the ceiling in the Oak Room. A narrow box room on the side elevation is three steps down from the landing to fit beneath the roof pitch, thus there are several 'split levels' on the upper floor, an architectural feature of many homes built in the same style and era.

In the front garden the winding path from the gate to the front door follows the original line, and a soakaway was found by the owner in the front garden in early 2020, which she has now converted into a 'water feature'. Sam Clegg would be very pleased to see the creative use of artistic talent in his old front garden! The back garden, though much reduced in size since the days when it stretched down as far as the railway embankment, incorporating an orchard and tennis court, is still enclosed by the original walls on the side boundaries and contains one apple tree from the early

Clegg days. A large enclosed veranda to the rear elevation now incorporates the outbuildings. The outside utility room is like a museum piece, with all original features including a copper for heating water, a fireplace, a 'steam door' outlet, a 'butler's sink', a hand pump (not now working), quarry-tiled floor, a pine shelf, pine door and sash window, and in a corner a covered well.

Although the Cleggs' physical connections with Sawley and Long Eaton were now finally broken Mary presented a large portrait photograph of her father, Sam Clegg, taken by Fred Attenborough, to Long Eaton Library, and to this day the portrait immediately catches the eye as one enters the library, thus maintaining a strong sense of the Clegg heritage in the town.

CHAPTER THIRTY-SEVEN

TRAGIC EVENTS OF 12 JULY 1961

On 13 July 1961 the *Leicester Mercury* reported with stark headlines, under a photograph of Mary:

Mrs. Attenborough killed in crash.

The report went on to say that:

Mrs. Mary Attenborough, mother of Richard Attenborough, the actor, and explorer David Attenborough, was killed in a car crash at Putney, London, yesterday. Mrs. Attenborough ... was driving her car down Putney Hill when it was in collision with a lorry. It then struck a stationary car and a motor coach and finally collided with a wall. Mrs. Attenborough ... was thrown from the car.

Typically Mary, at sixty-five years of age, was working in one of her voluntary roles when the fatal accident occurred. She was driving to a meeting of the London Marriage Guidance Council Executive. The MGC paid a full, generous and heartfelt tribute to one of the important figures in the early days of the organisation and offered:

the deepest sympathy of her friends to her husband and sons, Richard, David and John.

This tribute sums up very eloquently so much of the character and personality of Mary. Given the circumstances of her death, it seems appropriate and fitting to quote extensively from the article.

The author of the tribute explains how, as the wife of the principal of University College Leicester, Mary had been placed:

in a key position, with many responsibilities and social contacts. Despite this and the claims of her family – of which she was always the hub – she found time to become a magistrate and this quickened her interest in family life whose failure is so often reflected in the courts. When the Leicester M.G.C. was set up she was one of its founders and one of its earliest counsellors.

On retirement with her husband to Long Ditton, Surrey, and after an operation had restored Mr Attenborough's health, their home and garden was an unending interest which they shared. Their large Victorian house enabled them to welcome their sons and their families often at weekends. In the garden they never tired of growing new plants and, in the autumn especially, their borders were ablaze with dahlias and Michaelmas daisies. It was from this garden that she brought many of the flowers to beautify our headquarters for the Queen Mother's visit last February.

Mary Attenborough came to play a major part in the National and London headquarters of Marriage Guidance. Herself a trained marriage counsellor she had, until her untimely death at the age of 65, quietly helped many hundreds of troubled people. In policy-making she was a most valued and trusted member of Committees and she was especially concerned with counselling and publications. A very large slice of her leisure was devoted to Marriage Guidance, and the movement owes gratitude no less to her husband for sparing her so often when they loved to be together at home. Both of them were well-known throughout the movement through their attendance at Annual Conferences, and last May at Buxton Mary Attenborough took the Chair with brisk good sense and engaging humour at the final 'Any Questions' session.

The movement has much cause for gratitude and admiration for what she did. Yet it was the kind of person that she was that won the affection and trust in which she was everywhere held. Small of stature, she was full of courage, and determination. A forthright, warm but unassuming person, outstanding in perception and integrity, she was amused by the fame reflected on her by her distinguished sons, and used rather to imply that boys would be boys. She herself just got on with the job of helping others, with realism and humour. She combined firm beliefs with real tolerance, and only a few days before her death she wrote: 'I believe it is possible to stand by our principles without alienating those whom we are trying to help.'

No one in the marriage guidance movement typified its outlook better than Mary Attenborough, or made a more valued contribution to its counsels. We salute in her a gallant and inspiring person whose loss we mourn. Those who knew her well cannot doubt that their lives have been enriched by her friendship and example. Let this tribute speak for them, and for the many hundreds of her friends in the movement who admired her throughout the country, by recording our thankfulness for her life and our profound sympathy with her husband and family.

CHAPTER THIRTY-EIGHT
AFTER MARY'S DEATH

Fred Attenborough, at seventy-four years of age and in frail health, not surprisingly had great difficulty coming to terms with Mary's sudden death. Richard's son, Michael Attenborough, in a reference to his grandfather, told me that Mary's unexpected death:

cut him off at his knees.

David said that after Mary's death his father:

could not bear the house at Four Elms.

The three sons, by then all married and living in nearby Richmond, came to an arrangement with their father, whereby he would live with each of them on a strict rota for about ten weeks at a time. Each of them had a spare bedroom, which was set aside as Fred's room when he was staying with them. David said that the arrangement worked well, with all parties knowing that it was only temporary until their next turn!

Fred's health had been rather fragile since before his retirement from Leicester. On 20 March 1973, three days before what would have been the fifty-first anniversary of his marriage to Mary, he died in Putney Hospital at the age of eighty-five following a stroke suffered while staying at David's home. Fred was staying with David's wife, Jane, while David himself was in Borneo. David was informed that his father had been taken ill and immediately set off for the nearest settlement, which had a radio phone communication link. David's personal journal records:

> When I arrived, I was blandly told that only government people could make overseas calls and that therefore I could not, but my anger was so patent that they meekly changed their minds. After half an hour's wait, I got through to Jane and heard the news I knew I would. Father had died peacefully on Tuesday night having only regained consciousness transiently for a moment or so when Dick was with him.

David managed to get back home in time for the funeral the following Tuesday.

Frederick Attenborough's legacy in Leicester is well-honoured. The university college achieved full university status in 1957, the significant change being that the institution was now able to confer its own degrees. In the late 1960s, during a period of rapid physical growth on the main University of Leicester campus, plans were announced for the construction of a new tower block to house arts and social sciences departments on the edge of Victoria Park. This was to be known as the Attenborough Building to honour Fred's significant contribution to the development of the institution. Perhaps carried away by the sheer speed of development during the 1960s the original thoughts for development of the site included two other tower blocks alongside the proposed arts block. To the relief of many local citizens the plans for the additional blocks were abandoned. In October 1970, half a century after the foundation of the university college, the Attenborough Building, the tallest building on the campus and one of the tallest in the city, was finally opened by John Attenborough, in a ceremony attended by the whole Attenborough family except Fred himself, who was not well enough to attend in person. The occasion was also marked by the conferring of honorary degrees on both Richard and David Attenborough.

The ongoing incidental interaction between the Clegg–Attenborough family and Nikolaus Pevsner continued when, in the second (revised) edition of Pevsner's volume on *Leicestershire and Rutland* (1985), the Attenborough Building was described as:

eighteen monotonous storeys, prickly with window units angled out from top to bottom of the pre-cast concrete panels, a feature more successful inside than out.

In 2020 the Leicester Literary and Philosophical Society, of which Fred had been president during the war, decided to name one of its regular winter season lectures in honour of the Attenborough family, starting in 2021. Both David and Michael proposed that the lecture should be called specifically the 'F.L. Attenborough Lecture'. The inaugural lecture, to be given by Michael Attenborough in March 2021, is to be entitled: *Do the Arts have any Role in Education?* I detect a continuing theme here down the generations from Samuel Clegg to his great-grandson!

CHAPTER THIRTY-NINE

MARY'S SIBLINGS – THE LEGACY OF SAMUEL CLEGG

As we have already seen, Mary was the eldest of six children of Sam and Mary Clegg senior, five daughters and one son. Their third child, Dorothy, was born in 1899 and died in 1966 at the age of sixty-seven in West Kirby on the Wirral in Cheshire, where she had been living with her 'adoptive' family, cousin Irene Baxendale and her parents, Aunt Bernice and Uncle William, for the past thirty-five years following the death of both Sam and Mary Clegg senior in 1930. Dorothy's story has already been told above, as has the very short life of the fifth sibling, Eunice, who died from diphtheria, aged just seventeen months, in November 1907.

Mary's closest sibling in age was Margaret, born in 1897, consequently their schooling was the most contemporaneous. They were both travelling together for much of their respective day courses whilst studying for their external London degrees at University College Nottingham. Mary and Margaret remained very close. When Mary kept her daily diary at the Sorbonne in Paris in early 1914 she received her first letter from home after a fortnight on Friday 23 January, and noted:

Was very glad to receive a letter from home which I had been looking for all the week – was very disappointed not to hear a word from Mag.

The two sisters were then aged seventeen and sixteen respectively. Apart from Dorothy the younger siblings were Barbara, then aged eleven and

Alec, aged four, who were almost of a separate generation at that stage of their lives, so inevitably Mary and Margaret would have been closer, with more experiences in common. When Margaret married Gilbert Peaker in 1930 she was a high school teacher in Birmingham. Gilbert was five years her junior and had been a student of Fred Attenborough's at Borough Road College in the 1920s. Margaret and Gilbert had one child, Jane, born in 1936, who later met and married Tom Muirhead after they had both been dentistry students in Edinburgh. Jane and Tom now live in North Yorkshire. Jane had been a regular visitor as a young child to Mary and Fred during the war and remembered life with the family at College House with great affection. Jane was in fact evacuated from her family home in Wimbledon for weeks at a time on more than one occasion.

Gilbert Peaker had joined the Civil Service after university and from 1924 to 1927 was a cartographer in Nigeria with the Colonial Service. He was an assistant director of education at the age of twenty-eight in 1930 when he and Margaret married, and he later became an inspector of schools. After the war Gilbert resumed work as an inspector, mainly concerned with higher technical education. In his leisure time Gilbert was a keen climber and became a highly accomplished and respected Alpine mountaineer. When Gilbert died in 1983 the Alpine Club published a tribute by C. Douglas Milner in the *Alpine Journal*, describing him as:

> *A man of brilliant mind and vigorous body. At Cambridge he was awarded a First in Mathematics and a Half-Blue as a Marathon runner. He was elected to the Club in 1930, and his list of climbs from 1923 to 1929, all guideless, would be considered very fine today, and in those days astonishing.*

The author goes on to describe Gilbert's achievements in the European Alps during the 1930s and then:

> *When the war broke out, we both had the misfortune to be in reserved occupations, he in the Treasury and I in the Head Office of my bank so we had our holidays in Wales. In 1944 we had with us his nephew, David Attenborough, who was just about to go up to Cambridge. It was intended to teach him climbing, but he finished by leading us. I sometimes*

wonder if his experiences with his formidable uncle led him to the study of gorillas.

Gilbert's climbing career came to an end in 1957 when he was fortunate to survive a serious climbing accident in North Wales, which left him permanently lame.

Even so he eventually recovered sufficiently to walk with much of his old vigour and until just before his death he would regularly ascend towards Fairfield from the back of his Grasmere home.

Gilbert Peaker climbing Grey Slab, Glyder Fawr, Snowdonia

Gilbert died in 1983. Margaret outlived all of her siblings and died in 1989 at the age of ninety-one.

Mary's youngest sister, Barbara, was taller than her older sisters and was gifted in athletics and team games such as hockey. In the *Long Eaton School Magazine* Barbara showed an early interest in women's social history when she researched and wrote an article with her friend, Annie Allen, about the history of the first Women's Clubs in Sawley, self-help Friendly Societies, which were wound up early in the twentieth century when Prime Minister Lloyd George introduced the first national insurance schemes. The *Derbyshire Advertiser and Journal* on 5 August 1922 reported on the annual meeting of the Midland Agricultural and Dairy College held at Sutton Bonnington in south Nottinghamshire on 31 July 1922. The college was by then part of the University College Nottingham, and its successor is still located at Sutton Bonnington. After the formal business of the meeting certificates were given to successful students, and a College Diploma 2nd Class was given to Barbara Clegg. Whether this was Mary's sister is not certain, but as Barbara was just short of her twentieth birthday at that time it seems highly likely that it was the same Barbara Clegg following her older sisters with success at Nottingham. Barbara married in 1930, to Frank Barraclough, continuing the 'education dynasty' among Sam Clegg's children. Frank was a physicist, and he went on to become director of education in the North Riding of Yorkshire and died in 1974 at the age of seventy-three. Barbara survived him by eleven years and died in Darlington in 1985 at the age of eighty-three. Barbara and Frank had one son, David, who spent much of his career and his retirement involved with railways. He worked in Hong Kong for some time on the local mass transit system. David Barraclough died in 2017, aged eighty-two. Frank Barraclough's educational philosophy was very different from that of his brother-in-law, Alec Clegg, who was in charge of education in the neighbouring West Riding. One wonders how Barbara viewed this.

The youngest of Mary's siblings, and the only boy of the family, was Alexander Bradshaw Clegg, soon to be known simply as Alec. He was born on 13 June 1909 when Mary was already thirteen, half a generation older. This is reflected in the final entry of Mary's Sorbonne diary on Monday 9 February 1914 when she reveals a rare moment of homesickness during her busy life in Paris:

> Got the letter home at night. The picture of Alec is just lovely – it makes me want to see him and hug him all the more.

A recurring theme of Mary's story has been how she, and her own children, grew up in a milieu where education was revered per se, and where so many members of her own family committed their working lives to ensuring that as many children as possible from all backgrounds could benefit from this philosophy. Alec acknowledged the debt of his immediate family for his own learning about education:

> My immediate family and their wives and husbands … between us in one way or another … had experienced almost every kind of educational position from a reception class teacher in a direct-grant school to the vice-chairman of the governors of a school for disruptive girls, from a teacher in a technical college to an HMI. I gained further intimate experience from the fact that one of my sisters who died at the age of 67 [Dorothy] never developed intellectually beyond the age of six or seven.

Alec was educated initially at the same Long Eaton school as his siblings, where his father was head, but then moved to Bootham School in York. This is an independent Quaker school. It was suggested to me by Alec's son, Peter, that Alec may not have been thriving in an establishment where his father was head, and that the idea of applying for admission to Bootham School may have come from Sam Clegg's sister, Alec's aunt Isabella (Bell), herself a teacher in the family tradition, who later taught geography to Margaret Thatcher at Grantham Girls' Grammar School. Alec went on to gain a degree in modern languages at Clare College, Cambridge, and then went to the London Day Training College (LDTC), which had been established in 1902, for teacher training. During Alec's time there the London County Council and the University of London had approved, in principle, for the LDTC to be transferred wholly to the university. The transfer eventually took place in 1932 and, at this point, the teacher-training college changed its name to the University of London, Institute of Education.

Alec was still a student at Cambridge when both his parents died in 1930, and his 'home' base for a time was then with his older sister Mary and Fred until he was fully independent. Between 1932 and 1937 Alec taught French and games at St Clement Danes' Holborn Estate Grammar School in London. During the war years he worked for three education authorities, Birmingham, Cheshire and Worcestershire. It was presumably while working in Birmingham that Alec met Jessie Phillips. Jessie, the daughter of a schoolmaster, was born on 14 December 1916 in West Hartlepool, County Durham, just seventeen days after the second German Zeppelin raid on the town had damaged many shops and houses in the area. Alec and Jessie, aged thirty-one and twenty-three, were married on 14 September 1940 at the Parish Church of The Holy Ascension in Upton-by-Chester. Witnesses were Mary Attenborough, Jessie's father, Thomas Phillips, and Alec's close friend from his Long Eaton schooldays, who was possibly his best man, Alec Daykin. Alec was working for Cheshire when they married, but Jessie's home address was still in Selly Oak, Birmingham.

Alec and Jessie had three sons, Andrew, John and Peter. Eldest son Andrew recalls an interesting episode in which he claims that Mary's quick thinking and decisive action saved his life. He was almost three when his brother John was born in 1946. Andrew was staying with Mary and Fred

The wedding of Alec Clegg and Jessie Phillips, September 1940.
Left to right Mary, Alec, Jessie and Jessie's parents

for a couple of weeks in Leicester while his parents coped with the birth of their second child. Andrew became ill whilst staying with Mary and Fred, and Mary recognised symptoms of osteomyelitis, which she was then able to convey, accurately, to the doctor and speed up the response to Andrew's illness. How Mary gained the medical knowledge to recognise the symptoms is a mystery. Did she have some basic training during the First World War? Did she work, or even study, in some voluntary capacity in the next-door doctor's surgery in New Sawley? We may never know for sure, but Andrew certainly believes that Mary's knowledge and quick thinking saved his life as a young child.

After the war in 1945 Alec Clegg was made deputy chief education officer for the West Riding of Yorkshire, and within months, following the retirement of the incumbent postholder, he was appointed chief education officer at the age of thirty-six. He remained in post for almost thirty years, retiring in 1974 at the age of sixty-five, coinciding with the major restructuring of local government outside London in the same year. As part of the 1974 reorganisation the historic name of West Riding disappeared as a political entity in favour of the more prosaic West Yorkshire. During Alec's time in post the West Riding became in many ways an innovative and pioneering education authority. The early years of his tenure coincided with the major social and welfare reforms of the post-war Labour government. The introduction of middle schools as part of a three-tier system of education was a major change of direction, gradually copied by many authorities across the country. For his services to education Alec Clegg was knighted in the Queen's Birthday Honours List of June 1965.

In an after-dinner speech on 3 August 1972 at the conclusion of a summer vacation course for teachers at Bingley College of Education in West Yorkshire Sir Alec Clegg outlined key aspects of his educational philosophy. It is remarkable how much of what he said on that occasion could have been the basis of a similar speech, had it been given fifty years earlier, by his own father, Sam Clegg. Alec explained the omnipresent educational background in his own family:

> I am the son, son-in-law, grandson, husband, brother, brother-in-law, nephew, father and father-in-law of teachers.

Alec considered the qualities of the ten best headteachers he had known and distilled their philosophies into the following list:

- *that there is good in every child, however damaged, repellent or ill-favoured he may be*
- *that success on which a teacher can build must somehow be found for every child*
- *that all children matter*
- *that happy relationships between head, teachers, and pupils are important*
- *that the life of the child can be enriched by the development of his creative powers*

- *that encouragement is far more important than punishment*
- *that teachers just as much as pupils need support and thrive on recognition*

Those words could easily have been spoken by Sam Clegg fifty years earlier. In a further echo of his father's philosophy Alec looked ahead to how his grandchildren's generation might be:

> astonished ... that we don't yet understand how to develop discrimination and judgment and the enjoyment of things designed by civilised man to be enjoyed – painting, music, art and so on – all of which are just as much part of our education as history and geography, but we tend to undervalue them because we cannot mark them or have them externally examined.

His concluding comment perhaps sums up much of the philosophy and approach to life shown by the main personalities in this story:

> Let me close with a quotation I found early this year in Rome.
>
> When Michelangelo was going to Rome to see the Pope prior to his being employed to build the great dome of St. Peter's and paint the Sistine Chapel, he took a reference with him which said:
>
> 'The bearer of these presents is Michelangelo the sculptor. His nature is such that he requires to be drawn out by kindness and encouragement. But if love be shown to him and he be treated really well, he will accomplish things that will make the whole world wonder.'

Sir Alec Clegg died on 20 January 1986 at the age of seventy-six. Jessie Coverdale Clegg died in 2010 at the age of ninety-four.

CHAPTER FORTY

MARY'S LEGACY – HER CHILDREN

There is no intention whatsoever in this work to write 'biographies by proxy' of Mary's well-known sons. Richard, David and John Attenborough have all been mentioned at various points in the work as they are an integral part of Mary's story. David in particular has been a wonderful source of many family insights and anecdotes, which could never be found from any other sources.

Fred Attenborough, who, to quote Richard:

had pulled himself up by his own bootstraps

perhaps understandably in the early days had an expectation and hope of the boys following him into academia, or at the very least benefitting from a university education somewhere along the way.

Mary, whose own family experience and background led her to an understanding that everyone had different strengths, which should be given every opportunity and encouragement to flourish, was more relaxed about future careers for her sons but was determined to support them fully in whatever paths they chose. Mary's own philosophy must have been that if a cause or a chosen course was worth supporting and pursuing it was worth pursuing with energy, commitment and passion. She perhaps assumed these same qualities in her sons but sensed that the best way of nurturing them was to support them fully but less conditionally than Fred.

According to Sir David one of the attractions of the post at University College, Leicester, when Fred applied in 1931 was that there was a boys' state grammar school with a regional and national reputation for excellence almost next door to College House and effectively sharing a campus with the university college. All three boys duly attended Wyggeston Boys' Grammar School. David, whose time at the school coincided almost exactly with the war years, said that in some ways the quality of education was disappointing because many of the best younger teachers had been drafted into wartime duties elsewhere, and a number of elderly teachers, recently retired and summoned back reluctantly, took their places. This situation must have been mirrored across the country.

Another anecdote about his mother from David refers to life at the grammar school and illustrates, as he says:

Mary's preference for the sensible over the merely fashionable or conventional.

The school at the time apparently did not have a code about the boys having to wear school uniform:

However, it was a custom almost universally followed, to wear a blazer and shorts. The blazer was black with a white crest on the breast pocket. Almost all the boys in the school wore them, much encouraged by the local gents outfitter in (I think) Market Street. Mary did not approve. Blazers, jackets of any kind, were wholly unsuitable wear for ten-year-old boys. They should wear jerseys. Which explains why, in my earlier form photographs, I – to my mortification – am the only pupil in the picture wearing a V-neck jumper with the school colours confined to a stripe around the neck line.

Richard, as the eldest son, was the first to encounter Fred's expectations of academia. In Leicester Mary had two spells in the 1930s as president of the Leicester Drama Society at the Little Theatre, which was:

a vibrant and remarkably professional hotbed of amateur dramatics, according to Richard, who spent much of his time there at the expense of his schoolwork. Fred was at first disappointed that Richard had no wish to seek a university education, but he eventually probably accepted that his eldest son had inherited strong will from both his parents! He said that he would support his son's aspirations of a career in the dramatic arts only if Richard obtained a Leverhulme Scholarship to the Royal Academy of Dramatic Art (RADA), which would pay both tuition and living expenses. When Richard was called for an interview and audition at RADA in the early months of the war it was Mary who accompanied him:

> *A week before Christmas, taking our gas masks, identity cards and a shared suitcase, my mama and I set off for London.*

Richard was successful in his application for the scholarship, and the rest, as they say, is history. In January 1945 Richard married actress Sheila Sim, whom he first met at RADA.

David perhaps came closest to, but still a long way from, following his father's ideal of a career rooted in academia. From Wyggeston he gained a scholarship to Clare College, Cambridge, where he studied mainly geology and zoology for a degree in natural sciences. His early passion was for geology, and from College House he was able to cycle into the Leicestershire countryside to study first-hand the very contrasting surface geologies of Charnwood Forest to the north-west of the city and Tilton Cutting in the east of the county. The extensive grounds of College House and the site of the college also gave the young David opportunities to explore the natural world and collect and study specimens. In 1950 David married Jane Elizabeth Oriel. During the War, although college numbers fell at Leicester, the number of people operating on the campus actually increased as the university college found accommodation for several organisations, including a BBC unit. The largest influx of people came when King's College of Household and Social Science, London, decided to evacuate from the capital and accepted Leicester's offer of accommodation. Jane Oriel was a student at King's at the time, and this is how David and Jane met in Leicester. In 1952 David started a long career association with the BBC. At the time of writing he is still working with the BBC Natural History Unit at the age of ninety-four.

On 11 November 2018, on the centenary of the end of the First World War, David attended the annual Armistice Day commemoration at the Arch of Remembrance in Victoria Park, Leicester, within sight of College House. In a separate ceremony afterwards he formally dedicated a new open space, Centenary Square, on the university campus. In his speech he said, surely as a lasting memory and dedication to his own parents:

Mary and Fred at the wedding of David Attenborough and Jane Oriel, 1950

It is a proud boast that I have that I was reared on this campus. It is a wonderful university. This university has a wonderful reputation for humanity, for culture, for generosity as do the citizens of this ancient noble city.

John Attenborough followed David from Wyggeston to Clare College, Cambridge, where he studied modern languages, echoing Mary's aptitude for languages. John was always:

fascinated by anything mechanical

and went on to have a highly successful career as a managing director of Mann Egerton, as head of its Rolls-Royce division in Berkeley Street, Mayfair, and later as the head of the British operations of Italian car manufacturer Alfa Romeo. John married Janet Cleverdon, one of whose childhood homes in Cambridge, by pure coincidence, was just four doors away from the house in Tenison Road where the newly married Mary and Fred had lived from 1922 to 1925 and where eldest son Richard was born.

Three brothers with completely different career paths, but each pursued with a passion and the exemplary standards which the supportive

Mary would have fully endorsed and appreciated. Sam Clegg would also have felt vindicated that his grandsons enjoyed such varied and fulfilling lives.

| *Mary with grandchildren, Michael, Robert and Susan Attenborough at 'Four Elms', Surrey*

CHAPTER FORTY-ONE

WHAT CAUSES WOULD MARY BE FIGHTING IN 2020?

During the course of my research I often paused to ask myself the question:

If Mary had been born a century later, i.e. in 1996, what causes would she be espousing now as a young woman in her mid-twenties?

Here are some of my answers to my own question.

Almost a century after achieving full suffrage equality in this country I suspect that Mary would applaud the progress made by and for women in that time, but she would also be shocked at what has still not been achieved both in this country and around the world. If she had the same educational opportunities and experience in the twenty-first century Mary would certainly expect to have at least the realistic option of forging a career of her own, and if she took that option she would expect and fight for more equality of opportunity within the workplace which is still lacking in many areas of society. She would also be disappointed, though perhaps not surprised, to see that despite a raft of modern legislation to make illegal and to punish proven actions relating to social, racial, religious and sexual intolerance, legislation alone does not change human attitudes overnight, and she would be reflecting whether and how this might be possible to achieve. She would understand that this would be a long-term, even a lifetime's struggle, with no guarantees at the end, but given Mary's passion and commitment it is a fight which she would not shy away from.

Just seventy-five years after Helga and Irene's father was murdered for the simple fact of being Jewish in one of the most 'civilised' countries in Europe, and eighty-three years after young unaccompanied children were forced to flee their homeland with an uncertain future, unsure if they would ever see their families again simply because their parents' political views were at odds with those of a Fascist rebel leader, Mary would be appalled to see that militant anti-Semitism is still rife in Europe. She would be appalled to see that thousands of unaccompanied children all around the world are still fleeing for their lives in the face of civil wars, religious and racial intolerance and economic hardship, which is often the indirect result of discriminatory trade policies by the 'civilised' West.

Mary would be well aware that despite the impression deliberately purveyed in some quarters that the United Kingdom is the 'end destination' for all refugees from all over the world, ninety per cent of refugees actually flee over the border to their own neighbouring countries and place an enormous burden of responsibility on other nations, which are often facing their own hardships, and that even for those who do make it as far as Europe, the UK is not the first destination of choice for the great majority. She would probably be supporting organisations, which aim to improve conditions at source, such as Fair Trade movements, which often by definition help women's co-operatives to obtain a better deal to support their families and improve conditions in the long-term which may then avert the need for future mass migration.

On the home front Mary would be shocked at the level of child poverty in this country, one of the wealthiest nations in the world, yet one seemingly unable or unwilling to tackle a major issue which could be storing up problems for the future. She would surely be on the front-line in this battle.

Last but not least, Mary's humanitarian vision would surely recognise that one of the greatest threats to future world harmony and the battle against poverty on a global scale comes directly from the effects of global warming on man's ability to feed a burgeoning population. As a very pragmatic person she would be leading the fight against wastefulness in the capitalist economies, and she would surely be advocating the right of women to control their own lives and particularly the number of children they have, in order to limit poverty – a right we may now almost take for granted in the West, but it is a right which is not a universal given around the world.

CHAPTER FORTY-TWO

MARY'S PLACE IN HISTORY

The Attenborough name is forever associated with Leicester, well respected by the citizens of Leicester and well represented in several ways. As we have seen, in 1970, the university honoured its former principal by naming the tallest building on the campus after Frederick Attenborough in a ceremony performed by John Attenborough, and on the same occasion conferred honorary degrees on Richard and David. Twenty years later in June 1990 both Richard and David were made Freemen of the City of Leicester by the city council.

In March 2021 the Leicester Literary and Philosophical Society will hold the inaugural 'F.L. Attenborough Lecture', which will then become a part of its annual calendar of lectures.

In May 1997 Lord Richard Attenborough, accompanied by his close friend, HRH Princess Diana, just three months before her death, opened the Richard Attenborough Centre for Disability and the Arts, in Lancaster Road, on the edge of Leicester University campus. Richard was the chief patron of the project, which had been fundraising for six years, and he was very much involved with its planning. The centre is now known as the Attenborough Arts Centre and is run in partnership with the university, offering equality of access for people with disabilities to the creative arts and a range of live music, dance and theatrical events. Mary would surely be proud of the role of her own family in promoting equality of opportunity in the city where her young family grew up.

In September 2020, commenting on the long-term loan by Helga Bejach's daughters, who live in the United States, to the University of Leicester of the small but significant archive of documents and photographs, referred to in earlier chapters and including Helga's diary, president and vice-chancellor of the university Professor Nishan Canagarajah said:

> *Our University values are built on sacrifice, kindness, and a sense of duty – all of these can be traced back to the Attenboroughs. We're proud to be a University of Sanctuary, welcoming asylum seekers and refugees onto university courses and providing financial and personal support, and using the power of education to transform lives. The Attenboroughs' legacy lives on strong within our walls to this day, and will continue to lay the foundation for our future generations of scholars at Leicester.*

These words could almost serve as a preface for this biography.

So what of Mary Attenborough? There is so far no public recognition or acknowledgment of the life and work of Mary. Leicester prides itself on its diversity and its continuing role of welcoming refugees from adversity in desperate situations all over the world. The university is celebrating the centenary of its foundation with an emphasis on the unsung role of women in its early history. Surely now is an appropriate time for both the city council and the University of Leicester to acknowledge the wonderful humanitarian work which Mary undertook in the city between 1937 and 1946, rescuing young people from situations where their lives were threatened on account of the religious or political beliefs of their parents. Not only did she rescue these young lives but she cared for them as if they were her own, and she gave them the best chance of creating new lives and opportunities for themselves. Mary was also at the forefront of promoting and even founding organisations, both locally and nationally, which gave women a real voice after belatedly securing full suffrage in 1928.

Surely Mary deserves recognition and her rightful place in a history still dominated by the achievements of men.

SOURCES

SELECT BIBLIOGRAPHY

R. Adam (ed.), *Jewish Voices – Memories of Leicester in the 1940s and 1950s* (Leicester, 2009)

R. Aldrich, *The British and Foreign School Society, Past and Present*, History of Education Researcher, No. 91, May 2013

R. Attenborough and D. Hawkins, *Entirely up to You, Darling* (London, 2008)

G.F. Bartle, *A History of Borough Road College* (London, 1976)

British and Foreign School Society Archives Information Sheet No. 2, *A History of Borough Road College*, Brunel University Archives (May 2013)

P. Boylan (ed.), *Exchanging Ideas Dispassionately and without Animosity: The Leicester Literary and Philosophical Society 1835–2010* (Leicester, 2010)

H. Boynton, *The History of Victoria Park, Leicester* (Leicester, 2000)

C. Brown, *A Cultural Democracy: Education in Long Eaton, 1879–1930*, Derbyshire Archaeological Journal (1982), Vol. 102, pp.133–153

B. Burch, *The University of Leicester, A History, 1921–96* (Leicester, 1996)

A. Clegg, *About Our Schools* (Oxford, 1980)

S. Clegg, *Co-operation in Long Eaton* (Blackpool, 1901)

S. Clegg, *Drawing and Design* (2nd. Edition) (London, 1931)

R. David, *Child of Our Time: a Young Girl's Flight from the Holocaust* (London, 2003)

Education in England website www.educationengland.org.uk, *Sir Alec Clegg speech at Bingley College of Education*, 3 August 1972

Erewash Borough Council, *List of Buildings of Local Interest*

Exploring Beeston's History, www.beeston-notts.co.uk

H. Godwin, *Cambridge and Clare* (Cambridge, 1985)

A. Goode, *Emmanuel College Cambridge – An Historical Guide* (Sudbury, 2017)

R. Graves, *From Berlin to New York via Leicester: The Long Journey of the Attenboroughs' 'adopted sisters',* Parts 1 and 2, Leicestershire Historian, Vols. 50, 2014 and 51, 2015, Leicestershire Archaeological and Historical Society

R. Graves, *Leicester's Refuge for Basque Children from the Spanish Civil War,* Parts 1 and 2, Leicestershire Historian, Vols. 52, 2016 and 53, 2017, Leicestershire Archaeological and Historical Society

G.D.B. Gray, *Long Eaton Grammar School Jubilee Book 1960* (Long Eaton, 1960)

S. Greasley, *The Baptists of Derbyshire 1650–1914* (Ilkeston, 2007)

F. Harrison, *It All Began Here – The Story of the East Midlands Baptist Association* (1986)

J. Heath and A. Hooper, *A Brief History of Long Eaton and Sawley from 1750–1914 (Reprint)* (Long Eaton, 1967)

H.M.S.O., *Non-conformist Chapels and Meeting-houses, Derbyshire* (London, 1986)

Hucknall Torkard History, www.hucknalltorkardhistory.co.uk/industry.htm

W.G. Hoskins, *The Heritage of Leicestershire* (Leicester, 1950)

M. Lambert and J. Shipman, *The Unknown Cotswold Village: Eastcombe 1500–1980* (Eastcombe, 1981)

E. Leedham-Green, *A Concise History of the University of Cambridge* (Cambridge, 1996)

Leicester Literary and Philosophical Society, *Transactions, Vol. 104, 2010*

Leicester Rotary Club, www.rotary-leicester.org.uk

Long Eaton County School Annual (1912)

A. Newman and P Lidiker, *Portrait of a Community, A History of the Leicester Hebrew Congregation* (Leicester, 1998)

M. Pantling and E. Mitchell, *1920–2020 – 100 Years of Lady Magistrates in Leicestershire and Rutland* (Leicester, 2020)

D. Peters, *Curt Bejach – Berliner Stadtarzt und Sozialmediziner* (Berlin, 2010)

N. Pevsner, *The Buildings of England, Derbyshire* (London, 1953)

N. Pevsner and E. Williamson, *The Buildings of England, Leicestershire and Rutland (2nd. (rev.) Edition)* (London, 1985)

N. Pevsner, *The Leaves of Southwell* (London, 1945)

University of Southern California Shoah Foundation Visual History Archive, *Waldman, Helga. Interview 12009*, accessed at Royal Holloway, London, 12 November 2013

Wensleydale Railway News, *Rail Link, Ed.160, Oct 2017*

FAMILY PAPERS, CORRESPONDENCE, PRIVATE CONVERSATIONS

Sir David Attenborough

Janet Attenborough

Jane and Tom Muirhead

Michael Attenborough

Peter Clegg

Andrew Clegg

Denise Hopkins

Beverly Waldman Rich

Hilary Waldman

ARCHIVES, RECORDS AND MINUTES OF THE FOLLOWING INSTITUTIONS

University of Leicester

Emmanuel College, University of Cambridge

Royal Holloway, London

Senate House Library, University of London

University of Nottingham

Brunel University of London

Relate (formerly Marriage Guidance Council)

Leicester Magistrates' Court
Record Office for Leicestershire, Leicester and Rutland
Derbyshire Record Office
Derbyshire County Council, Long Eaton Library
Nottinghamshire County Council, Stapleford Library
Leicester Literary and Philosophical Society
General Register Office UK
The Alpine Club

NEWSPAPERS AND JOURNALS

Derby Daily Telegraph 4 Aug 1894, 25 Sep 1903
South Notts. Echo 13 Feb 1932
Nottinghamshire Guardian 15 Jan 1886
The New Age 1 Jan 1914
The Guardian 4 Jan 2014
The Derbyshire Advertiser 16 Oct 1914, 16 Jul 1909, 5 Aug 1922
London Gazette Aug 1877
Nottingham Evening Post 16 Sept 1899
Long Eaton Advertiser 21 Mar 1930, 24 Oct 1930, 2 Apr 1937, 14 Jun 1941
Leicester Mercury 27 Jan 1939, 27 Mar 1939, 6 Jul 1937, 2 Jun 1937, 5 Jun 1937, 9 Jul 1937, 30 Jul 1937, 2 Feb 1938, 8 Jun 1939, 5 Apr 1939, 21 Nov 1940, 10 Jul 1940, 21 Dec 1950, 13 Jul 1961
Leicester Evening Mail 11 Apr 1934, 1 May 1934, 17 Oct 1934, 14 Nov 1934, 12 Mar 1935, 28 Feb 1936, 21 Mar 1936, 2 Jan 1942, 4 Jun 1943, 8 Jun 1945, 6 Apr 1951